BEYOND THE VERSE
Talmudic Readings and Lectures
Emmanuel Levinas

Translated by Gary D. Mole

continuum

Continuum

The Tower Building   80 Maiden Lane
11 York Road   Suite 704
London   New York
SE1 7NX   NY 10038

www.continuumbooks.com

First published in Great Britain in 1994 by The Athlone Press,
1 Park Drive, London NW11 7SG

First published in France in 1982 by
Les Éditions de Minuit, Paris
as *L'au-delà du verset: lectures et discours talmudiques*

British Library Cataloguing in Publication Data
A catalogue record for this book is available from the British Library.

Library of Congress Cataloguing in Publication Data
A catalog record for this book is available from the Library of Congress.

ISBN 0826499031 (10)
     9780826499035 (13)

Typeset by BookEns Ltd, Royston, Herts.
Printed and bound in China by 1010 Printing International Ltd

To the memory of Léon Algazi, composer of music,
interpreter of verses and simple believer

Contents

Translator's Note

The following English translations have been used throughout this text: *The Babylonian Talmud,* under the editorship of Isidore Epstein, 34 volumes (London: The Soncino Press, 1935–1952) and *Midrash Rabbah,* under the editorship of H. Freedman and M. Simon, 10 volumes (London: Soncino Press, 1939). Biblical references have been taken from the Collins Revised Standard Version. However, biblical quotations within the Talmudic extracts conform to the versions given there. From Chapter 7 onwards Levinas does not quote in full the Talmudic extracts he is commenting upon, but biblical quotations still conform to the Talmudic versions except where the Talmud itself does not give such quotations in full, in which case the Revised Standard Version is used. Square brackets are used throughout in order to indicate Levinas's own variations or interpolations, or indeed to highlight discrepancies between the French and English versions. Such discrepancies are on the whole self-explanatory, but where thought necessary they have been explained in the notes. Existing English translations of other works that have been used in this translation have also been indicated appropriately in the notes, along with bibliographical references to those texts by Levinas to which he himself refers and which have been translated into English.

Author's Note

Apart from the studies whose origin or first publication are mentioned in the foreword of the present volume, the following indicates references relating to the other texts of this collection:

'The Name of God according to a few Talmudic Texts' appeared in the *Proceedings* from the Colloquium organized by the International Centre of Humanist Studies and the Institute of Philosophical Studies of Rome in 1969, under the title 'The Analysis of Theological Language'.

'Revelation in the Jewish Tradition' appeared in the collective volume entitled *Revelation* (Brussels: Facultés universitaires Saint-Louis, 1977).

' "In the Image of God", according to Rabbi Hayyim Volozhiner' appeared in 1978 in the *Mélanges* offered to Professor Herman Heering of Leyden (the Netherlands).

'Spinoza's Background', previously unpublished, is a lecture delivered at the Spinoza Congress in Jerusalem in 1979.

'The State of Caesar and the State of David' appeared in the *Proceedings* of the Colloquium of Rome in 1971.

'Politics After!' appeared in *Les Temps modernes* 398 (September 1979).

'Assimilation and New Culture' appeared in *Les Nouveaux Cahiers* 60 (Spring 1980).

The final section (pp. 108–15) of the study entitled 'On the Jewish Reading of Scriptures' appeared in 'Hommage à Georges Vajda', *Etudes d'histoire et de pensée juive*.

Foreword

1 Why beyond the verse?

Because the strict contours of the verses outlined in the Holy Scriptures have a plain meaning[1] which is also enigmatic. A hermeneutics is invited whose task is to extricate, from within the meaning immediately offered by the proposition, those meanings that are only implied. Do not these extricated meanings have enigmas themselves? According to other methods, they in their turn must be interpreted. And in the search for new teachings, hermeneutics incessantly returns even to those verses which, though already interpreted, are inexhaustible. A reading of Scripture, therefore, which is forever beginning again; a revelation which is forever continued.

The Talmud teaches a principle by R. Ishmael which is repeated eighteen times in the course of its Tractates: 'The Torah speaks the language of men'. Admittedly, this principle is always quoted so as not to compel the exegete to seek a metaphysical meaning behind every term of the biblical discourse. But this limitation in interpretation is always relative, and the limits are mobile. The great thought behind the principle consists in admitting that the Word of God can be maintained in the spoken language used by created beings amongst themselves. The marvellous contraction of the Infinite, the 'more' inhabiting the 'less', the Infinite in the Finite, as in keeping with Descartes's 'idea of God'. Hence, precisely, the enigmatic surplus of meaning for the reader; hence the implicit exegesis – and the call for exegesis already in the act of reading.

A contraction of the Infinite in Scripture, unless – and here there would be no impoverishment of the Cartesian idea, nor of the glory of God, nor of His religious proximity – unless it is the prophetic dignity of language, capable of always signifying more than it says, the marvel of inspiration where man listens, amazed, to what he utters, where he already *reads* the utterance and interprets it, where the human word is already writing. Scripture would begin with the line which is outlined in some way, and thickens or emerges as a verse in the flowing of language – no doubt of every language – in order to become text, as proverb, or fable, or poem, or legend, before the stylet or quill imprints it as letters on tablets, parchment or paper. A literature before the letter! No doubt there is instituted in this inspired essence of language – which is already the writing of a book – a commanding 'ontological' order which resembles neither the naturally necessary reality of history and things which – everyone hastens to find everywhere; nor the normative ideality of *having-to-be*; nor the utopian and 'unfathomable depth' of an interiority which in the waters of political realism, filling up good conscience – would be a mythical island, but where everyone suspects the subconscious, ideology or childishness. A religious essence of language, a place where prophecy will conjure up the Holy Scriptures, but which all literature awaits or commemorates, whether celebrating or profaning it. Hence, in the very anthropology of the human – and not only in the superstructure and fragility of its cultures – the eminent role played by so-called national literatures, Shakespeare, Molière, Dante, Cervantes, Goethe and Pushkin. Signifying beyond their plain meaning, they invite the exegesis – be it straightforward or tortuous, but by no means frivolous – that is spiritual life.

Aristotle's 'animal endowed with language' has never been thought, in its ontology, in terms of the book, nor questioned on the status of its religious relationship to the book. In the philosophical 'promotions' of categories, this relationship has never merited the rank of a modality as determining, and as essential and irreducible for the human condition – or uncondition – as language itself, thought, or technical activity. It is as if reading were only one of the stages in the circulation of information, and the book only one thing amongst others, demonstrating in handbooks – like a hammer – its affinity with the hand.

2 The enigma of the verse and the line is not, therefore, simply a matter of imprecision which – either inadvertently or in bad faith – gives rise to misunderstandings. It does not come from any insufficiency in the

linguistic instrument necessary for the communication of knowledge and, therefore, for the institution and maintenance of an objective, historical and political order. Language here no longer has the simple status of an instrument.

Language which has become Holy Scriptures, and which maintains its prophetic essence – probably language *par excellence* – the Word of God that is already audible or still muffled in the heart of every act of speech, is not solely a matter of the engagement of speaking beings in the fabric of the world and History, where they are concerned with themselves – that is to say, with their perseverance in being. In language a signified does not signify only from words which, as a conjunction of signs, move towards this signified. Beyond what it wants me to know, it co-ordinates me with the other to whom I speak; it signifies in every discourse from the face of the other, hidden from sight yet unforgettable: from the expression before words my responsibility-for-the-other is called upon, deeper than the evocation of any images, a responsibility in which arise my replies. My co-ordination with the other in language is the expression of commandments received: writing is always prescriptive and ethical, the Word of God which commands and vows me to the other, a holy writing before being sacred text. A word that is disproportionate to the political discourse, extending beyond information – a break, in the being that I am, of my good conscience of being-there. I hear it as my allegiance to the other. It brings into question the 'self-care' that is natural to beings, essential to the *esse* of beings. Consequently, there is a subversion of this *esse*, a dis-inter-es[se]tedness in the etymological sense of the word. A wind of crisis or the spirit, despite the knots of History which are retied after the breaks in which self-care needs justification. Is this implication of ethical responsibility in the strict and almost closed saying of the verse which is formed in language as if I were not the only one speaking when I speak and not already obeying, not the original writing in which God, who has come to the idea, is named in the Said? I am not just political and a merciless realist; but I am not, for all that, just the pure and voiceless interiority of a 'beautiful soul'. My condition – or my un-condition – is my relation to books. It is the very movement-towards-God [*l'à-Dieu*]. Is this an abstract expression? Language and the book that arises and is already read in language is phenomenology, the 'staging' in which the abstract is made concrete.

3 The extra-ordinary structure of the inspired texts of the Holy Scriptures is even more remarkable in that their reader is called upon not only in the good *common* sense of him being open to 'information', but in the inimitable – and logically imperceptible – uniqueness of his person and, as it were, of his own genius. The inevitable particularity of this individual approach to Scripture, like the particularity of every historical moment where the approach is attempted, does not at all signify a lack of objectivity and cannot be denounced as 'subjective' points of view which falsify and limit the truth. The act of reading does not solely concern the knowledge of objects. The truth of revelation, as we have said, also belongs to another spiritual process, and consequently signifies for the self in its non-interchangeable identity. The understanding that this self has of the truth of revelation determines a meaning which, 'in the whole of eternity', could not be attained without it: the irreplaceable part that every person and every moment contribute to the message – or to the prescription itself – which is received and whose wealth is thereby revealed only in the pluralism of persons and generations. This constitutes the foundation of the inestimable or absolute value of every self and all receptivity, in this revelation which is non-transferable, like a responsibility, and is incumbent afresh upon every person and every epoch.

But the contribution of each person and period is confronted with the lessons from everyone else, and from the whole of the past. Hence the way that readings continually refer to origins across history going from pupil to master; hence the discussion in gatherings between colleagues questioning one another from century to century, the whole thing integrating itself as tradition into commented Scripture, and always calling anew for a reading that is both erudite and modern. Hence the commentaries of commentaries, the very structure of the Torah of Israel, reflected even in the typographical feature of the Tractates overladen on all sides and all margins. The participation of him who receives the Revelation to the Work of Him who is revealed in prophecy. This, no doubt, is also what is meant in the verse from Amos 3: 8: 'The Lord God has spoken; who can but prophesy?' The reading of the prophetic text is still to a certain extent prophetic, even if all human beings are not open with the same attentiveness and the same sincerity to the Word which speaks in them. And who, nowadays, embraces tradition?

4 The 'Talmudic Readings' which make up the major part of the present collection – like all those which appeared in my other publications – are modest attempts to participate in the life of Scripture. The *Four Talmudic Readings*, and the five other readings in the volume entitled *From the Sacred to the Holy*, reproduced exclusively the lectures that had been given, over the last few decades, at the conferences of Jewish Intellectuals of France, organized by the French Section of the World Jewish Congress.[2] Amongst the Talmudic texts commented upon in the present collection, however, there is also 'On Religious Language and the Fear of God', an extract of a page from the Talmud with a commentary – dedicated to Paul Ricreur on the occasion of his sixty-fifth birthday – which appeared in French in 1980 in the 13th issue of the American journal *Man and World*. A further commentary, relating to a few lines in the Tractate Makkoth, written in a form which is less usual for me, is part of the study entitled 'On the Jewish Reading of Scriptures'. Published in 1979 in the 144th issue of the Lyon journal *Lumière et vie*, this study has been inserted here under the rubric 'Theologies', following on from that which, under the title 'Talmudic Readings', groups together the rabbinical commentaries produced in my usual format. 'Theologies' includes studies which certainly also refer to Talmudic particulars, but concern, more especially, exegetic methodology,[3] points of doctrine and religious philosophy. 'Theologies' in the plural removes, I hope, any dogmatic pretension from the general idea which this word harbours in my collection. Theologies: the search for a theo-logic, for a rational way of speaking of God.

The pages which open the present work, under the rubric 'Fidelities', recall and co-ordinate the motifs which seem to me to be living in Judaism today, and the memories in which the modern Jew recognizes himself. The article entitled 'Demanding Judaism', which these pages contain, is reprinted from the 5th issue of the journal *Débat*, which appeared in October 1979. Zionism could not be absent from these themes. If the three articles concerning it are placed at the end of the book, they are not, however, its conclusion. The present work attempts in all humility to pick up and update elements of the biblical and rabbinical tradition of Israel, without confining itself to the negation that simplistic and impatient minds – non-Israeli and Israeli – confuse with development and modernity. It does not simply result in the political forms which, at the risk of seeing Judaism disappear body and soul, had to be assumed by the ancient longing for 'Mount Zion [rejoicing]' of Psalm 48, where the 'right hand' of God is 'full of [justice]' and 'the daughters of Judah rejoice, because of [God's] judgements'. Land and Justice, Justice and Joy! Nobody has the intellectual right to speak lightly of this ancientness, and to pronounce it archaic and outdated in the name of some perfunctory ideas. The three studies grouped together under the title 'Zionisms' aim merely to show how the historical work of the State, which it is not possible to do without in the extremely politicized world of our time, a work of courage and labour which claims to be secular, is impregnated in Israel, from the beginning, and progressively, with young thoughts, but thoughts which issue from the Bible; how the continuation and development of this biblical culture showed itself to be inseparable from the temporal ends of the State, and extended beyond these ends. Israel's unrepentant eschatology. However, eschatology possesses a number of styles and genres, and it was the Jewish Bible which probably discovered the one which consists in feeling responsible in the face of the future one hopes for others. Yet ever since the creation, it was to be found in the humanity of man. It cannot be the cause of wars.

But who can ignore all that is lacking in this spiritualization, given the conflict between Israel and the Palestinians or Israel and the Arabs? One can and must think – at times in agreement with the most lucid thinkers from the opposite camp – that it is time to take the heat out of such adversity.

But are passions really nourished from the Holy Scriptures, as certain decidedly secular minds maintain? Are ideas capable of becoming key ideas of peace when they are separated from the Bible and the Koran, in their abstract nakedness? Do they not run the perpetual risk of alienation in the purely political game? Can democracy and the 'rights of man' divorce themselves without danger from their prophetic and ethical depths? The serenity sought for peace is not possible in simple indifference. It is inseparable from the recognition of the other in the love of one's neighbour taught by the Scriptures. Such love can be seen, but on condition, of course, that one does not approach the utopia of books from an antiquated philosophy of certain clichés such as 'pious but ineffectual predication', 'intolerant dogmatism', 'hegemonic monotheism'; on condition that one is at least as modern and philosophical towards utopia as Ernest Bloch the Marxist. Ah, the scandal of the Jews as the chosen people! Is being chosen a scandal of pride and of the will to power, or is it moral conscience itself which, made up of responsibilities that are always urgent and non-transferable, is the first to respond, as if it were the only one to be called?

Can we understand the suffering of others? Nobody could weigh up and compare sufferings which do not have, like the elements of matter, different 'atomic weights'. But can one deny, in the Passion of the Holocaust, the despair of all human sufferings! Can one compare Hegel's 'unhappy consciousness' with a millennial history of outrages and tears, of permanent insecurity and of the shedding of real, warm blood? That is where the concrete cause and real *raison d'être* of Zionism lies, not in any biblical exaltation of hope and domination, nor in an inversion of paranoia into persecution – too new a movement for a very ancient people.

Of course, it is the West, not the Arab world, which bears the responsibility for Auschwitz. Unless one accepts that the responsibility of men cannot be divided, and that all men are responsible for all others. In *Difficult Freedom* I published the following lines, written more than ten years ago:

> What is the suppression of national distinctions if not an indivisible humanity, that is to say, responsible in its entirety for the crimes and misfortunes of the few? ... Are all human relations reducible to the calculations of damages and interest, all problems to the settling of scores? Can anyone amongst mankind wash his hands of all this flesh gone up in smoke? ... The gesture of recognition which would come to Israel from the Arab peoples would no doubt be replied to by a brotherly zeal such that the problem of the refugees will lose its unknown elements.

Today, I will no longer say refugees, but Palestinians. Zionism is not at an end, for all that. It is not finished if Jews and Israelis recognize that if the State of Israel is to exist it needs the recognition of the Arab world and, for Israel, an entrance into the intimacy of this world. But the fundamental idea of political Zionism is not in the misapprehension of this world which, with its vast expanses and immense wealth, knows the plenitude of autonomous political existence. Its inalienable idea is the necessity for the Jewish people, in peace with its neighbours, not to continue being a minority in its political structure. This is not just demanded as the necessary environment of its supra-national and communicable culture – what I call, precisely, historical necessity – in order for the attack and murder of Jews in the world to lose their character of an uncontrollable and unpunished phenomenon. The great –

the greatest – ethical idea of existence for one's neighbour applies unreservedly to *me,* to the individual and the person that I am. An idea that cannot be thought to include demanding the existence of a people of martyrs, whose model many beautiful souls reproach Zionism for distorting.

I think of the last words of the verse from Genesis 30: 30: 'Now when shall I provide for my own household also?' In the biblical context they can mean neither that a self vowed, of itself, to others, is making a simple and sharp claim for its own interests, nor that the essential structure of the self is being denied. I think that in the responsibility for others prescribed by a non-archaic monotheism it reminds us that it should not be forgotten that *my* family and *my* people, despite the possessive pronouns, are my 'others', like strangers, and demand justice and protection. The love of the other – the love of one's neighbour. Those near to me are also my neighbours.

September, 1981

FIDELITIES

1
Demanding Judaism

Religion, independently of the metaphysical and eschatological positions expressed or implied in the discourses and rituals which represent it, can, of course, also express or support certain social structures. It can justify the particular interests of dominant groups and serve as an ideology in which their members acquire a good conscience necessary to their domination and to their thought as right-thinking people. Like other denominations, the Jewish religion is probably able, to a certain extent, to lend itself to the needs of the privileged class to which Jews can adhere in contemporary Western society, or which some of them were able to constitute even in the heart of the communities of the past which were separated and excluded, and always threatened. It is no less evident, for all this, that the religion to which the privileges possible in a ghetto would have been attached was the very pretext for enclosure, exclusion and an arbitrary rule which spared no one; and that – admitted late to what is acceptable as the condition of reality – Jewish society in our time, even in its allegedly satisfied middle classes, retains a feeling of uncertainty and instability. The Passion that is called 'Holocaust', and the whole past of trials whose memories this sacrifice will have forever updated, project on to the future the shadow of a question mark. Nothing in this religion of survivors resembles less the good conscience and security of an established order.

Of course, no religion can be exhausted in canons of conformism, domination and economic establishment. But it is probably the distinctive feature of the Jewish people to live and endure, already in its exceptional history and in the precariousness of its condition and dwelling on earth, the incompletion of a world experienced from the irreducible and urgent demand for justice which is its actual religious message. The crudeness of the world, if one may say so, of which Judaism is not only the conscience, but also the testimony, that is to say, the martyrdom; the cruelty where the burning of *my* suffering and the anguish of *my* death were able to be transfigured into the dread and concern for the *other man.* As if Jewish destiny were a crack in the shell of imperturbable being and the awakening to an insomnia in which the inhuman is no longer covered up and hidden by the political necessities which it shapes, and no longer excused by their universality. As a prophetic moment of human reason where every man – and all of man – end up refinding one another, Judaism would not mean simply a nationality, a species in a type and a contingency of History. Judaism, rather, is a rupture of the natural and the historical that are constantly reconstituted and, thus, a Revelation which is always forgotten. It is written and it becomes Bible, but the revelation is also continued; it is produced by way of Israel: the destiny of a people that is jostled and jostles through its daily life that which, in this life, is content with its natural or 'historical' meaning. A thought which precociously and untiringly denounces the cruel, excesses of power, and all arbitrary rule.

Even if it is understood as a system of beliefs and rituals by 'objective observers', Judaism has not changed much through the millennia and the planetary space of its 'dispersion', despite the absence of all central authority and all structuring which would have intentionally assured it unity and taken care of its permanence. An apparent conservatism which, in its constancy, expresses above all the obstinate negation of a political and social order which remains without regard for the weak, and without pity for the vanquished, and taking place, as a universal and inexorable History, in an apparently unsaved world – Judaism's original dissidence, a stiff-necked people with ulterior motives, resisting the pure force of things, and with the ability to disturb. The trauma of the 'bondage in the land of Egypt' which marks the Bible and the liturgy of Judaism would belong to the very humanity of the Jew and of the Jew in every man who, a freed slave, would be very similar to the proletarian, the stranger and the persecuted. By incessantly recalling this founding fact – or this myth – does not Scripture go so far as to make, of the inconvertible demand for justice, the equivalent of the spirituality of the Spirit and the proximity of God? Is this not the original circumstance in which this extraordinary word emerges and where, at least, one has it on the tip of one's tongue?

Perhaps a text, Isaiah 58, the character of which, significant for Judaism, is underlined by its central place in the liturgy of Yom Kippur, which is the pinnacle of the Jewish liturgical year, will permit us to illustrate this equivalence: 'Why have we fasted, and thou seest it not? Why have we humbled ourselves, and thou takest no knowledge of it?' So ask, in this prophetic passage of verse 3, the 'pious souls' who are already probably refined enough spiritually to solicit, by affliction and in humility, not the accomplishment of some vow, but divine proximity. And here, in the mouth of the prophet, comes the Lord's first reply: the proximity sought is not compatible with the pure and simple continuation of economic life, with all the conflicting movements which accompany it, brutality, hatreds, domination, perfidy:

> Behold, in the day of your fast you seek your own pleasure, and oppress all your workers. Behold, you fast only to quarrel and to fight and to hit with wicked fist. Fasting like yours this day will not make your voice to be heard on high. Is such the fast that I choose, a day for a man to humble himself? Is it to bow down his head like a rush, and to spread sackcloth and ashes under him? Will you call this a fast, and a day acceptable to the Lord?

Certainly, no religion excludes the ethical. Each one invokes it, but tends also to place what is specifically religious above it, and does not hesitate to 'liberate' the religious from moral obligations. Think of Kierkegaard. On the other hand, what we are told by the rest of this prophetic text is that the religious is at its zenith in the ethical movement towards the other man; that the very proximity of God is inseparable from the ethical transformation of the social, and – notably and more specifically – that it coincides with the disappearance of servitude and domination in the very structure of the social: 'Is not this the fast that I choose: to loose the bonds of wickedness, to undo the thongs of the yoke, to let the oppressed go free, and to break every yoke? . . .' The transformation of the very social being of society! But, as if the expression still had something impersonal about it, as if a solution that we would call 'bureaucratic' threatened to turn the original culmination of the ethical into its contrary, the prophet adds what is possible only in a personal relation with the other: 'Is it not to share your bread with the hungry, and bring the homeless poor into your house; when you see the naked, to cover him, and not to hide yourself from your own flesh?' An admirable ending in which the other is recognized not in the appeal of his face but in the nakedness and misery of his flesh!

From this point onwards, it is the accomplishment of the ethical which accomplishes the religious and, as it were, a change of plan in being:

> Then shall your light break forth like the dawn, and your healing shall spring up speedily; your righteousness shall go before you, the glory of the Lord shall be your rear guard. Then you shall call, and the Lord will answer; you shall cry, and he will say, Here I am.

Hence, perhaps, a feeling which certainly cannot be inscribed within a theological formula and 'does not hold' theoretically, but which marks the religiosity of Israel: the feeling that its destiny, the Passion of Israel, from the bondage in the land of Egypt to Auschwitz in Poland, its holy History, is not only that of a meeting between man and the Absolute, and of a faithfulness; but that, if one dare say so, it is constitutive of the very existence of God. Thought for itself, this existence remains as abstract as the conclusion, which is always problematic, of some syllogism or a more complex and more modern theorem of the proof of God's existence. An abstract idea that no negative theology or hyperbolical proposition can manage to fill with meaning. As if the meaning of this existence, the meaning of the verb 'to be' when applied to God, refused to let itself be explained, formulated or understood, or even approached outside holy History, through its contradictions, its declines and rises, sacrifices and doubts, fidelities and denials. As if the history of Israel were the 'divine comedy' or the 'divine ontology' itself; as if the trials of the just, capable, despite their weaknesses, of being faithful unto death, were a lived experience stronger than the death which denies it, a concrete experience or even the event of divine eternity, belonging to the semiotics of the word God or, as Jews say of their brothers who die for the Invisible, to the sanctification of the Name. Not that this destiny, Passion and History 'finally' provide the proof of God's existence which the philosophers lacked. Rather, they are the spreading out of this very existence, a concrete spreading out right into the Diaspora where, according to an enigmatic saying by the Talmudic scholars, God followed Israel.

It is justifiable to think that this modality of Jewish religiosity – whose metaphysical validity we do not intend to support or, of course, to contest here – explains, for the most part, the actual way in which Judaism concerns Jewish men, the paradoxical forms in which, in contemporary

Jewish society, it is still claimed or in which it imposes itself, and the difficulty that can be experienced in interpreting or classifying these ways of concerning or imposing.

At the heart – or in the margin – of the human groups who recognize themselves or who are recognized or who seek or flee from themselves as Jews, there are the strongly characterized – that is, orthodox – collectivities, where Judaism is felt as the obedience to God's will. For these communities of strict observance, the Torah, as it is interpreted in the monumental work of the Talmud,[1] is the highest expression of this will. Judaism is consequently lived as a rigorous ritualism, penetrating and regulating all the events and deeds of daily life. As the accomplishment of prescriptions and the respect for the interdicts in the Torah, and the study of this Torah within the perspectives opened up by the Talmud, life in its entirety would be liturgy and cult where an eminent value is attached to study. A difficult life, no doubt, for men who, in our time, cannot escape the material necessities of modernity. But there is nothing resembling a 'yoke of the Law'. Obedience to prescriptions, in the material acts that they entail, is fervour. It is as if the ritual acts prolonged the states of mind expressing and incarnating their interior plenitude, and were to the piety of obedience what the smile is to benevolence, the handshake to friendship and the caress to affection.

Outside the structure of these communities, orthodoxy is less strict. In our time Jewish people do not confess, in their huge majority, the ultra-orthodoxy that has just been described. Its beliefs, symbols, practices and texts have often been transformed into cultural contents: lifestyle, custom, literature. At least they are interpreted or confessed in good faith as such by those who adhere to them. For hundreds of thousands of Israelites assimilated to surrounding civilizations and to nations of the Diaspora, Judaism no longer even claims to be a cultural content. In the total lack of knowledge of its sources and foundations, and in a way of life that is totally foreign to that of orthodox communities, Judaism is reduced to vague memories of memories, and to a few words that have lost their original meaning and, in any case, their grammatical form as Hebraic words. Empty wrappings of musty perfumes. But in the essential hours of Jewish destiny – which all carry, in the years that we are living, the reflection of the flames of the Holocaust, and where the hopes created by the State of Israel are more and more deafened by the cries of its detractors – in these essential hours, for men who have lost all links which count socially with the Jewish people and its culture, these vestiges fill up with an overflowing meaning, one that is felt as the irresistible call to solidarity and to responsibilities, but also as election. All of this bears witness, simultaneously, to the exceptional depth in which, in human consciousness, holy History is played out, this 'Divine Comedy', this Passion of Israel and the incomparable strength of rituals which, in the material of the world, are its inscription, commandment and memory.

In the vast strata of Jewish society, even for those who oppose one another, and fight or ignore the ultra-orthodox communities, Jewish ritual, even if it is diffuse, retains strange virtues in continuing Israel and its supernatural adventure led in the form of daily life. These old practical prescriptions are a detour irritating for some, but unavoidable – made by the vocation of human fraternity and justice which, in the kerygma of Israel, certainly seduces fine minds more easily. Human fraternity and the thirst for justice on earth have not, in fact, in contemporary Jewish society, been 'subjective' feelings. Rather, they determined both the revolutionary commitments of a youth formed in the homes of Jewish life in Eastern Europe which it rejected for socialism, and the early dissidence in the resistance to Stalinist perversion and its aftermath; and the Zionist zeal which has never been separable – including within the Jewish State beleaguered since its resurrection – from the universal Messianic dream, nor from the subversion of the prophetic discourse defying kings and lords, and awakening men numbed by History to an order without victories or hegemonies, without wars or cruelties. An awakening that is sober enough not to be fooled by the crimes committed in the name of freedom, revolution and even love.

But it is the Torah, and the liturgical significance it confers on the material acts of life outside their natural finality, which is the surest safeguard and most faithful memory of Israel's ethics. And only the existence of the State of Israel ensures a similar function today. There is a mysterious energy in these antiquated gestures, but such is the experience of Israel and probably one of the meanings of the Talmudic saying which associates the Torah and the liturgical service with the 'good works' on which the universe would rest, and which, when listing these 'three things' that give stability to the real, mentions the Torah and the liturgy before the good works.

Despite everything that the medieval Jewish philosophers, who themselves were also disciples of the Greeks, thought of the Jewish faith whose credo they never ceased formulating and reformulating, one may wonder whether the major role of ritual practice, of obedience to the commandments, leaves as much room in Jewish spirituality as elsewhere for actual faith, for the belief which adheres to metaphysical propositions which are knowledge, whether it be less certain or more exalting in faith than in natural light. In this spirituality – and this, it should be stressed, is primordial – there is a certain passivity of belonging, the consciousness of an indisputable participation – and, in some way, prior to initiative – in the responsibilities of a holy History. A belonging despite oneself, as if one were being seized hold of. To have been seized 'by a lock' of one's hair, like the prophet in Ezekiel 8: 3! Not let go of even when the commandments are forgotten, or no longer heard, or rejected. The piety of non-believers! A seizing which, in the insult of anti-Semitism, shows itself when it resurfaces like a glory from the depth of the humiliation experienced. A consciousness of irremissible responsibilities that malevolence interprets as the pride of a people aspiring to be the chosen ones, or of some miserable person aspiring to be a slave. Admittedly, this is a paradoxical responsibility in the irremissible. But a paradox that is fundamental to the Bible. God holds you without letting you go, but without enslaving you: a relation in which, despite the subordination it formally outlines, the difficult freedom of man arises. It is even for this reason that God is God and not some logical term, and that the biblical ontology of the person departs from the subjectivity of the idealist subject. Is not the concrete nature of this heteronomy assuring an autonomy the occasion to ask whether the content of human lived experience is not able to break the formal quality of the purely theoretical? Does not the coming of the spiritual occur in this break, and is it not also in this that 'man goes infinitely beyond man'?

We do not intend here to decide on good philosophy. Yet in order to clarify the conception that has just been expounded, we do permit ourselves to resort to the collection of a few quotations. They will thus provide the opportunity to end by giving the reader an idea of the style assumed by a *sui generis* hermeneutics similar to the homily which is not only a type of liturgy, but also an essential form of human thought, and which is familiar to Jewish exegesis. Such are the unusual paths of the rational.

The recommendations given towards the end of Leviticus Chapter 25, with a view to assuring the redemption 'of your brethren reduced to bondage', find their justification in verse 55, which closes the chapter: 'For to me the people of Israel are servants; they are my servants whom I

9

brought forth out of the land of Egypt: I am the Lord your God'. As if the human self could signify the possibility of a belonging that is not alienating, and be exalted to freedom through this very subjection. And, in effect, according to the legislation of the Pentateuch (Exodus 21: 5–6), the slave who, for love of his master, renounces the freedom that is due to him, 'in the seventh [year]', '[shall be brought] before [the court]' and will have 'his ear [bored] through with an awl'. Commenting on this strange arrangement, the Talmud (Tractate Kiddushin 22b) notes its symbolic significance: mark for ever with infamy an ear that will have been capable of remaining deaf to the good news of verse 55 in Leviticus Chapter 25, in which, at the foot of Sinai, the end of the enslavement of man by man is announced. The man who, despite the Revelation, seeks a human master for himself, is not worthy of serving God – in other words, is not worthy of his freedom.

And the Tractate Baba Mezia (10b) extends this principle of freedom conditioned by allegiance to the Most High, to the daily problem of the rights of the day labourer. As a servant of God, he retains with regard to his employer an independence that even his contract cannot alienate; and he can, in certain circumstances, leave his master right in the middle of the day's work.

TALMUDIC READINGS

2
Model of the West
(Tractate Menahoth 99b–100a)

MISHNAH.[1] There were two tables inside the porch at the entrance of the House, the one of marble and the other of gold. On the table of marble they laid the Shewbread when it was brought in, and on the table of gold they laid the Shewbread when it was brought out, since what is holy we must raise (in honour) but not bring down. And within (the Sanctuary) was a table of gold whereon the Shewbread lay continually. Four priests entered, two bearing the two rows (of the Shewbread) in their hands and two bearing the two dishes (of frankincense) in their hands; and four went in before them, two to take away the two rows (of the Shewbread) and two to take away the two dishes (of frankincense). Those who brought them in stood at the North side with their faces to the South, and those who took them away stood at the South side with their faces to the North. These withdrew (the old) and the others laid down (the new), the handbreadth of the one being by the side of the handbreadth of the other, for it is written, *before me continually* (Exodus 25: 30). R. Jose says, even if these (first) took away (the old) and the others laid down (the new later on), this too fulfils the requirement of 'continually'. They went and laid (the old bread) on the table of gold that was in the porch. The dishes (of frankincense) were then burnt and the cakes were distributed among the priests. If the Day of Atonement fell on a Sabbath the cakes were distributed in the evening. If it fell on a Friday the he-goat of the Day of Atonement was consumed in the evening. The Babylonian (priests) used to eat it raw for they were not fastidious.

GEMARA. It was taught [a *baraitha*[2]]: R. Jose says, Even if the old (Shewbread) was taken away in the morning and the new was set down in the evening there is no harm. How then am I to explain the verse, *'before me continually'*? (It teaches that) the table should not remain overnight without bread.

R. Ammi said, From these words of R. Jose we learn that even though a man learns but one chapter in the morning and one chapter in the evening he has thereby fulfilled the precept of *'This book of the law shall not depart out of thy mouth'* (Joshua 1: 8). R. Johanan said in the name of R. Simeon b. Yohai, Even though a man but reads the *Shema* morning and evening he has thereby fulfilled the precept of *'(This book of the law) shall not depart'*. It is forbidden, however, to say this in the presence of *'am ha-arez* [an uncultured man]. But Raba said, It is a meritorious act [a *mitzvah*] to say it in the presence of *'am ha-arez*. – Ben Damah the son of R. Ishmael's sister once asked R. Ishmael, May one such as I who have studied the whole of the Torah learn Greek wisdom? He [R. Ishmael] thereupon read to him the following verse, *This book of the law shall not depart out of thy mouth, but thou shalt meditate therein day and night* (Joshua 1: 8). Go then and find a time that is neither day nor night and learn then Greek wisdom. This, however, is at variance with the view of R. Samuel b. Nahmani. For R. Samuel b. Nahmani said in the name of R. Jonathan, This verse is neither duty nor command but a blessing. For when the Holy One, blessed be He, saw that the words of the Torah were most precious to Joshua, as it is written, *His minister Joshua, the son of Nun, a young man, departed not out of the tent* (Exodus 33: 11), He said to him, 'Joshua, since the words of the Torah are so precious to thee, (I assure thee,) *"this book of the law shall not depart out of thy mouth"* (Joshua 1: 8)!'

A Tanna of the School of R. Ishmael taught: The words of the Torah should not be unto thee as a debt, neither art thou at liberty to desist from it.

Hezekiah said, What is the meaning of the verse, *Yea, He hath allured thee out of the mouth of straits into a broad place, where there is no straitness [and that which is set on thy table is full of fatness]* (Job 36: 16)? Come and see that the manner of the Holy One, blessed be He, is not like that (of men) of flesh and blood. A man of flesh and blood allures another out of the ways of life into the ways of death; but the Holy One, blessed be He, allures man out of the ways of death into the ways of life, as it is written, *'Yea, [I] have allured thee out of the mouth of straits'*[3] (Job 36: 16), that is, out of Gehenna [hell], whose mouth [entrance] is narrow so that its smoke is stored up within it. And lest you say that as its mouth [entrance] is narrow so the whole (of Gehenna) is narrow, the text therefore states (for the *Tofet* has long since been ready; it too has been laid out), *Deep and large* (Isaiah 30: 33). And lest you say that it is not made ready for a king, the text therefore states, *Yea, for the king it is prepared* (Isaiah 30: 33). And lest you say that there is no wood in it, the text therefore states, *The pile thereof is fire and much wood* (Isaiah 30: 33). And lest you say that this is the sole reward (of the Torah), the text therefore states, *And that which is set on thy table is full of fatness.*

> Rabbah b. Bar Hanah said in the name of R. Johanan, They were not Babylonians but Alexandrians, but because [they] hated the Babylonians they called (the Alexandrians) by the name of Babylonians.
> It was likewise taught [a *baraitha*]: R. Jose says, They were not Babylonians but Alexandrians, but because [they] hated the Babylonians they called (the Alexandrians) by the name of Babylonians. Said to him R. Judah, May your mind be at ease for you have set mine at ease.

Before beginning I must explain to my listeners my intentions and the nature of the Talmudic text whose commentary I am undertaking. I have four points to make clear.

– In front of a room in which I recognize so many people with such vast Talmudic knowledge, I am anxious to fix the limits of my aims. The public for whom I am speaking is admittedly cultivated, but it is a wide one, and no doubt I will have to make references and preliminaries which might seem superfluous to those who are familiar with the Talmudic Tractates.
– I am not claiming in this lesson to be able to make the whole of the Tractates vibrate in the text studied, as is demanded and as is natural in advanced study of the Talmud.
– My subject of enquiry consists in questioning the text, whose polysemy is evident and whose dimensions are multiple, in relation to the particular theme of our conference.
– Finally, what I am setting out to attempt to do consists, as usual, in extricating the unity of the various themes that can be distinguished in the passage looked at and whose diversity cannot but strike you on the

15

first reading of the translation in your hands. What I shall principally attempt to do is to seek out the coherence of the text and the harmony of the various themes evoked.

There will, then, be a lot of preliminaries. The immediate meaning of the text's particulars must first be explained. The text refers to two biblical passages which I shall read to you without quoting them in full: Exodus 25: 23–30 and Leviticus 24: 5–9.

I shall start with Leviticus – the logical order of the subject matter is more important than the 'chronological' order of the texts – which speaks of the liturgical service in the desert sanctuary. It mentions: (1) the making of the bread to be set down every Sabbath and exposed until the following Sabbath, which is called in the English translation 'Shew-bread';[4] (2) the setting down of this bread on a table 'before the Lord continually' and the eating of it every Sabbath by the pontiffs or priests, by the *cohanim*:

> And you shall take fine flour, and bake twelve cakes of it; two tenths of an ephah shall be in each cake. And you shall set them in two rows, six in a row, upon the table of pure gold. And you shall put pure frankincense with each row, that it may go with the bread as a memorial portion to be offered by fire to the Lord. Every Sabbath day [one] shall set it in order before the Lord continually on behalf of the people of Israel as a covenant for ever. And [this bread] shall be for Aaron and his sons, and they shall eat it in a holy place, since it is for him a most holy portion out of the offerings by fire to the Lord, a perpetual due.

It is the Lord's portion: the bread is entirely distributed and eaten by the *cohanim*.

The text from Exodus 25: 23–30 speaks of the making of the table which is to have the bread placed on it; this will introduce us directly into our Talmudic text, which begins by referring to a table:

> And you shall make a table of acacia wood; two cubits shall be its length, a cubit its breadth, and a cubit and a half its height. You shall overlay it with pure gold, and make a moulding of gold around it. And you shall make around it a frame a handbreadth wide, and a moulding of gold around the frame.

It concerns the same frame mentioned in the previous verse. Then the various utensils to be prepared are enumerated. And the final verse says: 'And you shall set the bread of the Presence on the table before me [continually]'. One has therefore to keep in mind the idea of a liturgical institution; of cakes, or bread, which are placed every Sabbath in the Temple and eaten after they have lain there for a week (this is old bread!) by the priests; the existence of a table covered in gold in the Temple itself where this bread is exposed; not forgetting the frame of gold mentioned in two verses; finally, the position of the bread on the table, continually before the Lord – 'before me [continually]', says the text.

It is the meaning of permanence, or the various models according to which this permanence is thought in our Talmudic text, that seemed to me to justify the dedication of this rabbinical page to the subject of our conference concerning 'the model of the West'. No doubt ironically. But in the theme of this conference the position of Israel *vis-à-vis* the modern world into which the West throws itself is of great interest to us. It is through the way they experience and are affected by time, the ultimate difference, that we can still, perhaps, distinguish brotherly humanities amongst which we rank Israel and the West.

What does permanence signify? What does the 'always' signify? How can the always have signification? How does Israel think the significance of the always? These are the questions we would like to ask.

Faced with the 'historical meaning' which dominates modernity, the meaning of becoming which, for the Westerner, certainly carries the real to its conclusion, but a conclusion which is unceasingly deferred in the false Messianisms of modern times (times, however, which are defined as times of conclusions); faced with the 'historical meaning' which thus calls into question, relativizes and devalues every moment or which, foreseeing a supra-temporal eternity of ideal, yet, in reality, incomparable relations, is capable of a mathematically perfect science in a badly made or un-made world; faced with all this historicism, does not Israel attach itself to an 'always' – in other words, to a permanence in time, to a time held by moments of holiness, by the way in which they have a meaning or are 'so close to the goal' – and where not one of these moments is lost, or to be lost, but they are all to be deepened, that is to say, sublimated? And instead of remaining word, a purely theoretical view or doctrinal affirmation, or some sort of coexistence of moments of time passing, do not this predilection and this signification of the always call for a whole structuring of concrete human reality and a whole orientation of social and intellectual life – perhaps justice itself – which would render only such a signification possible and significant?

But before entering into such a serious debate, I still owe an explanation to the critical minds present in this room, who might precisely be surprised that such serious and topical problems are being treated in the context of bread and tables (the fantasies of rabbis), which have long since disappeared!

I would like, in fact, to recall what, according to rabbinical tradition, the significance is, notably, of the ritual of the Shewbread and the table on which it remains exposed, and the thoughts into which such a ritual introduces us. As a point of departure, let us take a detail which I have already emphasized. In my quotation from Exodus 25, there was a golden frame around the table which can also be translated as 'crown'. Whether we read it as a frame or as a crown, the text of Exodus indicates yet one more: a crown or frame on the altar, and another on the Holy Ark of the sanctuary. I do not know if the furnishings of the sanctuary are present in your mind. There are five holy objects: the Ark, the table, the lampstand, the golden altar for the offerings of frankincense and the bronze altar in the court in front of the entrance. Well, the Ark, the bronze altar and the table have a frame. The *Midrash* – the parabolic exegesis of the Rabbis – would see in these crowns or frames symbols of sovereignty. The Tractate Aboth, in particular, says that there are three crowns, or three modes of sovereignty: the sovereignty of the priesthood or of the liturgy evoked by the frame of the altar; the sovereignty of the king or of political power symbolized by the frame of the table; and the sovereignty which is the highest of all, at the disposal of everyone and anyone who wishes to make the effort to take it: the sovereignty of the Torah, which is the frame of the Holy Ark. (In the Tractate Aboth, yet a fourth crown is mentioned: the crown of good reputation, which is, it seems, the highest of all, but it does not enter into our text.)

The crown of the table is thus the royal crown. The king is he who keeps open house; he who feeds men. The table on which the bread is exposed before the Lord symbolizes the permanent thought that political power – that is to say, the king, that is, David, that is, his descendant, that is, the Messiah – is vowed to men's hunger ... Not to the end of times, to the hunger of hungry men; kingship in Israel is always Joseph feeding the people. To think of men's hunger is the first function of politics.

That political power should be thought of from the point of view of men's hunger is rather remarkable. The bread in question, *lechem hapanim,* is translated as 'Shewbread'. Translating these words literally, one should say: 'bread of faces'. Why 'bread of faces'? Rashi says: bread which has two faces because of the shape in which it is baked, these faces being turned towards the two sides of the sanctuary. According to Ibn Ezra – who is probably less pious than Rashi, but has also said some extraordinary things – 'bread of faces' is the bread which is always before the face of God. I think the two interpretations are not dissimilar. What should bread before the eyes of God do, if not look at men? What other purpose should it have, if not to feed men? The horizontal direction of the look is the completion of the look descending from above. I know that 'horizontal' and 'vertical' are terms which are currently being discussed in the search for the meaning of the religious. The two directions, I believe, orientate the same movement. That in all these symbols there should exist the very problem of the relation between the Spirit and the food of men, that they should recall the political character of the problem which, despite the progress of thought and modern technology, the United Nations Organization and Unesco, Western politics has not managed to resolve, perhaps gives some topicality to the evocation of the table and the bread of faces. Let us also emphasize that the bread in question is not originally communion bread; it is first and foremost the bread of the starving, and only by being such is it, perhaps, communion bread. Is there agreement or discrepancy between the West's preoccupation with eating and the religious sensibility of Judaism inscribed in the structure of the sanctuary – that is, perhaps, inscribed in a deep innermost recess of the Jewish soul? I do not know. It is very similar, yet very different.

Let us end this preliminary section by pointing out that the two other sovereignties, those of the liturgy and that of the Torah, are equally going to appear in our text as the centres of permanence. From the table of the bread of faces we shall indeed move on to the table of study, to the Torah, to the 'permanence' of the Torah within us, which must not leave our mouths, just as the bread of faces must not leave the table of the sanctuary. We shall move on to the Torah in its unity with the liturgy, which is perhaps still essential in the structure of Judaism. But I am jumping ahead.

The first and the oldest part of the Talmudic text, in the *Mishnah,* seems at first glance just to give the description of a ceremony. The *Mishnah* describes the ceremony of the weekly changing of the Shewbread; on the day of the Sabbath, the old bread is removed and the new bread is brought in. But the *Mishnah,* in describing the ceremony of the Temple of Jerusalem, adds to the one table provided for in the Bible – only one table figures in the text from Exodus which I read, and it was placed inside the desert sanctuary – two tables which are supposedly found in a porch or interior space within the boundary of the sanctuary but outside the sanctuary itself. Let us read the first lines of the text:

> There were two tables inside the porch at the entrance of the House, the one of marble and the other of gold. On the table of marble they laid the Shewbread when it was brought in, and on the table of gold they laid the Shewbread when it was brought out, since what is holy we must raise (in honour) but not bring down. And within (the Sanctuary) was a table of gold whereon the Shewbread lay continually.

So there are three tables: one of marble at the door where the fresh bread is placed, and one of gold where the bread is put that has just been taken away from the table of gold situated inside the sanctuary. ... And why this order of marble, gold and gold? 'Since what is holy we must raise (in honour) but not bring down.' The bread was first on a marble table, then it was put on the table of gold which is inside the sanctuary: as Shewbread, holy bread, it has just been raised from marble to gold; the bread on the table of gold is removed to be taken out of the sanctuary; will it be placed on a table of marble? But it would thus be brought down. As Shewbread, holy bread, there must at least be a table of gold outside for it. It is in this way, in our opinion, that the principle which commands the becoming in the becoming worthy is affirmed. Admittedly, the true values are also changing; but they are not falling in value: the principle of their change is one of elevation. The principle of the permanence of the values in succession is their elevation. It is a rule of conduct symbolized by rituals. For example, at Hanukkah, must the lights of the lampstands be lit in increasing or decreasing progression? This is discussed by the school of Shammai and the school of Hillel. The school of Hillel, advocating increasing progression, has become *Halakhah,* for 'what is holy we must raise (in honour) but not bring down'.

A table of marble, a table of gold and a table of gold. It is a rule of teaching: never vulgarize what has been raised, always exalt it, always draw what can be sublimated from an ageing value. Is this a reactionary principle of non-dispute? Not at all! The pedagogical recommendation supposes an axiology of true values and of a holy history. The elevation is the proper signification of a value's duration. A duration which never wears out, a duration which is an opening out. Higher and higher, irreversibly. Is this not an interpretation of profound temporality, or of the very diachrony of time? The striving of the holy towards the holier, the 'more' already working at the heart of the 'less'. A structure of valuing which is very different from that which we give to valuing in our daily existence, and in our daily or non-daily philosophy. More exactly, perhaps, there is a distinction to be made between relative value and holy values which are defined precisely by this exaltation, by this transition from the good to the better; the life of value is a holy history. . . . Not only the discovery of history, about which Mr Serres spoke admirably the day before yesterday, but a certain elevation of history. Everything in history is not true history; everything does not count as history. Every moment counts, but everything is not a moment. Hence the Jewish independence concerning events that others take for history. The West professes the historical relativity of values and their questioning, but perhaps it takes every moment seriously, calls them all historical too quickly, and leaves this history the right both to judge the values and to sink into relativity. Hence the incessant re-evaluation of values, an incessant collapse of values, an incessant genealogy of morals. A history without permanence or a history without holiness.

The Jew, like the Westerner, is certainly without any illusion as to the 'relativity of certain values', but he makes a distinction precisely between values and holiness. The permanence of Israel is in this awareness of holiness which is exalted and in this possibility of judging history; this 'eternity' of Israel is not a privilege but a human possibility, and it is not unimportant that this temporality of holiness, this holiness as life, is said not in connection with some ethereal spirituality, with what is called in discourses 'spirit', but on the occasion of the bread of men. Let us read what follows: 'And within (the Sanctuary) was a table of gold whereon the Shewbread lay continually. Four priests entered, two bearing the two rows (of the Shewbread) in their hands . . .' The ceremony is described in detail:

> . . . two bearing the two rows (of the Shewbread) in their hands and two bearing the two dishes (of frankincense) in their hands; and four went in before them, two to take away the two rows (of the Shewbread) and two to take away the two dishes (of frankincense).

> Those who brought them in stood at the North side with their faces to the South, and those who took them away stood at the South side with their faces to the North. These withdrew (the old) and the others laid down (the new), the handbreadth of the one being by the side of the handbreadth of the other.

Consequently, there was no moment when the table was uncovered.

> For it is written, *before me continually* (Exodus 25: 30). R. Jose says, even if these (first) took away (the old) and the others laid down (the new later on), this too fulfils the requirement of 'continually'. They went and laid (the old bread) on the table of gold that was in the porch. The dishes (of frankincense) were then burnt and the cakes were distributed among the priests. If the Day of Atonement fell on a Sabbath the cakes were distributed in the evening.

The elevation of holiness continues: the marble, the gold, and the mouths of the priests – the mouth of the eater. An elevation to eating. The bread is eaten entirely by the priests, God simply being evoked by the frankincense which is burned. Nothing is put aside for the altar. The biblical text said that the frankincense will serve as a memorial. God will be thought of, and for this memory, there will be the frankincense, but the bread here will belong entirely to the men who eat it. 'Great is the act of eating', says R. Johanan; great is the act of eating for the person – one's neighbour – who is hungry. But does not the Atonement opportunely mentioned here by the *Mishnah* come and evoke a beyond the hunger that has been satisfied?

Let us now pay attention to the meaning of the permanence described in these lines of the *Mishnah,* to which R. Jose seems opposed at the beginning of the *Gemara.* The 'always' of the *Mishnah* is the continuity of time: a time without interruption; the bread exposed before God's eyes does not leave this table empty for a moment; but, curiously, a certain type of interpersonal relation is presupposed here in order to ensure this continuity. The faces – remember this detail of the text – are turned towards one another. The continuity is ensured by a movement of collaboration, but between collaborators who know and look at one another. This is the small society whose interpersonal relations constitute men's 'real presence' to one another. It is not society at large, where men live in anonymity.

But it is probably this that explains R. Jose's intervention at the beginning of the *Gemara*. This is what he adds to the *Mishnah*: permanence does not consist just in the continuity of time ensured by the face-to-face of men, by men showing their faces and seeking the face of their neighbour. The permanence of the human is ensured by the solidarity constituted around a communal work; by the same task being accomplished without the collaborators knowing or meeting one another. Much more wondrous is the brotherhood of men where the brothers are not even acquainted!

> If the Day of Atonement fell on a Sabbath the cakes were distributed in the evening. If it fell on a Friday the he-goat of the Day of Atonement was consumed in the evening. The Babylonian (priests) used to eat it raw for they were not fastidious.

I have already explained this evocation of Atonement in the account of the elevation of holy things. I am saying nothing about the male goat of Atonement. I shall say a word about that at the end. I shall go on to the *Gemara*.

'It was taught [a *baraitha*]' – that is to say, a *Mishnah* which has not entered into Rabbi Judah haNasi's collection –

> R. Jose says, Even if the old (Shewbread) was taken away in the morning and the new was set down in the evening there is no harm. How then am I to explain the verse, *'before me continually'*? (It teaches that) the table should not remain overnight without bread.

This *baraitha*, with which the *Gemara* begins, introduces us to R. Jose's argument which I have already commented upon, but also to the condition that R. Jose puts on his argument. There is permanence without temporal continuity provided that, of a night, there is no empty table. There is permanence, therefore, in a collaboration whose functions are organized, even if the collaborators were not to meet one another. Why the importance attributed to the night? What is feared of a night? I think that the night is the critical moment of great collectivities founded on the organization of functions rather than on personal contacts. At night, everyone goes home. It is private life. Disintegration and individualism. It is the night which threatens with disintegration and anarchy the large society built on economic solidarity, the society of our

23

great States, built, precisely, on economic solidarity – the society of our great modern States.

Let us read what follows:

> R. Ammi said, From these words of R. Jose we learn that even though a man learns but one chapter in the morning and one chapter in the evening he has thereby fulfilled the precept of '*This book of the law shall not depart out of thy mouth*' (Joshua 1: 8).

R. Ammi says: 'From the position adopted by R. Jose as to the commandment relating to the permanence of the bread on the table of the sanctuary, are we to draw a conclusion as to the commandment relating to the permanence of the Torah in the mouth of the Israelite? Does an analogy exist between the permanence of the bread on the table and the permanence of the Torah that "shall not depart out of thy mouth"?' Is reasoning by analogy valid when the order is changed? The Torah is not bread. Its crown is different. It is within reach of whomsoever wants it. The royal crown belongs to David and his descendants; the liturgy is the domain of Aaron and his descendants; the crown of the Torah belongs to him who devotes himself to its study – study, the daily exercise of the intellect; not intuition, which comes only once. The Torah's crown is within everyone's reach, but at the price of constancy and struggles.

Here, however, a new model of permanence is outlined: neither continuity in time, nor unity around the work of those who may not know one another. The permanence of daily regularity and the permanence of study. Indeed, there is no need here to assure oneself against the night where the members of communities would risk escaping into privacy, where society would dissolve. R. Ammi, while reasoning by R. Jose's analogy, does not, like him, demand a permanence of night. Do the parts of the Torah lead by themselves to the whole of the Torah? We shall see further on that something similar is implied by Raba. Here is an 'always' through study, a continuity of time which is constituted not by the social relations of men united through a work, but by knowledge in the rudiments of the Torah, in the unity of the true.

But in daily regularity which suffices for the study of the Torah, is not this 'always' of study similar to the 'always' of the cult, of the virtue of daily liturgical obligation, which to one doctor of the Talmud seemed to be the highest teaching of the Torah, more important than that of the love of one's neighbour, and which, without liturgical constancy, greatly risks remaining rhetorical? The most sublime verse of the Pentateuch, according to Ben Anas, approved by his master, teaches simply that 'One lamb you shall offer in the morning, and the other lamb you shall offer in the evening'. We are at the point in which liturgy and study are merged, the unique characteristic trait of Israel where intellectual life can become cult and the supreme form of spiritual life. Hence the opinion of R. Johanan: 'R. Johanan said in the name of R. Simeon b. Yohai ...' – R. Simeon b. Yohai is the father of Jewish mysticism –

> Even though a man but reads the *Shema* morning and evening he has thereby fulfilled the precept of *'(This book of the law) shall not depart'*. It is forbidden, however, to say this in the presence of *'am ha-arez* [an uncultured man]. But Raba said, It is a meritorious act [a *mitzvah*] to say it in the presence of *'am ha-arez.*

The twice-daily reading of the *Shema Yisra'el* is part of prayer. According to the rabbinical tradition, this prayer expresses the acceptance of the 'celestial yoke', the submission to the Law. Submission to the Law, permanence of service, acceptance of the ritual which comes between myself and natural instincts. It is an awakening: Hear Israel! But 'Hear Israel' is a text from Scripture. Here is the daily liturgy in its permanence coinciding with the permanence of a truth. It is the teaching of Jewish monotheism at its most rigorous: Elohim-God, the creative power and the principle of justice, and consequently the expansion or outpouring of this power and authority into creature, the Lord-Elohim is but the absolute unity of the Tetragrammaton; no 'difference' comes to affect the unity of the One! It is through daily ritual and truth regularly repeated, a ritual rooted in truth, that the somniferous course of natural life is shaken up. This is the secret of the life of Israel, the secret of its awareness of the 'always': the 'not to sleep', like the Guardian of Israel himself, 'who neither sleeps nor dozes'. It is through the regular return of these sovereign moments – the crown of the Torah being added to the crown of the liturgy – that the dispersion of time is brought back together and retied into a permanence.

But why not say this to the uncultured man? Does R. Johanan think he has taught the 'minimum' with which the uncultured man risks being forever content? Does he fear that ritual and truth, despite their power to awaken, also have 'soporific virtues' for an intelligence lacking in culture? Or, on the other hand, why would there be merit in saying this to the uncultured man? Does Raba have confidence in the dynamic character of ritual and study, and does he mean to give the uncultured man the possibility of making a start? For him too, is holiness, by itself, not always ascending higher?

> Ben Damah the son of R. Ishmael's sister once asked R. Ishmael, May one such as I who have studied the whole of the Torah learn Greek wisdom? He [R. Ishmael] thereupon read to him the following verse, *This book of the law shall not depart out of thy mouth, but thou shalt meditate therein day and night* (Joshua 1: 8). Go then and find a time that is neither day nor night and learn then Greek wisdom.

Does this mean that such an hour does not exist, and that Greek wisdom is being excluded from the Jewish universe? Is it, consequently, a refusal of the model of the West? Is it, on the contrary, an allusion to the hours of dusk, neither day nor night, hours of uncertainties where recourse to Greek wisdom would be possible, perhaps even necessary? An opinion to be considered. It would qualify a whole epoch of Jewish history; and perhaps it would even take into account the ultimate essence of Greek wisdom. This latter is excluded only from the hours where Israel is either master of its difficult wisdom, or blindly subjected to its tradition. It would be necessary in the hours of hesitation, capable as it is of reducing multidimensional questions to the disjunction of yes or no. And does not the seduction exercised on a whole epoch of Jewish history by this rationalism of yes and no measure the degree of our Jewish uncertainties?

But one may also wonder whether the exclusion pronounced by R. Ishmael is not a means of hiding R. Johanan's opinion from Ben Damah, in accordance with the caution he recommends. That Ben Damah should be uncultured will come as a surprise. Does he not know the whole of the Torah? Unless there are learned uncultured people! What is the deep meaning of *'am ha-arez*? He who considers that culture or the Torah has its time and its limits, that the Torah permits itself to be enclosed within a time schedule and that it leaves spare time for Greek wisdom; that there exists a Greek wisdom for the slack periods of holidays and Sundays. That being the case, R. Ishmael reminds an *'am ha-arez* of a permanence of the Torah in the sense of the continuity forbidding all interruption. The latter is unable to understand it in any other way.

But one may wonder, finally, what is meant, in this dialogue between Ben Damah and R. Ishmael, by Greek wisdom. It is surely not through its scientific and artistic splendours, through the clarity of its reasoning, that it can be brought into question. Indeed, it is not certain that Greek wisdom signifies these splendours in the Talmudic texts. Let us compare those texts in which the term appears: it would concern a certain language, that which is spoken at the court of kings; it concerns courtesy and diplomacy; everything that Greek civilization bespeaks of flattery and charm – everything that charms us in the Western model. It probably concerns rhetoric, the 'virtue' of illusion that a certain language possesses; it perhaps concerns what today we call, with distrust, humanism, in its powers to abuse and betray. It concerns the Greek wisdom open to humanist eloquence. It concerns whatever precisely is not mathematical in it (although the perfection of mathematics in an imperfect world has a rhetorical side). Rhetoric is all that is said too beautifully to leave us with what is true. Here is another aspect of it. Sotah 49b writes:

> When the Kings of the Hasmonean house fought one another, Hyrcanus was outside [outside Jerusalem] and Aristobulus within [within Jerusalem]. Each day they [those in Jerusalem] used to let down *denarii* in a basket, and haul up for them (animals for) the continual offerings. An old man there, who was learned in Greek wisdom, spoke with them in Greek, saying, 'As long as they carry on the Temple-service, they will never surrender to you'. On the morrow they let down *denarii* in a basket, and hauled up a pig. When it reached halfway up the wall, it stuck its claws (into the wall) and the land of Israel was shaken over a distance of four hundred parasangs. At that time they [the scholars] declared, 'Cursed be a man who rears pigs and cursed be a man who teaches his son Greek wisdom!'

And the text of Sotah makes it clear that the Greek language is one thing and Greek wisdom another; and it makes an exception for Rabban Gamaliel, to whom it authorizes this wisdom, for 'Rabban Gamaliel ... had close associations with the Government'.

Greek wisdom, therefore, is an opening, but it is also the possibility of speaking through signs which are not universally understood and which, as signs of complicity, thus have the power to betray. Greek wisdom, inasmuch as it is enveloped by ambiguity in a certain language, is thus a weapon of ruse and domination. In philosophy, it is the fact that it is open to sophistry; in science, that it places itself in the service of strength and politics. There would exist in purely human wisdom the power to invert itself into lie and ideology. That is why, in the reply to Ben Damah, the exclusion of Greek wisdom would be radical. Not because it would be knowledge, but because, in purely human knowledge without Torah, in pure humanism, this deviation already slips towards rhetoric and all the betrayals against which Plato himself struggled. Perhaps the Talmudic style whose interpretation is causing us so much difficulty is also precisely this struggle with rhetoric. Mr Hansel spoke to you yesterday about the opposition of Jewish wisdom to sorcery; it is opposed above all to the sorcery of language.

All sorcery, in any case, is the power of words. Is it possible to forget the danger of rhetoric? But is it possible to neglect science and art, and all that Greek wisdom contributes to science and art? Is it possible to cut Judaism off from the sources of the West? In the text that follows one can read an objection to R. Ishmael, or at least a toning down brought to the rigour of his statement. On condition that this reading is not done by an uncultured person, by an 'am ha-arez, it will be a reading which will not have been arbitrary.

> This, however, is at variance with the view of R. Samuel b. Nahmani. For R. Samuel b. Nahmani said in the name of R. Jonathan, This verse is neither duty nor command, but a blessing. For when the Holy One, blessed be He, saw that the words of the Torah were most precious to Joshua, as it is written, *His minister Joshua, the son of Nun, a young man, departed not out of the tent* (Exodus 33: 11), He said to him, 'Joshua, since the words of the Torah are so precious to thee, (I assure thee,) *"this book of the law shall not depart out of thy mouth''* (Joshua 1: 8)!'

The first meaning of the text is that Greek wisdom cannot be forbidden. In the verse from Joshua 1: 8, the verb is not in the imperative but in the optative. The person who hears the calling of the Torah is free to interpret this optative as a blessing.

The Hellenists are no longer infidels! But there is more. He who is not uncultured brings those values disseminated everywhere to their true meaning. The Torah is the blessing of all that comes from elsewhere, and things coming from elsewhere are admissible.

That the permanence of the study of the Torah, however, should not be a commanded duty, that it should be a blessing, may have a specific meaning in order to suggest a new model of permanence towards which, in different aspects, the last sequences of our text are also leading us.

That the permanence of the Torah should be a blessing and not an order certainly signifies that the permanence must not be understood in the sense of temporal continuity. But this teaching can be given only to the pupil who is not uncultured. It is reserved for those who love the Torah. The way in which the Torah covers, then, the totality of a life stems from an overabundance, from the fecundity of the Torah; what enters into the mind during the time that is devoted to it bears fruit in the intervals between the lessons: a free reward that reason reaps beyond its actual exercise. A notion of blessing expressed in another remarkable passage from the Talmud: in studying the Torah, its depths are given as a supplement. Sanhedrin 99b – in scanning, it is true, a verse from Proverbs 16: 26 in a very free way – teaches us that 'Man toils in one place, the Torah toils for him in another'. Rashi comments on this in the following manner: 'The Torah that man has learnt takes care of him and asks the Master of the Torah to reveal to man the ''whys'' of the Torah and its internal organization'. The more in the less! A beyond reason given to reason; a beyond reason which perhaps has a presence of another order than the presence of a theme which we are studying. We shall see this marvellous property in the very last part of our text. The Torah would not be one literary genre amongst others, but the place where, out of letters, propositions and verbs, a life begins. A dynamism which, perhaps, is also inscribed in the formula on the elevation of 'holy things'.

But is it certain that the blessing, despite its fecundity, is, in one respect, less than an obligation? Is it not more than a duty? And we come to the passage which gives to the permanence of the Torah the vision which seemed to me to be the highest: 'A Tanna of the School of R. Ishmael taught: The words of the Torah should not be unto thee as a debt, neither art thou at liberty to desist from it.'

The words of the Torah are not a debt, because a debt can be settled, whereas here we are faced with something which is always to be settled. In his commentary, Rashi introduces here the most original category of our text; to the overabundance of the blessing he adds a beyond of duty, which is not a mere setting free from duty. The Torah is a permanence because it is a debt that cannot be paid. The more you pay your debt, the more in debt you become; in other words, the better you see the extent of what remains to be discovered and done. A category that is to be transposed into the relation with the other man that the Torah teaches: the closer you get to the other, the greater your responsibility towards him becomes. The infinite of duty – which is perhaps the very modality of the relation to the infinite. Here again, there is a movement upwards ...

And we are approaching the final text. It seems at first glance to interrupt the presentation of these models of permanence:

> Hezekiah said, What is the meaning of the verse, *Yea, He hath allured thee out of the mouth of straits into a broad place, where there is no straitness [and that which is set on thy table is full of fatness]* (Job 36: 16)?

This is a verse which begins in Hebrew with the words *ve'aph hesitikha*. The second word can mean the act of taking away, of trailing from one place to another; but also the act of persuading, of convincing, of seducing with an idea, of alluring. Now here is Hezekiah's hermeneutic: 'Come and see that the manner of the Holy One, blessed be He, is not like that (of men) of flesh and blood. A man of flesh and blood allures another ...' – this time the *hesitikha* is used by the Hebrew of the *Gemara* itself to mean 'he will allure you' – 'out of the ways of life into the ways of death; but the Holy One, blessed be He, allures man out of the ways of death into the ways of life, as it is written ...'

Well, Mr Hansel showed you yesterday the way in which the Talmudist allows himself to proceed. He will use the quotation from Job in a sense that will apparently be completely distinct from its plain meaning. Here – which caps it all! – he will read together two different verses taken from two different books: he will comment on a verse from Isaiah and a verse from Job together. The verse from Job 36: 16 becomes: '*"Yea, [I] have allured thee out of the mouth of straits"*, that is, out of Gehenna [hell], whose mouth [entrance] is narrow so that its smoke is stored up within it'. Not at all so as not to be able to enter, but so that the smoke cannot get out! 'And lest you say that as its mouth [entrance] is narrow so the whole (of Gehenna) is narrow, the text ...' – another one, from Isaiah 30: 33! –

> therefore states (for the *Tofet* has long since been ready; it too has been laid out), *Deep and large* (Isaiah 30: 33). And lest you say that it is not made ready for a king, the text therefore states, *Yea, for the*

king it is prepared (Isaiah 30: 33). And lest you say that there is no wood in it, the text therefore states, *The pile thereof is fire and much wood* (Isaiah 30: 33). And lest you say that this is the sole reward (of the Torah), the text ...

– from Job this time, 36: 16 – 'therefore states, *And that which is set on thy table is full of fatness'.*

At first sight, there would be a threat of hell here. Nothing very new as a homily. The Word of God leads to heaven; the word of man as simply man, man's allurement, always leads to hell.

I am going to try to put a little order – or perhaps a little more disorder – into this text. For me, the main thing is the verb *hesitikha*: to persuade, to seduce someone with friendly remarks rather than with reasons, something which recalls rhetoric. The *Gemara* seems to apply this term to God. Here is God not teaching you by speaking to your reason, but teaching you and leading you to this 'table full of fatness' by seducing you. Man allures and it ends badly, but God allures, God seduces too, as if God had his rhetoric. What is this divine allurement? Is there an allurement which does not deceive, a word which is not pure reason, yet which truly reveals? But is everything that is not reason before reason? Is there not an 'after' reason, a beyond reason? Divine allurement is the Torah.

That there should be an element of after reason in the Torah is perhaps what is suggested to us here. This beyond reason would not be just a crude opinion, or an element of faith, but a beyond reason in rational truth itself: a personal relation in the universal and truth. It is in the Torah that you draw near to him who speaks to you personally. Get rid of ideas of malice, of ill will, of deception! The Torah appears here as pure truth, as universal truth, like a thing unique of its kind, unique to the world. It outlines the irreducible category of a teaching which leads beyond philosophy towards personal presence, towards the personal which perhaps can appear in its originary purity only through this text. A form of knowledge which leads to a relation to a person, to a relation which is no longer a form of knowledge. Hence, perhaps, the strange words of certain Talmudists, like Rabbi Hayyim Volozhiner, who say that the Torah is God. The Torah would be the text which leads us through truth to the personal *par excellence,* that of God. It involves an element of seduction without deception, a rhetoric which is holy, opposed to the human rhetoric of pure humanism against which, precisely, the preceding passages of our text stand.

All the rest of the text from this point onwards is easy to understand. That Isaiah and Job are used together, in the great art of Talmudist hermeneutics, is not what bothers us. How curious, on the other hand, is this hell where there is probably fire, yet where those doomed to hell do not suffer from the stake, but suffer from the smoke. You are smoked out in this infernal existence to which pure humanism, humanism without Torah, has led us. This is hell on earth: towns are smoked out, the culture being communicated is suffocating. The metaphor of smoke which is used here to speak of hell is remarkable. It is not an eternal martyrdom through fire, it is pollution; a pollution not as a local and contingent problem but as a modality of social life where one can no longer live. There is a lot of wood, there is all the paraffin you want, but it is to smoke out humanity. Are there any exceptions? Must the king pass through? The king also passes through. No condition puts you above this existence. Must we therefore believe in the absurd? No, all is not absurd. All is not in vain. The table for feeding the just is prepared. The table from the start of our text reappears at the end, conferring on our text something of a circular completion.

There, I have finished. Two more words: the only part that I have not managed to include in my reading of the text is the passage from the end of the *Mishnah* relating to the male goat of Atonement that had to be eaten raw when the Day of Atonement fell on a Friday. And I have not been able to say anything today about the land of Israel. Can this land not be evoked on the occasion of the goat of Atonement celebrated on Fridays? Nowadays, Atonement can no longer fall on a Friday; now we have calendars and we have managed to sort everything out. But in the past, when the neomenia demanded observances and testimonies, the end of Atonement could coincide with the beginning of the Sabbath. Consequently, the goat of Atonement which is eaten in the evening, at the end of Atonement, could not be eaten, for the beginning of the Sabbath forbade its cooking. Certain priests were therefore called who bore the name of Babylonians; they would eat the goat raw. They were not fastidious. The *Gemara* harks back to this story of eaters of raw food, and says:

Rabbah b. Bar Hanah said in the name of R. Johanan, They were not Babylonians but Alexandrians, but because [they] hated the

Babylonians they called (the Alexandrians) by the name of Babylonians.

It was likewise taught [a *baraitha*]: R. Jose says, They were not Babylonians but Alexandrians, but because [they] hated the Babylonians they called (the Alexandrians) by the name of Babylonians. Said to him R. Judah, May your mind be at ease for you have set mine at ease.

R. Judah was a Babylonian: he was very happy to learn that he did not belong to the category of these eaters of raw food. Those who ate raw meat were Alexandrians. Probably Greeks who came from Egypt. But then, why were the Babylonians so hated? The text does not say why. It is the Tosafist who explains to us that when the great *aliyah* from Babylon took place, on the return from the exile in Babylon, some of the priests in exile had no wish to return to the country where the new Judea was being built. Those who did not make the *aliyah* were hated. Even then! And the word 'Babylonian' has remained a pejorative term, an insult. The Alexandrians who ate raw food were called Babylonians.

In this way – is it rhetorical? – the land of Israel nevertheless finds itself honoured at the end of my speech.

3
Cities of Refuge
(Extract from the Tractate Makkoth 10a)

These cities (of refuge) are to be made neither into small forts nor large walled cities, but medium-sized boroughs; they are to be established only in the vicinity of a water supply and where there is no water at hand it is to be brought thither; they are to be established only in marketing districts; they are to be established only in populous districts, and if the population has fallen off others are to be brought into the neighbourhood, and if the residents (of any one place) have fallen off, others are brought thither, priests [*cohanim*], Levites and Israelites. There should be traffic neither in arms nor in trap-gear there: these are the words of R. Nehemiah; but the Sages permit. They, however, agree that no traps may be set there nor may ropes be left dangling about in the place so that the blood avenger may have no occasion to come visiting there.

R. Isaac asked: What is the Scriptural authority (for all these provisions)? – The verse: *and that fleeing unto one of these cities he might live* (Deuteronomy 4: 42) which means – provide him with whatever he needs so that he may [truly] live.

A Tanna taught [a *baraitha*]: A disciple who goes into banishment is joined in exile by his master, in accordance with the text, *and that fleeing . . . he might live,* which means – provide him with whatever he needs to [truly] live. R. Ze'ira remarked that this is the basis of the dictum, 'Let no one teach Mishnah [the Torah] to a disciple that is unworthy'.

R. Johanan said: A master who goes into banishment is joined in exile by his College [his *yeshivah*]. But that cannot be correct, seeing that R. Johanan said: Whence can it be shown (Scripturally) that the study of the

Torah affords asylum? From the verse: *Bezer in the wilderness* (Deuteronomy 4: 43) [that Moses chose], which is followed by: *This is the law which Moses set before the children of Israel* (Deuteronomy 4: 44). This (discrepancy) is not difficult (to explain). One (of his sayings) is applicable to the scholar who maintains his learning in practice, while the other saying is applicable to him who does not maintain it in practice. Or, if you will, I might say that 'asylum' means refuge from the Angel of Death, as told of R. Hisda who was sitting and rehearsing his studies in the schoolhouse and the Angel of Death could not approach him, as his mouth would not cease rehearsing. He (thereupon) perched upon a cedar of the school-house and, as the cedar cracked under him, R. Hisda paused and the Angel overpowered him.

R. Tanhum b. Hanilai observed: Why was Reuben given precedence to be named first in the appointment of (the cities of) deliverance? Because it was he who spoke first in delivering (Joseph from death), as it is said: *And Reuben heard it and he delivered him out of their hand* (Genesis 37: 21).

R. Simlai gave the following exposition: What is the meaning of the text, *Then Moses separated three cities beyond the Jordan, toward the sun-rising* (Deuteronomy 4: 41)? It means that the Holy One, blessed be He, said to Moses: 'Make the sun rise for (innocent) manslayers!' Some say (he explained it so): The Holy One, blessed be He, said to Moses (approvingly), 'You did make the sun rise for (innocent) manslayers!'

R. Simlai (also) gave the following exposition: What is the meaning of the verse: *He that loveth silver shall not be satisfied with silver, and who delighteth in multitude, [has] increase* (Ecclesiastes 5: 10)?[1] *He that loveth silver shall not be satisfied with silver,* might be applied to our Master Moses, who, while knowing that the three cities beyond the Jordan [which he had selected] would not harbour refugees so long as the (other) three in the land of Canaan had not been selected, nevertheless said: The charge having come within my reach, I shall give (partial) effect to it, now! (The second part,) *And who delighteth in multitude, [has] increase* (means): Who is fit to teach a '*multitude*'? – He who has all *increase* [of knowledge] of his own. This is similar to the interpretation given by R. Eleazar (b. Pedath) of, *Who can utter the mighty acts of the Lord, (who can) show forth all His praise?* (Psalms 106: 2) as, Who is fit to utter the mighty acts of the Lord? He (only) who is able to show forth *all* His praise! But the Rabbis, or some say Rabbah b. Mari, interpreted the same, *who delighteth in multitude* has *increase,* as, Whoever [that is, the master] delighteth in the multitude (of scholars) has increase (of scholars), and the eyes of the schoolmen turned on Rabbah the son of Raba.

R. Ashi said it meant that whoever loves *studying* amidst a *multitude* of (fellow) students has increase, which is to the same effect as what R. Jose b. Hanina said: What is the import, (he asked), of the words, *a sword upon the boasters [the solitary] and they shall become fools* (Jeremiah 50: 36)? May a sword fall upon the neck of the foes of Israel [that is, upon the neck of the 'scholars of the Law', designated thus ironically], that sit and engage in the study of the Torah, *solitary* and *apart*! Nay, furthermore, such wax foolish! Holy Writ has here, *and they shall become fools* [*veno'alu*] – and elsewhere it says, *wherein we have done foolishly* [*no'alnu*] (Numbers 12: 11); nay, furthermore, they also become sinners, as it is added there, *and wherein we have sinned*! If you prefer, (it is derived) from this verse, *The Princes of Zoan have become fools* [*no'alu*] (Isaiah 19: 13). Rabina explained (that former passage) thus, Whoever delighteth in teaching a multitude (of scholars) has increase, which is to the same effect as what Rabbi said: Much Torah have I learnt from my Masters, more from my fellow-students and from my disciples most of all!

R. Joshua b. Levi said: What is the meaning of the (Psalmist's) words, *Our feet stood within thy gates, O Jerusalem!* (Psalms 122: 2)? (It is this.) What helped us to maintain our firm foothold in war? The gates of Jerusalem – the place where students engaged in the study of Torah! R. Joshua b. Levi said also the following: What is the meaning of the (Psalmist's) words, *A Song of Ascents unto David. I was rejoiced when they said unto me: 'Let us go unto the house of the Lord'* (Psalms 122: 1)? David, addressing himself to the Holy One, blessed be He, said: Lord of the Universe! I heard men saying, 'When will this old man die and let his son Solomon come and build us the Chosen Shrine and we shall go up there (as pilgrims)?' and I *rejoiced* at that. Said the Holy One, blessed be He, to him, *A day in thy courts is better than a thousand!* (Psalms 84: 10). Better to Me one day spent by you in study of Torah than a thousand sacrifices that your son Solomon will (some day) offer before Me, on the altar!

1 City Compact Together with the Heavenly Jerusalem

In the text that I will comment upon, the name of Jerusalem does not appear until towards the end. This end mentions the first two verses of Psalm 122. The Psalmist here sings the joy of finding himself before the gates of Jerusalem. He exalts this place of pilgrimage and tribunals of justice. He wishes, as do we all, peace and prosperity on to the city. 'Peace be within your walls, and security within your towers!' It is the Psalm whose third verse, which is not quoted in our text, translated word for word, resounds so mysteriously: 'Jerusalem, built as a city which is bound firmly together'. This is an enigmatic verse whose translation from the French Rabbinate gives us the plain meaning as: 'Jerusalem which is built as a city of harmonious unity'.[2]

The *Gemara* of Ta'anith 5a comments on this by seeking the secret meaning. All of this is outside the text which has been handed out to you, but the digression here is an indispensable one. Let us devote a few minutes to it. R. Nahman says to R. Isaac: 'What is the meaning of the scriptural verse, *I will not execute the fierceness of mine anger, I will not return to destroy Ephraim: for I am God, and not man; the Holy One in the midst of thee: and I will not come* ba'ir? (Hosea 11: 9)'. According to Rashi, this last word would mean 'in hatred': 'I will not come in hatred'. According to the free translation of the Talmudic scholars, based on the similarity of the spelling, it would mean 'into the city': 'I will not come into the city'. And according to these scholars, the end of the verse: 'the Holy One in the midst of thee: and I will not come into the city' is separated from the beginning of the verse. But do the translation and the separation of 'the Holy One in the midst of thee: and I will not come into the city' retain a meaning? What city does it concern? This is what R. Johanan says about it: 'The Holy One, blessed be He, said, "I will not enter the heavenly Jerusalem until I can enter the earthly Jerusalem"'. Is there, then, a heavenly Jerusalem? Yes, for it is written – and our verse from Psalms 122: 3 is quoted by translating it as: 'Jerusalem, thou art builded as a city that is compact together'.

We have here one of the origins of the notion of a heavenly Jerusalem which was mentioned last night. The whole of this complex hermeneutic makes of the earthly Jerusalem the unavoidable antechamber of the heavenly Jerusalem. And that is what counts. In what sense? First, in the sense that we were concerned with last night: God followed Israel into exile, He will return unto Himself only by crossing, with Israel returning from exile, the earthly Jerusalem. This in its turn would mean, notably, that there is no spiritual plenitude for Israel without the return to the earthly Jerusalem. A rigorously Zionist reading of the Talmudic saying.

But it can also be read in other ways. If the Talmudic saying is so strange, it is not because it would take pleasure in stating in a complicated way what can be expressed in a simple way. On the contrary, it is because it leaves a multiplicity of meanings to its saying, because it calls for several readings of it. Our role, precisely, consists in looking for them. Here is a second reading: Jerusalem, an exceptional, unique city, twinned with the city of God, a city of all religions, a city twinned with its ideal, a city twinned with its model. The awareness of a Judaism that is essential to the world. The affirmation of the religious essence of the Jewish city.

There is a third meaning which brings us close to what will be the theme of the rest of our commentary: the impossibility for Israel – or according to Israel – of religious salvation without justice in the earthly city. No vertical dimension without a horizontal dimension. An unavoidable stage-of-justice for all elevation. An earthly Jerusalem must be accomplished – which in Talmudic terms means studying and practising the Torah or the justice of the Torah, and in a way moving, thanks to study, on to another level of practical conscience and attention through which the science called Torah is defined – so that the heavenly Jerusalem is filled with divine presence. There is no other access to salvation than that which passes through the dwelling place of men. That is the fundamental symbolism attached to this city.

It is perhaps surprising to begin with the end of the text, and even with a passage which lies beyond this end, and to speak straight away of Jerusalem as the gate of heaven (*sha'ar hashamayim*). It is to take Jerusalem straight away for a theological symbol, whereas our entire purpose consists precisely, as we have just seen, in remembering that this is a question of a real city, where men dwell, and where they are faced with concrete questions relating to their relations with their neighbours, with other men.

At least the beginning of the Talmudic extract that we have chosen gives us the sense of the problems faced in the cities in which men like ourselves live. It concerns, as you will see, cities which bear witness to a very high level of civilization, and to a humanism which is certainly authentic. But it is a completely different mode or potential of spirituality, a new attention to the human, and placed, as it were, above humanism which will enlighten us in the Jerusalem of the Torah, which is perhaps defined as a consciousness more conscious than consciousness. That the Jerusalem of the Torah on which our 'chosen piece' ends should appear in the context of this humanist urbanism of the cities of refuge will be revealed as extremely significant for the very notion of the Torah.

2 The Cities of Refuge

Our extract, indeed, concerns cities of refuge, a biblical institution discussed in Numbers 35. Permit me to present it to you.

When a murder is committed as an unwitting act of homicide; when, for example – a biblical example – an axe-head comes away from its handle during the work of the woodcutter and deals a mortal blow to a passer-by, this murder cannot be pursued before the court of judgement. This 'objective' murder is committed without intent to harm. However, a close relation of the victim, called an 'avenger of blood' – or, more exactly, a *go'el hadam,* a 'redeemer of spilt blood', whose 'heart is heated' by the murder committed (*ki yicham levavo*) – has the right to carry out an act of vengeance. A certain right, beyond the public right of the court, is thus recognized for the 'heat of the heart'. A certain right is granted to a simple state of mind! But only a certain right. Against this marginal right, there is the right proper to protect the manslayer. The law of Moses designates cities of refuge where the manslayer takes refuge or is exiled. Takes refuge or is exiled: there are the two. The 'avenger of blood' can no longer pursue the murderer who has taken refuge in a city of refuge; but for the manslayer, who is also a murderer through negligence, the city of refuge is also an exile: a punishment. The exile lasts – it is not eternal for those who are lucky enough to live a long time – until the end of the pontificate of the high priest contemporaneous with the murder; at the death of the high priest, the manslayer returns to his land of origin.

In the city of refuge, then, there is the protection of the innocent which is also a punishment for the objectively guilty party. Both at the same time. This already follows from the right to vengeance of the avenger of blood; but also from the affirmation – appearing in the lines which follow the Talmudic extract we are commenting upon, to which an allusion is made in this very extract – that there would be no absolute solution of continuity between the race of manslayers and that of murderers proper. Is our responsibility limited by negligence and lack of care? Are we conscious enough, awake enough, men already men enough? Be that as it may, there must be cities of refuge where these half-guilty parties, where these half-innocent parties, can stay shielded from vengeance.

3 The Cities of Refuge and Ourselves

Before reading the text through which I would have had the unusual idea, or the unusual audacity, to present Jerusalem in the context of these cities of refuge, or in contrast with these cities, I would like to mention what topical significance the institution of these cities and the recognition of the 'avenger of blood' might have for us, beyond the reminder of picturesque and outdated customs.

Do not these murders, committed without the murderers' volition, occur in other ways than by the axe-head leaving the handle and coming to strike the passer-by? In Western society – free and civilized, but without social equality and a rigorous social justice – is it absurd to wonder whether the advantages available to the rich in relation to the poor – and everyone is rich in relation to someone in the West – whether these advantages, one thing leading to another, are not the cause, somewhere, of someone's agony? Are there not, somewhere in the world, wars and carnage which result from these advantages? Without us others, inhabitants of our capitals – capitals certainly without equality, but protected and plentiful – without us others having wanted to harm anyone? Does not the avenger or the redeemer of blood 'with heated heart' lurk around us, in the form of people's anger, of the spirit of revolt or even of delinquency in our suburbs, the result of the social imbalance in which we are placed?

The cities in which we live and the protection that, legitimately, because of our subjective innocence, we find in our liberal society (even if we find it a little less than before) against so many threats of vengeance fearing neither God nor man, against so many heated forces; is not such protection, in fact, the protection of a half-innocence or a half-guilt, which is innocence but nevertheless also guilt – does not all this make our cities cities of refuge or cities of exiles? And while it is a necessary defence against the barbarity of heated blood, dangerous states of mind, and threatening disorder, is not civilization – our brilliant and humanist Graeco-Roman civilization, our wise civilization – a tiny bit hypocritical, too insensitive to the irrational anger of the avenger of blood, and incapable of restoring the balance? One may wonder whether spirituality is still wide awake, the spirituality expressed in the way we live, in our right intentions, in our acts of goodwill, and in the attention we pay to the real.

4 The Urbanism of the Cities of Refuge

Let us now read our text. The beginning tells of the way these cities of refuge are laid out so that the men who are 'subjectively innocent' may escape the illegal but understandable punishment of the avenger of blood. Let us admire first of all – I am not going to read it all – the evidently elevated level of this urbanism, and recognize in it the genius, or the source of genius, of the builders of Israel, of these Europeans who convert deserts into gardens, and are so open on this point to all the teachings of the West. They have learnt this in the West: they have had books which had opened their minds.

'These cities (of refuge) are to be made neither into small forts', because the avenger of blood might enter small forts and be tempted, without encountering any resistance, to succeed; nor are they to be made into 'large walled cities', for in large walled cities the avenger of blood may slip into the crowds and go unnoticed. They are to be made into 'medium-sized boroughs; they are to be established only in the vicinity of a water supply and where there is no water at hand it is to be brought thither; they are to be established only in marketing districts', so that murderers through negligence lack nothing. And they are to be established 'only in populous districts', again to protect the manslayer: so that, against the avenger of blood who would like to risk it, the person being attacked can call for help (one supposes in our text that the people in the streets of populous districts will defend you against aggression!). 'And if the population has fallen off others are to be brought into the neighbourhood, and if the residents (of anyone place) have fallen off, others are brought thither, priests [cohanim], Levites and Israelites', in order to ensure the man who has taken refuge a society preserving the structure of a normal Jewish society. 'There should be traffic neither in arms nor in trap-gear there', so that the avenger of blood does not come and buy his arms in the city of refuge, nor can he bring any without attracting attention. 'These are the words of R. Nehemiah', our text goes on to say: R. Nehemiah is extremely prudent! 'But the Sages permit ...' the sale of arms and trap-gear, probably because a city must have arms against wild beasts which can appear there, and against attackers other than the avenger of blood. 'They, however, agree that no traps may be set there nor may ropes be left dangling about in the place', so that the avenger of blood seeking the man who has taken refuge does not have the possibility of catching him with the help of traps that have been permanently installed. All of this 'so that the blood avenger may have no occasion to come visiting' in the city of refuge.

5 Humanitarian Urbanism

So much for the description of the cities of refuge. On what Scriptural facts is it founded? A question which is often asked in the *Gemara:* what verse is to be quoted? It is not only so as not to affirm without foundation, but also so that the verse throws light for us on the spirit of the institutions attached to it.

> R. Isaac asked: What is the Scriptural authority (for all these provisions)? – The verse: *and that fleeing unto one of these cities he might live* (Deuteronomy 4: 42) which means – provide him with whatever he needs so that he may [truly] live.

Life can thus mean only life worthy of the name; life in the full sense of the term: exile, of course, but no prison, no hard labour, and no concentration camp. Life which is life. The humanism or humanitarianism of the cities of refuge! A principle also found a little further on in the text of our *Gemara*: 'R. Simlai gave the following exposition: What is the meaning of the text, *Then Moses separated three cities beyond the Jordan, toward the sun-rising* (Deuteronomy 4: 41)?'

Nothing, apparently, is clearer than the meaning of this verse, but this is what R. Simlai draws from it: 'It means that the Holy One, blessed be He, said to Moses: "Make the sun rise for (innocent) manslayers!"'

The word sun would not figure in this verse in order to locate the place of the city or to indicate the direction it faces. It is mentioned in order to affirm that a life must have some sun. 'Some say (he explained it so): The Holy One, blessed be He, said to Moses (approvingly), "You did make the sun rise for (innocent) manslayers!"'

'You have done well.' According to the first version, an order from God was needed to think of the sun necessary to those in exile; according to the second, Moses thought of it all by himself and was approved. But perhaps the second version agrees with the first: is not the spontaneous movement of the prophetic soul the very path that the divine word follows?

Life as life to the full. Needs satisfied, clarity of the sun, but also Torah:

> A Tanna taught [a *baraitha*]: A disciple who goes into banishment is joined in exile by his master, in accordance with the text, *and that fleeing … he might live,* which means – provide him with whatever he needs to [truly] live.

Can one live without culture? Can one truly live without Torah? And so the Torah makes its appearance in the city of refuge. The Torah for cultural needs, perhaps, and the Torah which is not its ultimate essence, that which it will have in Jerusalem. 'R. Ze'ira remarked that this is the basis of the dictum, "Let no one teach Mishnah [the Torah] to a disciple that is unworthy"'.

To teach an unworthy disciple is to risk finding oneself in exile one day because of the murder that this disciple will have committed. A very important point. It teaches us the following: the person who commits a murder through negligence is certainly not a criminal, but he is nevertheless not a worthy man. This is the relationship about which I was speaking at the beginning, between the race of manslayers and the race of murderers proper. The murderers through negligence are recruited from among the young who are a little suspect. The continuity in the scale of murderers is affirmed from now on by this detail. As I was saying earlier, this idea will be expressed in a more direct manner: there would be only one race of murderers, whether the murder is committed unwittingly or intentionally. Our conscience is not yet wholly conscience. It is a twilight. The transition from the non-intentional to the intentional is noticeable. We are not awake enough.

The master is thus exiled when the disciple needs Torah. What happens if a master is exiled? 'R. Johanan said: A master who goes into banishment is joined in exile by his College [his *yeshivah*].'

The relationship between master and pupil is a strict social structure. The disciple has the right to demand that the master join him in the city of refuge, and the master, that the disciples follow him. The spiritual relationship between master and pupil is as strong as the conjugal relationship.

6 The Torah and Death

There now comes an objection: how is it possible that a master of the Torah should need to exile himself in order to be protected against the avenger of blood? Is not protection provided by the Torah itself which he practises? Is the Torah not a city of refuge? Is this not known by the following 'questionable' hermeneutic:

> But that cannot be correct, seeing that R. Johanan said: Whence can it be shown (Scripturally) that the study of the Torah affords asylum? From the verse: *Bezer in the wilderness* (Deuteronomy 4: 43) [that Moses chose], which is followed by: *This is the law which Moses set before the children of Israel* (Deuteronomy 4: 44).

Because these two verses from Deuteronomy 4: 43 and 44 follow on from each other and begin in an analogous way, and because the former indicates the first city that Moses has chosen as a city of refuge, the latter should indicate another city of refuge. Now the plain meaning of verse 4: 44 consists in naming the Torah of Moses; the hermeneutic of the *Gemara* wants the Torah of Moses to be a city of refuge. But if the Torah is a refuge, how is it that the person who practises it and has committed manslaughter must be exiled? Has he not taken refuge in the Torah itself? That is the question. Of course it has a meaning independently of the succession of verses from which a specious hermeneutic seems to be drawing it. Is the Torah being treated in the cities of refuge as answering only to cultural needs, like the sun and water necessary to our physical condition? Is it not also eternal life itself, a pure act of the intellect and consequently indifference to death, and thus a Torah that is stronger than death? A complete awakening of the soul! A life which is never in phase with the world's acts of violence. And, subsequently, perhaps beyond the protection against the avenger, a life which is already the origin of all 'incapacity' to murder? But is this awakening without interruption?

> This (discrepancy) is not difficult (to explain). One (of his sayings) is applicable to the scholar who maintains his learning in practice, while the other saying is applicable to him who does not maintain it in practice.

One is protected, one is above death and murder, during the lesson, or when asking questions and listening to replies. But there are interruptions. Who can be pure mind? Ah, the Torah of the diaspora, the Torah of the dispersion, taught even on our days off! Dispersion from all points of view: the thousand thoughts which interrupt the lesson while rehearsing it. The Torah of exile, the Torah of the solitary. Is it still stronger than death? And if one broadens the notion, if one understands by Torah a thought which precisely goes beyond 'cultural activity', an occupation among others, if one understands by this a thought which gets to the truth and demands a flawless conscience in its pupils, it must be said that it is in fact always interrupted. We are vulnerable. Instead of expecting our devalued Torah to protect him against death, the manslayer, while still being a student in Torah, would do better to come into a city of refuge!

7 Stronger than Death, Weaker than the Just Avenger

But there is another reply to the question as to why the man of the Torah seeks the protection of a city of refuge when the Torah is stronger than death. 'Or, if you will, I might say that "asylum" means refuge from the Angel of Death . . .' and not from the avenger of blood. As if the scandal of murder, even if it is committed in innocence, were stronger than the power of death itself. Anyone who wishes to take refuge in the Torah in order to forget this involuntary yet objective sin remains exposed to the avenger of blood. He must seek protection – and expiation – in the city of refuge. It is as if nothing could silence the demand for justice. The iron of the intellect, the pure act of reason, offer no passivity to death. But do not hope to take refuge in spiritual life in order to forget a murder, even if it were manslaughter. The avenger of blood is stronger than the Angel of Death.

8 The Pure Act

The iron of the intellect, the pure act of the mind stronger than death. We have been jumping ahead. Let us read the following text: 'As told of R. Hisda who was sitting and rehearsing his studies in the school-house and the Angel of Death could not approach him, as his mouth would not cease rehearsing'.

The Angel of Death resorts to deception: 'He (thereupon) perched upon a cedar of the school-house and, as the cedar cracked under him, R. Hisda paused and the Angel overpowered him'.

The assiduous study of the Torah will find its reward. This is the edifying meaning of this text. But it can also be understood as we have been trying to do: the Torah is an act in the full sense of the term, its study is not some state of consciousness. There is no passivity in it, and the person who unites with it in study cannot receive death. In the world of violence which is our own, intellectual life is a mode of being such that it never puts itself in phase with the causality of the world. The violence of death has no hold over it.

Perhaps in all of this there is yet another thought: the spirituality of the true study of the Torah excludes oversight and absent-mindedness. A meaning which has importance for the rest of the commentary and for this whole theme of manslaughter, city of refuge and Jerusalem which we are approaching in the final passage, and which we shall enter after we have reflected on the good study of the Torah. The Torah is justice, a complete justice which goes beyond the ambiguous situations of the cities of refuge. A complete justice because, in its expressions and contents, it is a call for absolute vigilance. The great awakening from which all oversight, even that of manslaughter, is excluded. Jerusalem will be defined by this Torah, a city consequently of extreme consciousness. As if the consciousness of our habitual life were still sleep, as if we had not yet got a foothold in reality.

We are approaching the gates of Jerusalem. The text is already speaking of the true study of the Torah, and of the new attentiveness to the other.

9 The City of Refuge and Human Fraternity

An incidental question (but is it a problem?): why, in designating the cities of refuge in Deuteronomy 4: 43, does Moses name in the first place a town situated in the patrimony of the tribe of Reuben:

> R. Tanhum b. Hanilai observed: Why was Reuben given precedence to be named first in the appointment of (the cities of) deliverance? Because it was he who spoke first in delivering (Joseph from death), as it is said: *And Reuben heard it and he delivered him out of their hand* (Genesis 37: 21).

This return to Genesis 37: 21 – to Reuben, the son of Jacob, who took pity on Joseph threatened with death by his brothers – is a connection which naturally goes further than its literal signification. The ancient status of the city of refuge – the ambiguity of a crime which is not a crime, punished by a punishment which is not a punishment – is related to the ambiguity of human fraternity which is the source of hatred and pity.

Is it not so that another humanity can be better gauged, one which is sketched out on the horizon of our passage through which Jerusalem and the Torah which fills it are defined? The Torah of Moses, a book which contains, precisely, everything, including the noble lesson of the city of refuge, its indulgence and its forgiveness.

10 The True Torah

Jerusalem is very near. The text which follows indicates, in its fashion, the true way to study the Torah. A study which is not limited to the acquiring of knowledge. According to the Jewish tradition – and without being confused with another mystical practice – this study is the highest level of life where knowledge is no longer distinguished from imperatives and practical impulses, where science and conscience meet, where reality and justice no longer belong to two distinct orders. It is as if the human were to rise to it by attaining a new condition, a new mode of the spirituality of the spirit.

> R. Simlai (also) gave the following exposition: What is the meaning of the verse: *He that loveth silver shall not be satisfied with silver, and who delighteth in multitude [has] increase* (Ecclesiastes 5: 10)? *He that loveth silver shall not be satisfied with silver,* might be applied to our Master Moses, who, while knowing that the three cities beyond the Jordan [which he had selected] would not harbour refugees so long as the (other) three in the land of Canaan had not been selected, nevertheless said: The charge having come within my reach, I shall give (partial) effect to it, now!

Once more, we have an unusual interpretation of a biblical verse that has been 'incorrectly' translated! The parallelism of the two hemistiches is destroyed. The correct translation, the plain translation, should say: 'He that loveth silver shall not be satisfied with silver, nor he that loveth wealth with increase (or gain)'. Now, in the second hemistich, the negation expressed in the Hebrew word *lo* written with *aleph* is read as if it were written with *vav* and meant 'to him'. The *Midrash* allows itself to be guided, when it wishes, by the physical form of the words. A way of reading which resembles the processes of 'dissemination' in use today in certain avant-garde circles. The *Midrash,* on the other hand, thus obtains two hemistiches which no longer echo each other. 'He that loveth silver shall not be satisfied with silver' would mean that obedience to the commandments of the Torah, instead of being experienced as a subjected yoke of the Law, becomes desire, the desire to accomplish more than it commands. This noble desire is compared to passion, to the insatiable greed of the miser, with the infinite that vice opens for itself beyond natural inclinations. A gratuitous fervour suggested deliberately, as it were, by the image of money. It is not out of keeping to underline the fecundity of the *mitzvah*: Moses creates the cities of refuge before they can be used. He would have said to himself: as soon as a divine commandment 'comes within reach', it must be grasped and given effect.

The second part of the verse from Ecclesiastes which has been transformed, 'he that loveth wealth has increase', would announce a methodology of true study. We shall quickly list a few of its features.

> (The second part,) *And who delighteth in multitude, [has] increase* (means): Who is fit to teach a *'multitude'*? – He who has all *increase* [of knowledge] of his own. This is similar to the interpretation given by R. Eleazar (b. Pedath) of, *Who can utter the mighty acts of the Lord, (who can) show forth all His praise?* (Psalms 106: 2) as, Who is fit to utter the mighty acts of the Lord? He (only) who is able to show forth *all* His praise!

In order to teach the Torah, it must be possessed in its entirety. Be wary of the teaching given by those who are ignorant and amateurs! But above all and without doubt, in return for personal access to the truth and to Scripture – which is probably the *raison d'etre* of the very multiplicity of human beings aroused by the scintillating infinite of the *one* truth – there is the recourse to the tradition which is renewed only when it is received beforehand.

> But the Rabbis, or some say Rabbah b. Mari, interpreted the same, *who delighteth in multitude* has *increase*, as, Whoever [that is, the master] delighteth in the multitude (of scholars) has increase (of scholars), and the eyes of the schoolmen turned on Rabbah the son of Raba.

The master teaching the multitude: the excellence of universal teaching, or of teaching adapted to the many or of teaching capable, before a multitude of pupils, of responding to the uniqueness of every soul. And the excellence of the disciple capable of loving the master of the multitude; capable of a private conversation in a large crowd; or capable of a private conversation with the person of the master – capable of loving him – through the universality of the true. No doubt we have here a universality structured differently from the universality of the general and the abstract.

> R. Ashi said it meant that whoever loves *studying* amidst a *multitude* of (fellow) students has increase, which is to the same effect as what R. Jose b. Hanina said: What is the import, (he asked), of the words, *a sword upon the boasters [the solitary] and they shall become fools*

(Jeremiah 50: 36)? May a sword fall upon the neck of the foes of Israel, that sit and engage in the study of the Torah, *solitary* and *apart*! Nay, furthermore, such wax foolish! Holy Writ has here, *and they shall become fools* [*veno'alu*] – and elsewhere it says, *wherein we have done foolishly* [*no'alnu*] (Numbers 12: 11); nay, furthermore, they also become sinners, as it is added there, *and wherein we have sinned*! If you prefer, (it is derived) from this verse, *The Princes of Zoan have become fools* [*no'alu*] (Isaiah 19: 13).

According to R. Ashi, the fecundity of study 'amidst a multitude' would mean study that is not done alone. True thought is not a 'silent dialogue of the soul with itself' but the discussion between thinkers. The verse from Jeremiah 50: 36, whose plain meaning would be: 'A sword (or war) upon those who traffic in lies (upon those who invent), that they may lose their head', is read – according to the method that we have called 'dissemination' – in such a way as to hear in *badim* (traffickers in lies or inventors) the word *bodedim* (the solitary): 'A sword (or war) upon the solitary, that they may become fools' (or lose their head). A remarkable substitution of 'liar' for 'solitary thinker'! The meaning of 'and they shall become fools', in Hebrew *ve-no'alu,* is attained by bringing together various verses. The conjunction *ve* ('and') in *ve-no'alu* would signify a gradation: 'Nay, furthermore, such wax foolish'. Again the pluralism is affirmed of the truth that is, however, *one,* of the truth from out of the personal: 'Be wary of the aberrations of the solitary who do not verify their "inspired ideas" by calling to the other!' Be wary of the mindless state of the solitary person, and of his sin of pride!

> Rabina explained (that former passage) thus, Whoever delighteth in teaching a multitude (of scholars) has increase, which is to the same effect as what Rabbi said: Much Torah have I learnt from my Masters, more from my fellow-students and from my disciples most of all!

Pluralism is not only teaching between equals. The disciple is even better at enriching the thought of the master than a fellow-student. Teaching is a method of research. These are the words of Rabbi, who is Rabbi Judah haNasi, Rabenu Hakadosh, our Holy Master, the redactor of the *Mishnah*: 'Much have I learnt from my Masters, more from my fellow-students and from my disciples most of all'.

11 We Are Entering Jerusalem

> R. Joshua b. Levi said: What is the meaning of the (Psalmist's) words, *Our feet stood within thy gates, O Jerusalem!* (Psalms 122: 2)? (It is this.) What helped us to maintain our firm foothold in war? The gates of Jerusalem – the place where students engaged in the study of Torah!

The Torah, which elsewhere does not even permit the protection against the avenger of blood, has it that here, in Jerusalem, we 'maintain our firm foothold in war'. Is it a war where the Torah would permit victory? Justice will undoubtedly conquer, and the science of justice, in Jerusalem, includes the justice of acts. But in the context of the cities of refuge, this can also be read differently. There are cities of refuge because we have enough conscience to have good intentions, but not enough not to betray them by our acts. Hence the manslaughters. Reality is not transparent to us; we take a confusion of feelings for a conscience and hatreds for fraternity. Before the stream of things, we lose our footing. In Jerusalem, the city of the authentic Torah, it is a more conscious consciousness, completely brought down to earth. It is the great awakening. We have a footing. We are no longer submerged by events, we no longer fear the avenger of blood, there is no longer an avenger of blood. We no longer risk committing the murders which give rise to the blood avengers. We escape the disorder where every person existing is concerned with his existence to enter into an order where the other man is finally visible.

The end is still quite remarkable.

> R. Joshua b. Levi said also the following: What is the meaning of the (Psalmist's) words, *A Song of Ascents unto David. I was rejoiced when they said unto me: 'Let us go unto the house of the Lord'* (Psalms 122: I)? David, addressing himself to the Holy One, blessed be He, said: Lord of the Universe! I heard men saying, 'When will this old man die and let his son Solomon come and build us the Chosen Shrine and we shall go up there (as pilgrims)?' and I *rejoiced* at that.

I rejoiced at hearing people wishing me dead, says David, because what 'pushed them to wishing my death, was the joy of coming into the Temple, into the Chosen Shrine, whose builder will be my son'.

Said the Holy One, blessed be He, to him, *A day in thy courts is better than a thousand!* (Psalms 84: 10). Better to Me one day spent by you in study of Torah than a thousand sacrifices that your son Solomon will (some day) offer before Me, on the altar!

The science and the culture of the Torah would thus be more important than the liturgy. The excellence of Jerusalem is its Torah. Ah, the loftiness of these places, the unequalled light and azure of this sky! The lighting. The science.

The study of the Torah. After so many subtle distinctions – and obscurities – have we not ended up with a commonplace? Was a Talmudic reading necessary to define Jerusalem by the values of orthodoxy and tradition? Is this not the Jerusalem of popular imagination, the Jerusalem of folklore? In reality, our text, through all its movements, only makes us rediscover this notion that has become banal through use and through our trials, has become one scholarly subject among others, a knowledge among knowledges. A notion that is capable, possibly, of satisfying an intellectual need, and of conferring sagacity on our logic, but one which responds, satisfaction among satisfactions, like the sun and the air, to vital needs. Remember that in our text the promise of the Torah to the cities of refuge is inserted between that of water and the sun. But it is within the gates of Jerusalem, beyond places of refuge, that the Torah, according to our text, attains its veritable essence. Here in Jerusalem, it resists violence: it permits us 'to maintain our firm foothold in war' in keeping with the image of the Psalmist. It is a question of the salvation of the world; of man's return to his true humanity.

It is precisely in contrast to the cities of refuge that this claim of the Torah through which Jerusalem is defined can be understood. The city of refuge is the city of a civilization or of a humanity which protects subjective innocence and forgives objective guilt and all the denials that acts inflict on intentions. A political civilization, 'better' than that of passions and so-called free desires, which, abandoned to the hazards of their eruptions, end up in a world where, according to an expression from the Pirqe Aboth, 'men are ready to swallow each other alive'. A civilization of the law, admittedly, but a political civilization whose justice is hypocritical and where, with an undeniable right, the avenger of blood prowls.

What is promised in Jerusalem, on the other hand, is a humanity of the Torah. It will have been able to surmount the deep contradictions of the cities of refuge: a new humanity that is better than a Temple. Our text, which began with the cities of refuge, reminds us or teaches us that the longing for Zion, that Zionism, is not one more nationalism or particularism; nor is it a simple search for a place of refuge. It is the hope of a science of society, and of a society, which are wholly human. And this hope is to be found in Jerusalem, in the earthly Jerusalem, and not outside all places, in pious thoughts.

4
Who Plays Last?
(Tractate Yoma 10a)

R. Joshua b. Levi in the name of Rabbi said: Rome is designed to fall into the hand of Persia, as it was said: *Therefore hear ye the counsel of the Lord, that He hath taken against Edam; and His purposes that He hath purposed against the inhabitants of Teman: surely the least of the flock shall drag them away, surely their habitation shall be appalled to them* (Jeremiah 49: 20).

Rabbah b. 'Ullah demurred to this: What intimation is there that *'the least of the flock'* refers to Persia? (Presumably) because Scripture reads: *The ram which thou sawest having two horns, they are the kings of Media and Persia* (Daniel 8: 20). But say (perhaps) it is Greece, for it is written, *And the rough he-goat is the king of Greece*? (Daniel 8: 21). When R. Habiba b. Surmaki came up, he reported this interpretation before a certain scholar. The latter said: One who does not understand the meaning of the passage [from Scripture] asks a question against Rabbi. What does, indeed, *'the least of the flock'* mean? The youngest of his brethren, for R. Joseph learnt that Tiras is Persia.

Rabbah b. Bar Hana in the name of R. Johanan, on the authority of R. Judah b. Illa'i, said: Rome is designed to fall into the hands of Persia, that may be concluded by inference *a minori ad majus*: If in the case of the first Sanctuary, which the sons of Shem (Solomon) built and the Chaldeans destroyed, the Chaldeans fell into the hands of the Persians, then how much more should this be so with the second Sanctuary, which the Persians built and the Romans destroyed, that the Romans should fall into the hands of the Persians.

Rab said: Persia will fall into the hands of Rome. Thereupon R. Kahana and R. Assi asked of Rab: (Shall) the builders fall into the hands of the destroyers? He said to them: Yes, it is the decree of the King. Others say: He replied to them: They [the Persians] too are guilty for they destroyed the synagogues. It has also been taught [a *baraitha*] in accord with the above, Persia will fall into the hands of Rome, first because they destroyed the synagogues, and then because it is the King's decree that the builders fall into the hands of the destroyers.

[R. Judah said in the name of Rab]: The son of David will not come until the wicked kingdom of Rome will have spread (its sway) over the whole world for nine months, as it is said: *Therefore will He give them up, until the time that she who travaileth hath brought forth; then the residue of his brethren shall return with the children of Israel* (Micah 5: 3).

1 The Theme

The short extract from the Tractate Yoma 10a which I mean to comment upon concerns Persia and Rome. It concerns the possible war which should end History and which would be played out – if wars are played out – between these two empires.

Whatever thoughts today's events may provoke in your minds in counterpoint to my talk, please believe me when I say that I was not thinking of those events.[1] My text was chosen a few months ago, well before the present conflict which is filling newspapers and radio news bulletins. I thought that all this was not a sufficient reason to change subjects, nor to redo in another spirit a talk which had already been sketched out. Those who know me know that I regard the Talmud as a very lofty way of thinking, but I do not regard it as an oracle.

This extract, simple in its construction, concerns a reflection on the outcome of the political history of the world, an outcome which entails a war – the final war – between great empires. The result of this war which brings History to an end and which our text discusses – without imposing, strictly speaking, a conclusion – as well as the empires it names, perhaps suggest a certain idea on the meaning of political life and on its relations with religion. On the meaning of political life which, admittedly, is not always war, and which can become rivalry, competition and even pure emulation, during periods of peaceful coexistence between powers, but where these powers remain in any case on their guard and, thus, as it were, turned towards the outside, in all the forms of a State's inner life.

The great empires which are named in this text, empires with hegemonic or universal pretensions, are those of Antiquity: Persia and Rome. The name of Greece, probably designating in the Talmudic tradition the empire of Alexander the Great and his successors, evokes Hellenism in general. It is uttered in our text, but as if in passing. We shall try to find a reason for that too.

It is evident, on the other hand, that we are not concerned, in commenting on this half a page, with undertaking a historical and geographical study of Persia, Rome and Greece. This can be done, but it is not my intention to do it. Do these nations of Antiquity appear in our Talmudic fragment in their concrete historical reality? There is certainly an allusion to Mediterranean humanity here. But these proper names represent above all certain notions of power and the State according to the political thought of the rabbinical scholars who are the interlocutors of the dialogue which is reproduced. We need to see concepts in it, perhaps even categories, and it is as such that our extract may be of interest to us. The conceptual character attached to all these names of States does not, perhaps, exclude certain characteristic traits of the nations which have disappeared. They are not what is essential here, nor are they in many other Talmudic texts in which they appear. They allow us to be more specific about the political conceptions of traditional thought rather than bearing witness as historical documents.

Finally, outside Persia, Rome and the fleeting evocation of Greece, there figures, in the final part of our passage, a fourth entity which does not appear as a partner of the warlike play about which we are being told: there are the Jewish people who remain, from one end of the text to the other, outside the fighting. They await the coming of the descendant of David – that is, the Messiah; a coming which is to signal the end of the political history of the great empires, but which, as such, still belongs to History.

The text ends on the foreseen triumph of the Messiah, a religious and historical event. He will have the last word. Through him will begin an order which will be different to that of warring nations and to politics determined through conflicts. But the moment of this coming – and it is this that is interesting – is not politically indifferent, nor politically indeterminate. Contrary to received opinion, our extract, like many passages which echo it, seems to suggest that the coming of the Messiah cannot occur at just any moment. Our text includes, in a very visible way, a reference to a certain political situation, conditioning the Messianic end of History – even if this argument is not shared by all rabbinical scholars who can also think of Messianism without historical conditions.

One of the aspects of the relationship between politics and religion will thus be able to appear in the commentary we are attempting.

2 The Framework

On the whole, the text is simple but, as always, allusive and signifying through its minute particularities; consequently, it calls for interpretation.

The four paragraphs of my translation describe or reflect three moments of the reflection, or the dialectic proposed to us. Paragraphs 1 and 2 represent the first moment, paragraph 3 the second, and paragraph 4 the third.

Paragraphs 1, 2 and 3 announce the victory of Persia over Rome as the final event of the political history of the world.

Let us read the beginning of paragraph 1 and the beginning of paragraph 3:

> R. Joshua b. Levi in the name of Rabbi said: Rome is designed to fall into the hand of Persia ... Rabbah b. Bar Hana in the name of R. Johanan, on the authority of R. Judah b. Illa'i, said: Rome is designed to fall into the hands of Persia.

Rome will fall into the hands of Persia: the event is the same. But why two versions and two different traditions? How does R. Joshua b. Levi's argument differ from that of Rabbah b. Bar Hana?

In the last paragraph, the argument is reversed: Rome conquers Persia. 'Rab said: Persia will fall into the hands of Rome.'

I do not know if the Persia of our text is still Persia or is no longer Persia, but Rome is certainly no longer in Rome.

3 The Victory of Persia: Animal Strength

Let us resume the reading: 'R. Joshua b. Levi in the name of Rabbi said' – that is, in the name of the redactor of the *Mishnah*, the master of great authority – 'Rome is designed to fall into the hand of Persia'.

How does he know? He knows from a verse in Jeremiah.

> As it was said: *Therefore hear ye the counsel of the Lord, that He hath taken against Edom; and His purposes that He hath purposed against the inhabitants of Teman: surely the least of the flock shall drag them away, surely their habitation shall be appalled to them* (Jeremiah 49: 20).

It does not seem to be a question of Persia in the text of Jeremiah, even if Edom – which in the Bible designates Esau, Jacob's brother – had, according to a traditional convention of rabbinical exegesis, to symbolize Rome, a symbol also attached to Teman, which is the name of Esau's grandson (Genesis 36: 15).

Why Persia, then? Rome is identified, but why Persia? This is the question with which paragraph 2 begins. Indeed, 'Rabbah b. 'Ullah demurred to this: What intimation is there that *"the least of the flock"* refers to Persia?'

The reply is that it is intimated through a verse from Daniel which must allow verse 49: 20 in Jeremiah to be decoded. '(Presumably) because Scripture reads: *The ram which thou sawest having two horns, they are the kings of Media and Persia* (Daniel 8: 20).'

The end of Rome is predicted, despite everything, in a remarkable way! The prophet Jeremiah and Daniel would have chosen zoological symbolism: it is the 'meek' small livestock which will 'drag away' the proud Roman legions. What a defeat for Rome! And it will be the sheepfolds of the flocks which, by collapsing, will crush the eternal City, the great Western metropolis! The ram with two horns, seen in a prophetic dream, is identified with Persia and Media, and it will get the better of Roman power.

Let us pay attention to the beginning: it says nothing of the reasons which would justify the destruction of Rome; no motive is given to explain the victory and henceforth the definitive power of Persia. That a verse or a combination of verses permit the event to be predicted certainly indicates that, for the authors of the text, the events are not happening without providence's knowledge. But in the case in point, and above all compared to the second version of the argument stating the end of Rome, the initial statement is striking in its moral neutrality: divine will remains transcendent to that which it lets happen according to its own nature. There would be no internal reason for the predicted superiority of Persia.

... Unless – and this is my hypothesis – the very animality of the symbols used to predict the events expresses, moreover, the nature of these events. The animality of the symbols might, indeed, suggest a philosophy of war: war would be a confrontation of purely biological forces, of the brutality of animals; its outcome would be predetermined by the imbalance between the vitality of the initial energies of beings; politics would already be inscribed in chromosomes.

Admittedly, one might also venture to explain the zoological symbol by the persistence of totemic memories in the Bible and Talmud. I reject this. Bible and Talmud, prophecy and critical spirit, signify precisely the break with mythologies. Recourse to totemism can tempt, I think, only young men enamoured with what they call every other minute 'modernity', who – as R. Habiba b. Surmaki will say further on in our text – 'do not yet understand the meaning of the passage [from Scripture]', but already dare to oppose tradition.

I think, then, that the recourse to animal symbolism signifies for R. Joshua b. Levi, who is speaking in the name of Rabbi, that pure politics, in which the peoples of the earth are held together, is only the display, with a view to mutual repression, of the animal energies of the attachment to being. Energies deposited in the genes of the living person, vital energies, energies which are definitively yet unequally – that is, unjustly – distributed, sustaining weak races and strong races, and whose confrontation signifies nothing other than the very confrontation of forces which resist all equalization, an energy of which only the appearance is revealed by the theories, cultures or ideologies of human beings.

Animal energy would control the secret of the social, the political, the struggle, defeat and victory, an energy from which the rigour of logic itself would stem, the strength of reasoning and all 'ideas the right way up'. The life of the States predetermined animalistic ally without moral questions! The persistence of the animal in being, the *conatus*, remains indeed indifferent to all justification and all accusation. It cannot be questioned.

This idea of biological forces triumphing in the victory of Persia over Rome is again underlined by the insistence on youth. Let us read the end of the second paragraph again: 'What does, indeed, *"the least of the flock"* mean? The youngest of his brethren, for R. Joseph learnt that Tiras is Persia.'

The animals that will crush the vanquished Romans will be the youngest of the flock, and Tiras – a name mentioned in Genesis 10: 2, which R. Joseph identifies with the mythological ancestor of Persia – is the youngest.

I wonder, indeed, whether Judaism does not signify in the mind of Rabbi, who foresees this triumph of one empire over another without being able to invoke anything in favour of the victor – a very sombre vision of universal politics – whether Judaism and its Messianic vocation do not signify, for Rabenu Hakadosh, our holy Rabbi, the calling into question or the 'denucleation' of these variable life-atoms with atomic weight which are unequally – or unjustly – distributed. A questioning of natural inequalities, a questioning that one can call precisely religion, the creation of a society in which these inequalities, should they exist, are compensated for. I wonder whether it is not this that is opposed to the political vision of R. Joshua b. Levi; whether the initial revelation of Judaism is not a questioning of the incontestable right of the *conatus* itself, of the right to the perseverance in being, without any *raison d'être* other than causality. There are eminent Spinoza specialists in the room. I know the scandal entailed in their eyes in calling the *conatus* into question. A questioning against nature, against the very naturalness of nature! But is justice to be found in the perseverance in being, which is analytically, animalistically inherent in being, a requirement which is natural and without justification, a requirement for living space? A justice which does not imply the idea of a law which is 'abstractly' obligatory, juridical or mathematical, but the preliminary revelation of the human face, of the face of one's neighbour and the responsibility for the other man. The Law itself follows from this responsibility, the Law against a politics of the 'outgoing force',[2] a force which unfurls all on its own.

In this I agree with Bernard-Henri Lévy's book, *Le Testament de Dieu* – a sombre book, like the first paragraph of our text; a book which has said so many remarkable things on the Law, on the harsh Law which does not immediately give us, as certain young men who are too easily optimistic promise, the joys of 'nascent dawns', a harsh Law, for our part, we who are a people of a just Law; for our part, which is the best! But I have wondered whether he was not too hard on Greece, with which he envisaged, as a concession, that a dialogue was possible. I was asking for more, out of respect for science and Plato. I thought that, beyond the dialogue with Greece, its language was already necessary to us in our internal discourse. The temptation of Greece which has not yet been surmounted! Yet is not Bernard-Henri Lévy right in the face of all those who seek to appropriate such a brilliant heritage, to see in it also an excellence of vital forces which would be capable of such great delicacies without losing anything of their merciless arrogance?

It so happens that Greece appears in our Talmudic extract from the second paragraph onwards. Episodically, but it appears. Let us read on: 'Rabbah b. 'Ullah demurred to this: What intimation is there that "*the least of the flock*" refers to Persia? ... But say (perhaps) it is Greece, for it is written ...' – in this famous verse from Daniel which allows the text to be decoded – '*And the rough he-goat is the king of Greece*?'

The young animals in Jeremiah 49: 20 can also, therefore, signify Greece. Nothing forces us to identify the young animals with the ram with horns, any more than with the rough he-goat.

Greece, the empire of Alexander; the philosophic and artistic civilization which Hellenized the Mediterranean basin, one of the essential moments of the West. That, too, may therefore be the work of the young animals. The vital forces, in their play without regard for others, would be susceptible to turning into delicacy and refinement, without any ethical intention; they may become 'victory of the mind', and thus go further than crude acts of violence. But of course, the superiority of those who reach this level over those who have less 'vital force' remains the greatest superiority. At the moment there are thinkers who assure us precisely of this: the 'animal minds' are not crude driving forces; their violence is a subtle one. They can even conquer without violent battles and without lethal weapons. Has not Rome, which had conquered Greece, been conquered by Greece? No doubt it is the philosophers of this day and age – or this philosophy that is constantly being renewed – which are already being thought of by Rabbah b. 'Ullah and this 'certain scholar' who figures in our text, and who asks R. Habiba b. Surmaki for confirmation of his seductive argument without thereby separating the glory of Greece from its vitality as the rough he-goat. R. Habiba b. Surmaki rejects the hypothesis put forward: 'One who does not understand the meaning of the passage [from Scripture] asks a question against Rabbi'.

The hypothesis of Greece as the conqueror of Rome would, admittedly, announce a less sombre situation than Rome conquered by the sole virtue of brute force and without any more elevated justification. Conquest by civilization, by the excellence of arts, letters, science, already entails the triumph of certain values. One can understand the young man preferring Greece to Persia in this final struggle. If R. Habiba b. Surmaki immediately rejects the young man's hypothesis, it is because he does not want a Greece which is expressed in zoological symbols. He reproaches his interlocutor for his hermeneutic naivety: all that a text suggests does not enter the text, is suitable neither for the letters of the text nor for tradition. But, in content, R. Habiba b. Surmaki's firmness is even more revealing. The Greece suggested by the symbol of the rough he-goat is not much different from Persia. Cultural concepts, if they are based through these suggestions of zoological images on the pure display of biological forces, without the morality of a law coming from elsewhere to muzzle these forces, will end up regaining their brutal origin. The victory of Greece understood in this way will be equivalent to the victory of Persia. The culture without morality will have been a sham, a fragile and deceptive superstructure, a mystification and a camouflage. Aesthetics by itself is not, in the last analysis, reliable or sufficient. There is in it – Talmudists have always thought so – a possibility of rhetoric and pure courtesy, a 'courtly language' which veils cruelties and malevolence, the extreme fragility of all this refinement capable of ending up in Auschwitz.

There is, perhaps, another reason for rejecting the hypothesis of the 'young man'. The delicacy of a culture which is based on the power of young animals more talented than others must be rejected, for it will lead back to a society in which inequality reigns; the excellence of some will separate them from others. The inequality of natural talents is, by itself, a form of violence which can be curbed only by a sociality returning to sources other than biological ones. It is this sociality, capable of maintaining society despite the blind determinisms of nature, which must be compared to the idea of religion. The conquest of Rome by a Greece incapable by itself of being a peaceful society is equivalent to a conquest of warriors.

4 Morality in History

We have interpreted the first two paragraphs, which see Rome conquered by Persia, by opposing them to paragraph 3, which states the same argument but finds a moral reason in this victory. The second statement of the same argument does not quote verses but speaks of History. It invokes the moral superiority of Persia over Rome. Up to now, not one word of morality could be found in the text commented upon. The novelty of the second argument lies in this very precise motivation. Its presence underlines in some way the absence of this motivation in the first two paragraphs, which has led us to give them their own specific significance.

With Rabbah b. Bar Hana there appear, beyond the vital forces and their play, the just and the unjust. The history which would be only political is over with! From now on, the just will triumph over the unjust!

Rabbah b. Bar Hana in the name of R. Johanan, on the authority of R. Judah b. Illa'i, said: Rome is designed to fall into the hands of Persia, that may be concluded by inference *a minori ad majus*: If in the case of the first Sanctuary, which the sons of Shem (Solomon) built and the Chaldeans destroyed, the Chaldeans fell into the hands of the Persians, then how much more should this be so with the second Sanctuary, which the Persians built and the Romans destroyed, that the Romans should fall into the hands of the Persians.

The Chaldeans – or the Babylonians – demolished the first Temple built in Jerusalem by King Solomon. The kingdom of Babylon is defeated by the Persians. Persia will thus have refuted the destroyers of the Temple which it had not built. In the light of this, the credit for the return from exile in Babylon and the construction of the second Temple is due to Cyrus, King of the Persians. Is it not for him to punish Rome, the destroyer of the second Temple built by the Persians? Yes, all the more reason for this victory to belong to the Persians. Consequently, the destruction of Rome by Persia, foretold by the Prophets, finds its justification.

What, then, do opposing forces matter, if morality controls events? At least in the end. A justice would thus be immanent in politics! A new vision of politics! Yet is the religious vision which announces itself in this way self-sufficient? Has it nothing to expect from a politics which is irreducible to morality? We shall see this shortly, in the last part of our text.

Let us note that in the passage commented upon, Israel is not the actor of this politics dominated by morality. It does not participate actively in it as Israel as such, even if it remains, in some way, the criterion for the morality of a politics: political powers are judged according to the attitude they adopt towards the Temple of Jerusalem – as either builders or destroyers of the Temple. 'What is good for Israel is good' – or, in a less trivial way, the ultimate distinction between good and evil on the social and political plane would stem from the possibility, for a social and political order, of coexisting with the ethical demands of Israel. We must not speak here, prematurely or lightly, of nationalism. The Temple of Jerusalem in Jewish thought is a symbol which signifies for the whole of humanity; it is not simply a national institution. The biblical message and the history of a people of survivors, and the Passion of Israel through the history which they evoke, all belong to holy History. This latter does not immediately triumph over universal History, which inexorably unfurls; but it does allow it to be judged.

5 The Victory of Rome

Let us examine the last paragraph: Rome will triumph over Persia. 'Rab said: Persia will fall into the hands of Rome.'

But, that being the case, is not the moral administration of History, which seemed assured according to Rabbah b. Bar Hana's argument, brutally contested? A scandal expressed by the intervention of R. Kahana and R. Assi: 'Thereupon R. Kahana and R. Assi asked of Rab: (Shall) the builders fall into the hands of the destroyers?'

Rab replies in the affirmative. But two versions of his reply are handed down. According to the first version, he is said to have invoked a 'royal will' which decides in favour of Rome. Is it a question of divine decree? Or, in the absence of any motivation of this 'royal will', is it not a question of the inexorable reality which, indifferent to good and evil, unfolds with sovereign power and demands, by its intrinsic causality, the triumph of the strongest, Rome?

'He said to them: Yes, it is the decree of the King.' The ethical administration and outcome of human history would thus be utopian! How would ethics manage to impose itself on the order of nature which is indifferent and determined, or arbitrarily decided by an all-powerful God asserting himself in a *Sic volo, sic jubeo?* How would it impose itself on the causality of social nature, on the necessity specific to events, founded on the perseverance of beings in their being, whose rights raise no question and from which politics draws its technique or its art?

But could Rab understand in this sense the notion of royal will which he invokes? Could this sense, perfectly plausible in itself, accept Rab's spiritual universe? Let us read the other version of the reply which Rab gave to R. Kahana and R. Assi: 'Others say: He replied to them: They [the Persians] too are guilty for they destroyed the synagogues.'

Rab would thus not have doubted the attention paid by a moral God to human history. But for him, Persia's hands are not pure enough to carry out divine plans. Persia contributed to the rebuilding of the Temple, but it nevertheless destroyed the places where its spirit spread. Nothing can be expected from a politics which is pure violence! The role assigned to politics in the economy of human salvation would not, therefore, amount to eradicating evil through war. Messianism does not consist in entrusting to nations, guilty themselves, the function of punishing other nations.

But royal decree docs not contradict morality. With morality in mind, would it not have a completely different political aim? Here is the

63

quotation from a *baraitha* in which can be found – but put together as two motifs of the same reply – the two versions of Rab's reply, except that their order is reversed. That of the second version figures as the first motif; that of the first as the second motif.

> It has also been taught [a *baraitha*] in accord with the above, Persia will fall into the hands of Rome, first because they destroyed the synagogues, and then because it is the King's decree that the builders fall into the hands of the destroyers.

What can be the intention of the King in making this decision in favour of Rome? The words of R. Judah, again speaking in the name of Rab, make a connection between the universal extension of Roman power and the coming of the 'son of David'. No more than this is said:

> [R. Judah said in the name of Rab]: The son of David will not come until the wicked kingdom of Rome will have spread (its sway) over the whole world for nine months, as it is said: *Therefore will He give them up, until the time that she who travaileth hath brought forth; then the residue of his brethren shall return with the children of Israel* (Micah 5: 3).

Is not the King's intention anxious for the ultimate conqueror of political history to be precisely Rome? A wicked State, but most certainly a State. The exceptional success of violence managing to balance itself out. A State which would not have reached the ethical law which ensues from the life of a man for the other man: but a law which will have gone through animality to end up dialectically in the formal universality of the law itself, out of a condition in which 'man is a wolf for other men'. The appearance of moral law, but, formally, law; both in this appearance and in this formalism. This is probably what is expressed in a *Midrash* (Bereshith Rabbah 65: 1) which compares Edom – that is, Rome – to a swine whose hoofs are parted without it being a ruminant and, as a consequence, impure and unfit for consumption according to the Torah; a swine which 'in lying down, puts out its [legs and shows its] hoofs as if to say: "[Behold], I am clean", so does this wicked State rob and oppress, yet pretend to be executing justice'. A remarkable way of veiling and sheltering its 'wickedness' in the law while showing concern for equality.

From here onwards, there are two possibilities. The first hypothesis is that the universal power of Rome would precede the coming of the 'son of David', for it would be necessary for the harsh law of wicked origin and essence to spread its sway over the whole world. It would be necessary for men to drain the cup of suffering to the last dregs. The Messiah will come into a desperate world. A theme which can be found elsewhere in the Talmud (although mixed with diametrically opposed views). And here, to that effect, is a characteristic passage from the Tractate Sanhedrin 98a, reading the signs of the impending deliverance in the extreme misery of men:

> R. Eleazar said: [There can be no more manifest (sign of) redemption than this], as it is written, *For before these days there was no hire for man, nor any hire for beast; neither was there any peace to him that went out or came in because of the affliction* (Zechariah 8: 10). What is meant by, '*neither was there any peace to him that went out or came in because of the affliction*'? Rab said: Even for scholars, who are promised peace, as it is written, *Great peace have they which love thy law* (Psalms 119: 165), '*There (shall) be no peace because of the affliction*'. Samuel said: 'Until all prices are equal'. R. Hanina said: The son of David will not come until a fish is sought for an invalid and cannot be procured.

But one can venture another hypothesis: the last judgement and the destruction of evil belong only to the descendant of David. This triumph of justice requires a religious act which is precisely the coming of the Messiah. But why the King's cruel decree delivering Persia to Rome beforehand, and spreading the Roman Empire to the furthermost bounds of the earth? The extension of Rome into the world would be necessary to justice and to Messianic peace itself. In its wickedness, it begins the Order of the West. It is more and better than the unfurling of warrior forces and the opening out of being in its wild vitality. 'For nine months in which she who travaileth hath brought forth', our text says. Nine months, or nine years, or nine centuries of preparation for the coming of the Messiah. A world pregnant with a new future! Politics, such as Rome represents it, is a preliminary gestation for Messianic generosity itself. It will give being to the law which, issued from animality, keeps in check the animality of human hordes. Roman legalism is the positive effect of its negativity. 'Pray for the State; without it, men would swallow each other alive', declares a venerable *Mishnah* from the Tractate Pirqe Aboth taught at the height of the oppression of the Roman Empire. Here, to the same effect, is another surprising text from Bereshith Rabbah 9: 13:

> R. Simeon b. Lakish said [concerning Genesis 1: 31]: 'And God saw everything that he had made, and behold, it was very good'. 'It was very good' alludes to the kingdom of heaven. But the 'behold' which precedes 'it was very good' signifies the Roman empire. Is then the Roman empire very good? How strange! Rome earns that title because it exacts justice for men.[3]

Rome is the great order which began governing in the Mediterranean, and became the West. It is the Rome whose noise, already heard from afar, troubled the great among the great, R. Akiba and his companions, in the fine apologue which closes the Tractate Makkoth 24a.

A political West about which no illusion, certainly, is permitted. But the coming of the son of David demands, perhaps, that the union is made beforehand, the Western union – not straight away according to the law inspired by the love of the other man, but already on a preparatory basis according to the law where evil will give itself the appearance of good. A world organized entirely around the Law, which politically will have a hold over it. The necessity of a planetary West for the coming of the Messiah.

5

The Pact
(Tractate Sotah 37a–37b)

... They turned their faces towards Mount Gerizim and opened with the blessing etc. Our Rabbis taught [a *baraitha*]: There was a benediction in general and a benediction in particular, likewise a curse in general and a curse in particular. (Scripture states): *to learn, to teach, to observe* [to keep] and *to do;* consequently there are four (duties associated with each commandment). Twice four are eight and twice eight are sixteen. It was similar at Sinai and the plains of Moab; as it was said, *These are the words of the covenant which the Lord commanded Moses [to make with the people of Israel in the land of Moab, besides the covenant which he had made with them at Horeb]* (Deuteronomy 29: 1), and it is written, *Keep therefore the words of this covenant* etc. (Deuteronomy 29: 9). Hence there were forty-eight covenants in connection with each commandment.

R. Simeon excludes (the occasion of) Mount Gerizim and Mount Ebal and includes that of the Tent of Meeting in the wilderness. The difference of opinion here is the same as that of the teachers [the Tannaim] in the following [a *baraitha*]: R. Ishmael says: General laws were proclaimed at Sinai and particular laws in the Tent of Meeting. R. Akiba says: Both general and particular laws were proclaimed at Sinai, repeated in the Tent of Meeting, and for the third time in the plains of Moab. Consequently there is not a single precept written in the Torah in connection with which forty-eight covenants were not made. R. Simeon b. Judah of Kefar Acco said in the name of R. Simeon: There is not a single precept written in the Torah in connection with which forty-eight times 603,550 covenants were not made. Rabbi said: According to the reasoning of R. Simeon b. Judah of

Kefar Acco who said in the name of R. Simeon that there is not a single precept written in the Torah in connection with which forty-eight times 603,550 covenants were not made, it follows that for each Israelite there are 603,550 commandments (and forty-eight covenants were made in connection with each of them). What is the issue between them? R. Mesharsheya said: The point between them is that of personal responsibility and responsibility for others [responsibility of responsibility].

1 The Formal Law

The problem of the community that concerns us in this conference is certainly a topical one, owing to the unease felt by man today in a society which has become, in a certain sense, planetary, and in which – owing to modern means of communication and transport, owing to the worldwide scale of economy in industrial society – everyone has the impression of being simultaneously related to humanity as a whole, but also solitary and lost. With each radio broadcast and each day's newspapers, we admittedly feel implicated in the most distant of events and related to men everywhere; but we also notice that our personal destiny, freedom or happiness, depend on causes which strike with inhuman energy. We notice that technical progress itself – to repeat a commonplace – which relates everyone to everyone else, brings with it necessities which leave men in a state of anonymity. Impersonal forms of relation replace direct forms – 'short connections', as Ricœur calls them – in a world in which everything is programmed to excess.

The structure of the States and nations is admittedly less abstract than that of the planet, but it is still too broad, and the universal ties of the law guarantee that men come together side by side rather than face to face. Even within the family, human relationships are less alive and less direct because of the multiplicity of systems in which each person is caught. But the parental structure has perhaps never fully satisfied man's social vocation; hence the search for a more restricted society whose members would know one another. Some think that in order to achieve this, it is necessary to spend time together, to see one another regularly. Is this really the solution? A concrete yet marginal society, establishing itself only on the edges of a real society which, despite its impersonal structures, is based in the 'order of things'. Will our sociality find fulfilment in a society of Sundays and leisure activities, in the provisional society of the club?

If these structures of a more intimate social life are to make people aware of community life, one which is exalted in the recognition of one person by another, is it not necessary, in fact, for these structures to be non-artificial? Normal society is one in which is reflected and breathes a humanity which is in contact with the world. Today's professional life, with the points of concentration it determines, its towns, industry and crowds – but also its intercontinental dispersion – retains an understanding of the serious side of the things that count. It is not the result of lack of care or a mistake. It is the very essence of modernity. The solidarity of the modern world, a solidarity planned through Law and regulations, all these 'long connections' which it establishes, are what make reality function these days; even if these connections make us walk together rather than turning men's faces towards one another. Are we thus not back to the starting point of our problem?

2 Our Talmudic Extract

But also, perhaps (and this is what brings me to the Talmud), we have not measured all the implications of the Law which Western society welcomes too formally, and which have got lost within it.

This, perhaps, is one reason to question one of Israel's old texts. The Talmudic text we have chosen is a relatively simple one, though, as always, it is unusual. It concerns the problem we have just mentioned. It deals with a covenant, and interprets it in its fashion, which consists in apparently not touching on it. It interprets the covenant concluded between the Eternal of Israel and the children of Israel. It is through this covenant that the society of Israel is instituted by legislation and the Torah. I have entitled the proposed passage which has been translated for you 'The Pact', and it is an extract from the Tractate Sotah 37a–37b from the Babylonian Talmud. It is very short: just half a page.

I should situate the passage in its context. The sequence of the *Gemara* from which it is taken prolongs a *Mishnah* relating to a different theme altogether. This *Mishnah* deals with the question of whether Hebrew or profane languages are suitable for certain liturgical expressions such as 'benedictions', 'oaths', etc. The *Mishnah* is followed by several pages of *Gemara*. The small sequence which has been handed out to you is taken from these pages of the *Gemara*. This sequence is only a digression in relation to the thematics of language, in which the problem of Greek always arises. The theme of language will appear at a certain moment in our extract. This theme of language about which the *Mishnah* speaks is in no way without interest. In it is announced – or dissimulated – the problem of the relation between the particularism of Israel and the universality of men. We shall find an echo of it again in the commentary on our extract.

3 From the Bible to the Talmud

This text appears to be a commentary on Deuteronomy Chapter 27, but it also refers to Joshua Chapter 7. By recalling these texts, and also by returning to the text of the *Mishnah* which refers to them – in an even more complete way than the first sentence with which our extract begins – we shall first be able, by way of example, to measure the distance which can separate the written Law from the oral Law.

Deuteronomy Chapter 27, indeed, sets out the recommendations given by Moses to Israel for a ceremony which has to take place later, when – after his death, and at the end of their travels in the wilderness – the people will enter the Holy Land. Here are a few of the verses. The end of verse 2 and the beginning of verse 3: 'And on the day you pass over the Jordan ... you shall set up large stones, and plaster them with plaster; and you shall write upon them all the words of this law.' It concerns all the words of the Torah. Verse 4: 'You shall set up these stones, concerning which I command you this day, on Mount Ebal.' The location where this ceremony has to take place is specified – there are two mounts: Mount Ebal and, next to it, Mount Gerizim. Having set up stones there, and written the Torah upon them, there is a second recommendation in verse 5: 'And there you shall build an altar to the Lord your God, an altar of stones; you shall lift up no iron tool upon them.' Let us appreciate the suggestive symbol: whole stones, unhewn ones, stones which will have been untouched by iron. Iron, probably the principle of all industry, is, in any case, the principle of all warfare. Burnt offerings will be offered on the altar, and peace offerings sacrificed. And verse 8 takes up the initial theme of the inscription of the Torah on the stones, but it specifies how it should be written. It is not the question of language which is raised but, for the moment, that of the graphic quality of the inscription: 'And you shall write upon the stones all the words of this law "very plainly" (*ba'er hetev*).' From verse 11 onwards, we have the recommendations of Moses relating to the dividing of the people on Mounts Ebal and Gerizim, and to the 'ceremony of the Covenant' anticipated by Moses. Six tribes will stand upon Mount Gerizim 'to bless the people', and six others 'shall stand upon Mount Ebal for the curse'. Thus, whether they are blessed or cursed, are not the people as a whole visible to all? During the whole of this anticipated ceremony, the members of the society can see one another. It is extremely important for the theme of our conference devoted to the problem of the community. From verse 14 onwards: 'And the Levites shall declare to all the men of Israel with a loud voice', verses of cursings sanction the transgression of certain interdicts, 'And all the people shall say, "Amen"'. From verse 15 to verse 26 the interdicts in question are listed – there are eleven of them – to which is added the general interdict of transgressing the 'words of this law' (verse 26). These interdicts certainly represent the essential principles of the pact, but they coincide with the Ten Commandments of Sinai on only a few points. There is the prohibition of idolatry, the interdict of treating one's father and mother with contempt, the interdict of moving the boundaries of a piece of land (not to encroach on one's neighbour's property), the order not to mislead a blind man, not to pervert the justice due to the sojourner [stranger], the widow and the orphan; the prohibition of various forms of incest, the interdict of 'slaying one's neighbour in secret' (this is principally how calumny is prohibited), and the interdict of taking a bribe so that an innocent person can be slain. No doubt these are the founding principles of society. Yet they do not cover the content of the Torah as a whole: hence the last verse of the chapter which specifies the whole of these principles. No doubt the evocation of curses and blessings in the first verses of Deuteronomy 27 signifies the blessing for him who respects the interdict, and the curse for him who does not. But in fact it is only the negative version, the curse, which is given in this passage. All the people, after every curse of the Levites, will reply 'Amen'. The words of the Levites are heard by all: all the people are present to all the people. Everyone will say 'Amen'. A veritable pact is thus concluded, and in the presence of the people as a whole, of a society – as I keep emphasizing – in which everyone looks at everyone else.

Let us recognize the fact that the text from Deuteronomy leaves vague many of the points concerning the staging of the ceremony of the pact to which the first sentence of the Talmudic text I am commenting upon seems to refer – or which, at least, it seems to imply.

In fact, this sentence: 'They turned their faces towards Mount Gerizim and opened with the blessing ...' speaks of a 'blessing' which Deuteronomy does not formulate. The sentence refers to another presentation of the scene played out between Mounts Ebal and Gerizim, to the summary given of it in the Book of Joshua (Chapter 8, verses 30 to 35). I shall read it to you, specifying the difference between the two versions. This second account is more precise, and also shorter, and I am reproducing it in its entirety. It appears to be an account of the ceremony such as Joshua, faithful to the recommendation of Moses in Deuteronomy 27, would have carried out. It refers expressly to the recommendations of Moses:

> Then Joshua built an altar in Mount Ebal to the Lord, the God of Israel, as Moses the servant of the Lord had commanded the people of Israel, as it is written in the book of the law of Moses, 'an altar of unhewn stones, upon which no man has lifted an iron tool'; and they offered on it burnt offerings to the Lord, and sacrificed peace offerings. And there, in the presence of the people of Israel, he wrote upon the stones a copy of the law of Moses, which he had written. And all Israel, sojourner as well as homeborn, with their elders and officers and their judges, stood on opposite sides of the ark before the Levitical priests who carried the ark of the covenant of the Lord, half of them in front of Mount Gerizim and half of them in front of Mount Ebal, as Moses the servant of the Lord had commanded at the first, that they should bless the people of Israel. And afterward he read all the words of the law, the blessing and the curse, according to all that is written in the book of the law.

For every prescription of the book of the Law, there was the formula for the curse and the formula for the blessing! 'There was not a word of all that Moses commanded which Joshua did not read before all the assembly of Israel, and the women, and the little ones, and the sojourners who lived among them.'

You will notice that all twelve tribes are present, with women and children, in full, even with the strangers, the *gerim* who are among us. You will see that the meaning of this pact is expanded in relation to the first description we found in Deuteronomy. The picture is a little different – the disposition of the actors is specified, the 'staging' is not quite the same – but there are still the stones untouched by iron, stones which belong to the order of peace and not to that of warfare; and above all there is a remarkable insistence on the totality of the people present at the ceremony: women, children, strangers. There is also an insistence on the totality of the Mosaic text which is read beyond the eleven verses mentioned in Deuteronomy 27. Finally, there is the insistence on the rigorous fidelity to the word of Moses, the servant of God: yet everything that differs here in relation to Deuteronomy 27 is from Moses. Even though Moses spoke differently!

Allow me now to give you the last version of this scene taken from the *Mishnah* itself (32a) to which the *Gemara,* from which our text is extracted, refers, and to which belongs the proposition which figures at the head of my translation with its 'et cetera'. This *Mishnah,* as I have already told you, deals with the authorized or forbidden languages in certain liturgical or ritual formulas, and where our description of the pact simply finds a distant pretext. Here it is:

> Six tribes went up to the top of Mount Gerizim and six tribes went up to the top of Mount Ebal. And the *cohanim* (the priests) and the Levites and the Ark stood below in the midst [as in Joshua]; and the priests surrounded the Ark and the Levites surrounded the *cohanim,* and all Israel were on this side and on that, as it is written in Joshua [the *Mishnah* expressly says that this description conforms to the account found in Joshua], *And all Israel and their elders and officers and their judges stood on this side of the Ark and on that.* They turned their faces towards Mount Gerizim [the text of Joshua 8] and began with the blessing. Blessed be the man that maketh not a graven or molten image. And both these and these answered, 'Amen!' [quotation from Deuteronomy]. They turned their faces towards Mount Ebal and began with the curse, 'cursed be the man' who makes a graven or molten image. And both these and these answered, 'Amen!' – until they completed the blessings and the cursings. And afterward they brought the stones and built the altar and plastered it with plaster. And they wrote thereon all the words of the Law in seventy languages, as it is written 'very plainly' [*ba'er hetev*].[1]

What was a question of writing is now a question of language! This third version of the pact refers to the account of Joshua but takes up the formulas from Deuteronomy. Here the universality of the pact opens up, a pact which in Deuteronomy is concluded with all the tribes before an altar whose stones – already in the ancient texts of a civilization which aspires to have no wars – have not been touched by iron, and which in

Joshua is a pact encompassing women, children and strangers but whose law, according to the text of the *Mishnah,* is proclaimed in seventy languages. A message addressed to all humanity! Thought through to its conclusion, this particular ceremony of a people whose members can look upon one another, a concrete community capable of being taken in at a gaze, permits the whole of humanity to be included in the legislation in whose name this pact has been concluded.

This transition, then, from Hebrew to the universality which I call Greek is quite remarkable. It is the formula *ba'er hetev,* 'very plainly', recommending the clarity and distinction of Scripture, which begins to signify complete translatability. The process of liberation and universalization must therefore be continued. We have not yet finished translating the Bible. The Septuagint is incomplete. Nor have we finished translating the Talmud. We have hardly begun. And as far as the Talmud is concerned, it must be said how delicate the task is! What up until now was a patrimony reserved for oral teaching passes, perhaps too quickly, into foreign languages without losing its unusual features in its new forms.

This universality is thus born, in some way, from a society which, moreover, is entirely visible to its members assembled on two mounts, visible as if on a stage. Right from the beginning, the society which aspires to intimacy between twelve tribes looking at one another, this society of a community, is already present to the whole of humanity, or opens on to the whole of humanity.

You have had here a specific example of the development of an idea passing from the written Law to the oral Law. The oral Law claims to speak about what the written Law says. But the oral Law knows more. It goes further than the plain meaning of the passage studied, but it does so in the spirit of the global meaning of Scripture.

4 The Various Dimensions of the Law

But let us return to our text. It is now going to show us various dimensions in this pact of the Torah, dimensions which ought to guarantee that a community whose members are practically face to face should keep its interpersonal relationships when its members look outwards towards humanity. The distinction between community and society testifies only to a social thought that is not yet mature. The adoption of the Law on which this society is based would entail, for those men who adopt it correctly, the possibility of remaining face to face with one another.

> Our Rabbis taught [a *baraitha*]: There was a benediction in general and a benediction in particular, likewise a curse in general and a curse in particular. (Scripture states): *to learn, to teach,* to *observe* [to keep] and *to do;* consequently there are four (duties associated with each commandment). Twice four are eight and twice eight are sixteen.

The arithmetic is undeniable! But what is being spoken about here? In the text from Deuteronomy, the same laws are proclaimed and followed by curses for the person who transgresses them and blessings for the person who obeys them. For the person who undertakes to keep it, this cursing and blessing therefore constitute two independent ways of adhering to the same Law. In the covenant made on Mounts Ebal and Gerizim, there were thus two acts of will made to the same Law. 'Yes' was said twice over. If we look at the text of Deuteronomy 27, we will see that the interdicts are expressed in a particular form, but that according to the last verse they are included in the invocation of the 'words of this [whole] law'. The Torah is thus expressed in a general form and in a particular form. This makes two more acts of adherence. Two acts of adherence assenting to the curses, and two acts of adherence consenting to the blessings. So there are four acts of adherence. Four not as two plus two, but four as two times two.

But we know, moreover – if we refer to Deuteronomy 5: 1 and Deuteronomy 11: 19 – that the Torah entails four general obligations: the need to learn it (*lilmod*), to teach it (*lelamed*), to observe [to keep] it (*lishmor*), to do it (*la'asot*). Four covenants are included in the Covenant. Now we have just seen that every adherence to the Covenant entails four modes of adherence; there are thus sixteen covenants in the Covenant, sixteen pacts in the pact. The arithmetic may be surprising. I shall come back to it shortly. Let us say, generally, that in what we simply call adherence to the law, the rabbinical scholars distinguish sixteen dimensions.

Sixteen dimensions. But there are more! The Torah is said to have been taught three times, if we refer to the rabbinical calculations: according to Exodus, the first time at Sinai; the second time, according to Deuteronomy, in the plains of Moab; and for the third time – as we have just seen – between Ebal and Gerizim. Each time, as we have said, there were sixteen adherences, which makes forty-eight adherences in all. Let us stay at forty-eight for the moment. You will see that there are even more.

I shall try to explain the signification of these distinctions and calculations. Some people must certainly have been surprised that in the adherence to a law which implies a blessing for the person who obeys it and a curse for the person who transgresses it, two different acts can be discerned, as if the blessing and the curse were not the two faces, the positive and the negative, of the sanction which all law entails. In concrete terms, the difference between these two faces is a real one. Already, in passing a law, forgiveness can be reckoned with in the case of transgression. We can tell ourselves that things will always sort themselves out! Thank God, forgiveness is not unknown in Israel. Only in Israel it is not taken into account at the moment the Law is adopted. If forgiveness is to have a meaning, it should not already be accepted at the moment of adherence to the Law. We know the distrust that Judaism has in relation to forgiveness granted in advance. We know where it can lead.

Can adherence to the Law as a whole, to the Law in its general terms, be distinguished from the 'yes' which accompanies the statements of each law in particular? Naturally, a general adherence is necessary. The general spirit of a legislation should be drawn out. The spirit of the law should be deepened. Philosophy is not forbidden, the intervention of reason is not unwelcome! If there is really to be an inner adherence, this process of generalization cannot be put aside. But why distinguish from it the access to the particular expressions of this general spirit? Because the meaning of a legislation in its general spirit remains unknown as long as the laws which it embraces have not been recognized. There are two processes here, and their distinction is justified from several points of view. We are all sensitive to Judaism being reduced to a few 'spiritual' principles. We are all seduced by what can be called the angelic essence of the Torah to which many verses and commandments are reduced in an immediate way. This 'interiorization' of the Law charms our liberal soul, and we are inclined to reject what seems to resist the 'rationality' or 'morality' of the Torah. Judaism has always been conscious – rabbinical literature testifies to this – of the presence within it – and this is necessary for great spiritual quality – of elements which cannot be interiorized straight away. Next to the *mishpatim*, the laws of justice in which all are recognized, there are the *chuqim*, the unjustifiable laws which are Satan's joy when he mocks the Torah. He claims that the ritual of the 'red heifer' in Numbers 19 is meaningless and tyrannical. And what about circumcision? Will a little psychoanalysis explain it away? It was certainly not foreseen, and it has to be wondered whether it even works! What about many other ceremonial or ritual preparations described in the Torah? Consequently, in the law of Israel there are points which demand, beyond assenting to the general or 'deep' spirit of the Torah, a special consent to the particularities which are all too easily regarded as transitory. There is constantly within us a struggle between our adherence to the spirit and adherence to what is called the letter. That the latter is as indispensable as the former is what is signified in seeing two distinct acts in the acceptance of the Torah. This is also Jacob's struggle with the Angel: to overcome in the existence of Israel the angelism of pure interiority. Note with what effort victory is given here! Yet is it in fact given? No one prevails! And it is Jacob's religion which remains a little lame when the Angel's grip is released. This struggle is never over. But remember, the Angel is not the highest creature: as a purely spiritual being, it does not achieve the condition that life according to the Torah presupposes. It has neither to eat, to take, to give, to work, nor not to work on the Sabbath! A principle of generosity, but nothing but a principle. Admittedly, generosity entails an adherence. But adherence to the principle is not sufficient, and it entails a temptation; it calls for care and for our fight.

There is in the particular yet another reason for it to appear in the Law as an independent principle in relation to the universality reflected by all particular laws. It is precisely the concrete and particular aspect of the Law and the circumstances of its application which command Talmudic dialectics: the oral law is casuistic. It concerns itself with the transition from the general principle incarnated by the Law to its possible execution, its concretization. If this transition were purely deducible, the Law, as a particular law, would not have required a separate adherence. But it so happens – and this is the great wisdom the awareness of which animates the Talmud – that the general and generous principles can be inverted in their application. Every generous thought is threatened by its Stalinism. The great strength of the Talmud's casuistry is to be the special discipline which seeks in the particular the precise moment at which the general principle runs the danger of becoming its own contrary, and watches over the general in the light of the particular. This protects us from ideology. Ideology is the generosity and clarity of the principle which have not taken into account the inversion which keeps a watch on this general principle when it is applied; or – to pick up on the image used a short while ago – the Talmud is the struggle with the Angel. This is why adherence to the particular law is an irreducible dimension in all allegiance, and you will see that R. Akiba thinks not only that it is as important as that of adherence to the Law in its general form, but also that the place dedicated to its study – ultimately, the *yeshivah* – is one of the three places where the pact is made, and that the dignity of this place equals that of Sinai, where the Torah is revealed, and that of the plains of Moab, where it is repeated by Moses.

In the apparently strange calculation of the forty-eight covenants which our text discerns at the heart of the pacts made around the Law, the number four has been brought in, representing the four promises that all adherence to the Law entails: the promise to learn it, to teach it, to observe it and to do it. Without the theoretical activity of study, without the obligation of listening and reading, without the *lilmod,* nothing can enter us. But it is also necessary to teach what has been learnt in order to transmit it. The transmission, the *lelamed,* is an obligation distinct from the pure receptivity of study. For humankind entails the risk of a fossilization of acquired knowledge, depositing itself in our consciousness like some inert matter and being handed down in this ossified form from one generation to another. This congealment of the spiritual is not the same as its true transmission, whose essence lies elsewhere: in vitality, inventiveness and renewal which occur precisely through being taken up by way of tradition, or of a lesson taught to the other and assumed by the other. Without this method of procedure, it is not possible for true revelation – that is, a thought authentically thought – to take place. Transmission thus involves a teaching which is already outlined in the very receptivity for learning it. Receptivity is prolonged: true learning consists in receiving the lesson so deeply that it becomes a necessity to give oneself to the other. The lesson of truth is not held in one man's consciousness. It explodes towards the other. To study well, to read well, to listen well, is already to speak: whether by asking questions and, in so doing, teaching the master who teaches you, or by teaching a third party.

In the last four books of the Pentateuch one verse constantly appears: 'And the Lord said to Moses: "Say to the people of Israel *lemor* ('in these terms')"'. A prestigious master I had after the Liberation used to claim to be able to give one hundred and twenty different interpretations of this phrase whose plain meaning, however, is devoid of mystery. He revealed only one to me. I have tried to guess a second. The one he revealed to me consisted in translating *lemor* by 'so as not to say'. Which amounted to signifying: 'Say to the people of Israel so as not to say'. The unspoken is necessary, so that listening remains a way of thinking; or it is necessary for the word to be also unspoken, so that truth (or the Word of God) does not consume those who listen; or the Word of God has to be able to lodge itself, without danger to mankind, in the tongue and language of men. In my own reading of this verse, *lemor* would signify 'in order to say': 'Say to the people of Israel in order for them to speak'; teach them sufficiently in depth for them to begin to speak, for them to hear at the point of speaking. The one hundred and eighteen other significations of the verse remain to be discovered. My master carried their secret to his tomb.

Let us move on to the third obligation: to observe [to keep]. *Lishmor.* There are two possibilities: *lishmor* would signify the observance of the negative commandments, the interdicts. Here, where the difference between negative or positive commandments is not made, this interpretation is impossible. *Lishmor,* then, would signify the new thing which is necessary once one has learnt: not to forget – that is, to repeat the lessons. Studying is never over in its very reception.

Finally, *la'asot,* 'to do'. This requires no explanations. The depth of our text consists in thinking of the four points as going together, as liable to isolation and not perversion. Each of these moments of study requires a special adherence and special care. There were, then, sixteen covenants in each pact. Now the pact was made in these three places – on Sinai, in the plains of Moab, and between Ebal and Gerizim – which makes forty-eight covenants around the Law. But on this point there was a disagreement. As you will see, R. Akiba does not agree to consider the ceremony between Mounts Ebal and Gerizim as counting as one of the three occasions. I personally am very happy that R. Akiba should have had a doubt here. I shall tell you why later.

5 The Three Occasions

That the pact of the Covenant was made three times is indicated at the heart of the Talmudic text we are commenting upon in the account of the ceremony near Mount Gerizim, and by the 'it was similar at Sinai and the plains of Moab'. Here is the text in full: 'It was similar at Sinai and the plains of Moab; as it was said, *These are the words of the covenant which the Lord commanded Moses to make with the people of Israel in the land of Moab'*, besides the pact he had made with them at Horeb. '*Keep therefore the words of this covenant.*'

But here is someone who contests a point in this calculation: 'R. Simeon excludes (the occasion of) Mount Gerizim and Mount Ebal and includes that of the Tent of Meeting in the wilderness.'

Admittedly, R. Simeon also thinks that the covenant was made three times, but for him the ceremony which took place between Mounts Gerizim and Ebal does not count. In order to arrive at the number three, R. Simeon considers the covenant to have been made in the meetings between Moses and the people, of which Exodus Chapter 33 verse 7 speaks: 'Now Moses used to take the tent and pitch it outside the camp, far off from the camp; and he called it the tent of meeting. And every one who sought the Lord would go out to the tent of meeting, which was outside the camp.' The number of forty-eight covenants is thus guaranteed. But R. Simeon prefers to confer the dignity of the covenant's conclusion not on the simple ceremony which, for him, the rite between Mounts Ebal and Gerizim really was, but on the discussion concerning the Lord's Law, on the study of the Law which is supposed to be done inside the 'tent of meeting in the wilderness', where Moses welcomes those who have questions or problems. The Covenant is not staged so that everyone can see everyone else; the Covenant is where the pupils, as individuals, question the master. It was in the tent of meeting, precisely, in the *yeshivah* of Moses, that the voice of God is heard, and it is there, after Sinai and before the plains of Moab, that the Covenant is made for the second time.

For R. Simeon, then, the ceremony is replaced by study. An important decision. We shall see straight away that this was also R. Akiba's opinion. What are R. Simeon's motives? Rashi obviously asks this question. R. Simeon would have told himself that the text of Deuteronomy 27, announcing the ceremony on Mount Gerizim, lists only a few of the laws of the Torah. The whole of the Torah as such does not appear. The ceremony cannot, therefore, count as a 'complete' covenant. I do not wish to dispute Rashi's word. But was not R. Simeon also shocked by the fact that the laws mentioned in Deuteronomy 27 are proclaimed only in a repressive manner? Only curses are indicated. Admittedly there were blessings, but their formulation is missing.

Be that as it may, R. Simeon's intervention disputing the validity of the covenant at Mount Gerizim raises an important question. It is closely akin to a discussion which had taken place between the giants of the

Talmud: the Tannaim, R. Ishmael and R. Akiba, R. Simeon's master. Here is the text:

> The difference of opinion here is the same as that of the teachers [the Tannaim] in the following [a *baraitha*]: R. Ishmael says: General laws were proclaimed at Sinai and particular laws in the Tent of Meeting. R. Akiba says: Both general and particular laws were proclaimed at Sinai, repeated in the Tent of Meeting, and for the third time in the plains of Moab. Consequently there is not a single precept written in the Torah in connection with which forty-eight covenants were not made.

The difference of opinion expressed by R. Simeon thus dates back to an older discussion between Tannaim, between R. Ishmael and R. Akiba. R. Ishmael thought that the ceremony which took place between Mounts Ebal and Gerizim is included among the three ceremonies which should be counted as making the pact. What did he mean by this? Perhaps he thought that besides Sinai and the plains of Moab there was no other rite for the Covenant. For him only the particularities of the Law were taught in the tent of meeting, and the general laws at Sinai, such that Sinai and the tent of meeting count together as one single covenant. The plains of Moab are the second covenant, and Mounts Ebal and Gerizim the third. Moreover, perhaps R. Ishmael thought that something I will not discuss today – which is a possible problem – should be discussed: perhaps R. Ishmael was disputing this total equality between the study of the generalities and the particularities of the Law. Certainly he thought that the particular and the general are both important. If he had not, he would not be a master of the Talmud. But he considered that despite everything, the general laws are more important. Is he more liberal than R. Akiba? We should ask the Talmudists in the room who are more competent than me. Perhaps R. Ishmael considers that the ceremony in which everyone can see everyone else is an important ceremony. Perhaps he also had similar ideas to those formulated on the distinction between society and community, and consequently, for him, the experience of the community must have been an essential moment of revelation.

R. Akiba seems opposed to these ideas. He affirms the absolutely equal dignity of the general and the particular. He seems to exclude the ceremony in which everyone can see everyone else. Perhaps he thinks that the concrete presence of men is not what constitutes the true face-to-face.

We have come to count forty-eight covenants. We have tried to understand this calculation as the affirmation of the various dimensions of the Law, which go beyond the formal qualities of the anonymous law that would be at the origin of the crisis of modern society.

6 The Law and Interpersonal Relations

Forty-eight covenants? There are even more. 'R. Simeon b. Judah of Kefar Acco said in the name of R. Simeon' – in the name of the same R. Simeon who disputed the importance of the ceremony at Gerizim – 'There is not a single precept written in the Torah in connection with which forty-eight times 603,550 covenants were not made.'

The number of covenants made in these three ceremonies would thus be 603,550 multiplied by 48. Where does the figure 603,550 come from? It represents the number of Israelites standing at the foot of Sinai. But why multiply by this number? Because the Covenant made around the revealed Law, instead of appearing as an impersonal abstraction of a juridical act, is greeted as establishing living links with all those who adopt the Law: everyone finds himself responsible for everyone else; in every act of the Covenant more than six hundred thousand personal acts of responsibility are outlined. The forty-eight dimensions of the pact become 48 × 603,550. Obviously this may raise a smile. It is a lot. But it is still not an infinite number. The Israelites – or, more exactly, the men of mankind – are answerable for one another before a truly human law. In this making of the Covenant we have non-indifference concerning the other. Everyone looks at me! We do not need to meet on Mount Ebal or Gerizim and gaze at one another eye to eye to be in a position where we all look at one another. Everyone looks at me. Let us not forget the seventy languages in which the Torah is proclaimed. The Torah belongs to us all: everybody is responsible for everybody else. The phrase 'Love your neighbour as yourself' still presupposes self-love as the prototype of love. Here, the ethical signifies: 'Be responsible for the other as you are responsible for yourself'. We avoid the presupposition of self-love – self-esteem – which can be taken as the very definition of the personal. But we have not yet finished.

'Rabbi said . . .' The Rabbi who is speaking now is Rabenu Hakadosh, who gave the *Mishnah* its written form and is the highest Talmudic authority after, or next to, R. Akiba. 'Rabbi said: According to the reasoning of R. Simeon b. Judah of Kefar Acco who said in the name of R. Simeon . . .'

What a lot of references! Those of you who are perhaps attending a Talmudic lesson for the first time should not be surprised at this piling up. There is always a lot of care taken in the Talmud to specify who said what: a true lesson taught is that in which the universal nature of the proclaimed truth allows neither the name nor the person of him who said it to disappear. The scholars of the Talmud even think that the Messiah will come at the moment when everybody quotes what they learn in the name of the very person from whom they learnt it. Rabbi, then, says:

> There is not a single precept written in the Torah in connection with which forty-eight times 603,550 covenants were not made, it follows that for each Israelite there are 603,550 commandments (and forty-eight covenants were made in connection with each of them).

Is he not repeating the truth we have just seen? The *Gemara* asks itself the question. 'What is the issue between them?' It is R. Mesharsheya who locates the issue. 'R. Mesharsheya said: The point between them is that of personal responsibility and responsibility for others [responsibility of responsibility].'

Not only are we responsible for everyone else, but we are also responsible for everyone else's responsibility. Forty-eight, then, has to be multiplied by 603,550, and the result multiplied again by 603,550. This is extremely important. We saw a short while ago something that resembles recognition of the other, love of the other. To such a degree that I am answerable for the other, for the other's adherence and faithfulness to the Law. His concern is my concern. But is not my concern his? Is he not responsible for me? Consequently, can I be answerable for his responsibility for me? *Kol Yisra'el 'arevim zeh lazeh*, 'Everyone in Israel is answerable for everyone else', signifies: all adherents to the divine Law, all men who are truly men, are responsible for one another.

This must also signify that my responsibility stretches to the responsibility that the other man can assume. I always have, myself, one responsibility more than the other, for I am still responsible for his responsibility. And, if he is responsible for my responsibility, I am still responsible for the responsibility that he has for my responsibility: *en ladavar soph*, 'it is never-ending'. Behind the responsibility attributed to everyone for everyone, there arises, *ad infinitum,* the fact that in the society of the Torah I am still responsible for this responsibility! It is an ideal, but an ideal that implies the humanity of mankind. In the Covenant, when it is fully understood, in a society that deploys all the dimensions of the Law, society is also community.

6

On Religious Language and the Fear of God
For Paul Ricœur

The Word of God, to speak to God, to speak of God and of the Word of God – Holy Scripture, prayer, theology: what the multiple expressions of religious language have in common is the claim to be inexhaustible in references to the world from which the signification of words, propositions and discourses is woven. How do we open to language the borders of the given reality in which we live? Paul Ricœur has shown us the resources of the imagination, which would not be a simply reproductive faculty, doubling the perception of objects to which it owes everything except its powers of illusion. On the contrary, it would be the deepest dimension of the human psyche, immediately functioning in the element of poetic language, the 'mysterious root' of all the forces of the mind which are similar to the sur-real: 'Poetic language alone restores us to a sense of belonging to an order of things, which precedes our ability to distinguish ourselves from these things as objects facing a subject'.[1] In the poetic imagination, the unheard can be heard, called out to and expressed; a text can be opened up to the hermeneutic process more widely than the precise intentions which had determined it; metaphor can lead beyond, the experiences which seem to have created it; and symbol would give cause for thought on a speculative level. When it is marked by the exceptional character of the messenger, the imperative or teaching which comes from outside would be able to vouch for itself in the mind of the listener: this ability to bear witness, linked to that of the poetic word, would be the very depth of the psyche. The transcendent would be able to seduce and open up the imagination rather than constraining the will. There would be a mediation here connecting freedom to a certain obedience, a 'dependence without heteronomy' reconciling transcendence and interiority.

In connection with this, we shall try to present, by way of commentary, a short passage from the Babylonian Talmud. We shall try to bring to light a description of religious language which admittedly, in the last analysis, relates it fundamentally to a thought which is already a discourse (reading and studying the Torah) but which, between the Torah and the discourse allowing transcendence to signify, brings in attitudes of will as carriers of meaning, a psyche of obedience 'older' than thought living on poetic imagination, a discipline which is heteronomous to the point of depending on an educational community, and anterior to the specific possibilities of language play.

Our passage, taken from the Tractate Berakoth 33b, is related to the norms of the religious language constituted by prayer.[2] The text certainly does not exhaust the problem with which it is concerned. Nor is it the only one of its kind in the Talmud, nor the most famous, nor the most exclusive of texts where the emphasis on the themes they evoke may be placed differently, and where other themes that are perhaps less severe may arise in discussion. The one we have chosen is literally repeated in another Tractate (Megillah 25a). It is thus important in the flow of thoughts to which it belongs.

Commentary is necessary to the very presentation of this extract, for like all Talmudic texts, its specific structure is unusual on first reading. Compact, elliptical, allusive and, as it were, challenging all rhetoric and all magic of the word (for it to be intelligible, a simple translation requires the addition of syntactic particles and even implied sentence members), it is made up of arguments, questions and answers, objections and replies to the objections, all chronologically separated from one another, sometimes by centuries, yet brought together by the logic of the purpose whose mediate inferences are not all explicit. It has an incessant concern for attributing every saying to its historical author. Hence the constant evocation of personal names of the rabbinical scholars who have spoken or who, in such and such a circumstance, behaved in such and such a way. This is not to offer the reader a purely anecdotal interest; it is there for the purposes of teaching. Finally, in the presentation of the discussions there is very often a way of leaving them open, which would not fail to surprise those who believe in the false reputation of the dogmatism attached to the Talmudic Tractates.[3]

Like all Talmudic texts, and all commentaries on those texts, our text, modest as it may be, is for traditional Jewish thought both a religious discourse and a relation to God that is at least as intimate as prayer. A quality which – for our purpose, in any case – would come as an added bonus; the explanation of the text is sought in what is said – and in the suggestions of what is not said – only inasmuch as it contributes to the thoughts on religious language instigated by Paul Ricœur.

Here is the text:[4]

MISHNAH. If one (in praying) says 'May thy mercies extend to a bird's nest', 'Be thy name mentioned for well-doing' or 'We give thanks, we give thanks', he is silenced.

GEMARA. We understand why he is silenced if he says, 'We give thanks, we give thanks', because he seems to be acknowledging two Powers; also if he says, 'Be thy name mentioned for well-doing', because this implies, for the good only and not for the bad, and we have learnt, A man must bless God for the evil as he blesses Him for the good. But what is the reason for silencing him if he says, 'Thy mercies extend to the bird's nest'? Two Amoraim in the West,[5] R. Jose b. Abin and R. Jose b. Zebida, give different answers; one says it is because he creates jealousy among God's creatures, the other, because he presents the measures taken by the Holy One, blessed be He, as springing from compassion, whereas they are but decrees. A certain (reader) went down (before the Ark) in the presence of Rabbah and said, 'Thou hast shown mercy to the bird's nest, show Thou pity and mercy to us'. Said Rabbah: How well this student knows how to placate his [heavenly] Master! Said Abaye to him [Rabbah]: But we have learnt, 'he is silenced'? Rabbah too acted thus only to test Abaye. A certain (reader) went down in the presence of R. Hanina and said, O God, the great, mighty, terrible, majestic, powerful, awful, strong, fearless, sure and honoured. He [R. Hanina] waited till he had finished, and when he had finished he said to him, Have you concluded all the praise [glorifying] your Master? Why do we want all this? Even with these three that we do say [in prayer], had not Moses our Master mentioned them in the Law and had not the Men of the Great Synagogue come and inserted them in the *Tefillah* [the ritual], we should not have been able to mention them, and you say all these and still go on! It is as if

87

an earthly king [a king of flesh and blood] had a million *denarii* of gold, and someone praised him as possessing silver ones. Would it not be an insult to him? R. Hanina further said: Everything is in the hand of heaven except the fear of heaven, as it says, *And now, Israel, what doth the Lord thy God require of thee but to fear* (Deuteronomy 10: 12). Is the fear of heaven such a little thing? Has not R. Hanina said in the name of R. Simeon b. Yohai: The Holy One, blessed be He, has in His treasury nought except a store of the fear of heaven, as it says, *The fear of the Lord is his treasure* (Isaiah 33: 6)? Yes; for Moses it was a small thing; as R. Hanina said: To illustrate by a parable, if a man is asked for a big article and he has it, it seems like a small article to him; if he is asked for a small article and he does not possess it, it seems like a big article to him. 'We give thanks, we give thanks, he is silenced.' R. Zera said: To say 'Hear, hear', (in the *Shema)* is like saying 'We give thanks, we give thanks'. An objection was raised: He who recites the *Shema* and repeats it is reprehensible. He is reprehensible, but we do not silence him? There is no contradiction; in the one case he repeats each word as he says it, in the other each sentence. Said R. Papa to Abaye: But perhaps (he does this because) at first he was not attending to what he said and the second time he does attend? He [Abaye] replied: Can one behave familiarly with Heaven? If he did not recite with attention at first, we hit him with a smith's hammer until he does attend.

1 The Three 'Interdicts'

Our *Mishnah* denounces as improper three formulations of prayer which, paradoxically, appear to be pious.

The first alludes to Deuteronomy 22: 6–7:

> If you chance to come upon a bird's nest, in any tree or on the ground, with young ones or eggs and the mother sitting upon the young or upon the eggs, you shall not take the mother with the young; you shall let the mother go, but the young you may take to yourself; that it may go well with you, and that you may live long.

Let us leave aside the multiple explanations that rabbinical hermeneutics, at its various levels, gives of these biblical verses: their letter, their details, their possible symbols. We are not concerned with them here. The meaning as prayer would understand it, paradoxically prohibited, consists in glorifying the compassion of God which seems to extend his protection to the animal kingdom which is, however, subordinate to man (Genesis 1: 28).

The prohibition of the second formulation may seem even stranger. It would forbid mentioning God's name by justifying this mention through the good that is done.

The third 'impropriety' (and this surprises us too) would stem from repeating the terms 'We give thanks', which begin one of the blessings that appear in the daily prayer of the Israelite ritual called the 'Eighteen Benedictions'.[6]

The expression 'he is silenced' which closes the *Mishnah* is clarified in the *Gemara* by the behaviour of Rabbah and R. Hanina which it recounts.

2 From Man to God: The Confession of God's Unity and the Love of God

Why these three prohibitions? What binds them together? The *Gemara* begins by explaining the last two to us.

He who repeats 'We give thanks' seems to be addressing two divine Powers instead of confessing strict monotheism. We see here the extreme concern for form in respect of monotheism's exclusivity and the extreme importance attached to the psychological effects of the symbolism of attitudes, gestures and words – a discipline which is a typical feature of Jewish culture, and on which a true language would also depend. But in multiplying the 'giving of thanks', 'pouring out a stream of thanks', expressing gratitude to all those who are good to us, do we not move outside actual ritual life, and acknowledge or create for ourselves numerous cults, lose the distinction between levels, whereas God (the Most High, *El 'Elyon*) is unique?

But can this cult of the unique resist the insurmountable dualism of good and evil? The temptation here is to betray monotheism by invoking the Name of God only for the good that comes from him, and by imagining the forces of evil as independent of the divine will. The danger of a heresy that does not have a purely intellectual position as its aim, but the fundamental real-life experience of the relation to God. In what sort of piety, then, is speaking-to-God or prayer actually possible? This is the real theme of our text, which appears to have only formal concerns. From this point on in our text, the question arises of the place in this lived experience for the love of God, and the nature of this religious love. Is it in the acknowledgement of the satisfaction of our needs, or in the gratitude for proximity? In fact, our *Gemara* evokes a teaching of the Tannaim, a *Mishnah* according to which 'it is incumbent on a man to bless God for the evil in the same way as for the good' (54a of our Tractate). Here is the translation, followed by the translation of the *Gemara* which refers to it (60b). It constitutes a second text to be interpreted:

> It is incumbent on a man to bless God for the evil in the same way as for the good, as it says: *And thou shalt love the Lord thy God with all thy heart, and with all thy soul, and with all thy might* (Deuteronomy 6: 5). 'With all thy heart' means, with thy two impulses, the evil impulse as well as the good impulse;[7] 'with all thy soul' means, even though he takes thy soul (life); 'with all thy might' means, with all thy money [all thou possess].[8] Another explanation of 'with all thy might' is, whatever treatment he metes out to thee.[9]

Now here is the *Gemara* which 'explains' this *Mishnah*:

> What is meant by being bound to bless for the evil in the same way as for the good? Shall I say that, just as for the good one says the benediction 'Who is good and bestows good', so for evil one should say the benediction 'Who is good and bestows good'? But we have learnt: For good tidings one says, who is good and bestows good: for evil tidings one says, blessed be the true judge? Raba said: What it really means is that one must receive the evil with gladness. R. Aha said in the name of R. Levi: Where do we find this in the Scripture? *I will sing of mercy and justice, unto Thee, O Lord, will I sing praises* (Psalms 101: 1); whether it is 'mercy' I will sing, or whether it is 'justice' I will sing. R. Samuel b. Nahmani said: We learn it from here: *In the Lord* [written as the Tetragrammaton] *I will praise His word, in God I will praise His word* (Psalms 56: 10). *In the Lord* [written as the Tetragrammaton, signifying divine Mercy in the rabbinical tradition] *I will praise His word:* this refers to good dispensation; *In God* [which in the same tradition signifies God's rigorous Justice] *I will praise His word:* this refers to the dispensation of suffering. R. Tanhum said: We learn it from here: *I will lift up the cup of salvation and call on the name of the Lord; I found trouble and sorrow, but I called upon the name of the Lord* (Psalms 116: 13 and 116:

3–4). The Rabbis derive it from here: *The Lord gave and the Lord hath taken away; blessed be the name of the Lord* (Job 1: 21).

What lies behind this display of erudition? Above all, through the apparent attachment to the letter, there is the extreme attention paid to the spirit of the biblical text and a hermeneutic which puts a passage from Deuteronomy back into the context of (with a view to deepening) the totality of the Bible. For a commentary on this commentary to be comprehensive it would have to pick up on each of these biblical references and specify the difference of the ideas which are hidden beneath the variety of quotations. Without undertaking this task, let us note the last opinion attributed to the Rabbis (which often indicates the most authoritative opinion). It is enough, in fact, to refer to the context of Job 1: 21 to see that the blessing of the Lord at the hour of misfortune is not the mark of insensibility, nor of a simple inversion of natural sensibility. Rather, it is something in sorrow which is stronger-than-sorrow, something beyond sensibility.

For us readers of Berakoth 33b, under the obligation to 'silence him who gives thanks to God by evoking only the good that is done', for us who discover love at the heart of piety, the *Mishnah* 54a and the *Gemara* 60b clarify the notion of this love. It transcends the preferences of our natural inclinations, as if, above and beyond the good deeds which satisfy us, and are in keeping with what is within us to do and what we are capable of doing, that is, in keeping with our needs, the good of a disinterested attachment – the ethical good – were possible, reconciling the contradictions of human nature and demanding the sacrifice of what we are and what we have. An attachment which is also a sense of gratitude felt in the consciousness of a proximity at a level that is higher than the intimacy of satisfaction. A sense of gratitude for proximity-itself lived in gratitude, and as if the very meaning of the word God and the possibility of evoking and invoking it – the transcendent discourse – were to arise in this attachment. This proximity and this gratitude called love characterize monotheism, as if the possibility of the ethical good, above and beyond the difference between natural good and evil deeds, were the opening to transcendence and the source of religious language.

What is the path or the state of mind that leads to this transcendent love? We shall see from the rest of our text that this is its primary concern. But meanwhile, we have shown the way in which the impropriety of evoking God 'uniquely for the good that is done' is very much like that which consists in compromising monotheism by the dispersion of gratitudes.

3 From God to Man: Preference or Justice?

But why is the evocation of divine compassion stretching to the bird's nest said to be reprehensible?

R. Jose b. Abin fears the jealousy that this formulation – or this thought – would be capable of arousing in the work of Creation. God's creature is subject to rigorous justice. Compassion puts one creature aside. Would not this be to favour one above others? Does not the phrase 'to a bird's nest' simultaneously imply that this small creature does not have, in principle, the right to compassion, and that preference can replace justice? Compassion which is not the same for everyone arouses jealousy – that is, war. It cannot be said of God. Only the idea of a divine justice which is higher than compassion, then, can correspond in thought and discourse to the love that man owes to God – which, as we have just seen, is not something that is felt.

4 Obedience and Human Disinterestedness

We are now at the point of extending the ideas implied in the two interdicts that we have already presented. R. Jose b. Zebida's opinion is taken up here too: how do we think the relation of God to man? The way in which he understands it allows us to push the dis-interestedness of human love as far as it can go.

According to R. Jose b. Zebida, the evocation of the compassion that God is said to have felt before the bird's nest is improper not because it would express a preference but because it expresses a feeling. God's commandments – the relation of God to man – are the decrees of his will. In the realm of justice, admittedly, but in the realm of an unjustifiable justice which man cannot enter with the natural feelings which compassion still resembles. A justice whose laws are revealed only in their form as pure commandments, and which consequently demand an obedience of pure heteronomy. Man's love for God is thereby described positively, above and beyond its negative characteristic of a love which is not felt. An obedience which answers to a totally exterior will where man does not even discover the formal universality of Kant's categorical imperative. We learn from what follows that this obedience, experienced as the 'fear of heaven', is not 'in the hand' of heaven. The total exteriority of the divine will – the absolute heteronomy of its decrees – does not, therefore, constrain man in terms of force. Does not the *Gemara* come to suggest that it is in the privileged phenomenon of an almost blind obedience to a total heteronomy – but an obedience whose very disinterestedness shields it from all constraint, be it seduction or fear – that the exceptional nature of divine transcendence takes on meaning? In this heteronomy, to speak of God is, admittedly, already to expose oneself to the derision of rational beings,[10] but it is also, for man, to reach the greatest intimacy and the recognition of the highest of heights – or, more exactly, it is to reach the very meaning of the word God. This is an essential moment of Jewish piety.

But it is probably for this reason that the category of the fear of God is soon to appear in the central part of our *Gemara*. Does it not prove to be the unavoidable – and most difficult – stage of the actual love of God?

5 The Impossible Praises

This central part of our *Gemara* is preceded by two brief accounts which constitute teachings.

First of all we have the intervention of Rabbah, before whom a believer ('a disciple of the Rabbis') evokes in his prayer precisely God's compassion for a bird's nest. The master's intervention does not consist in interrupting the prayer but in disapproving of it when it has finished in order to avoid repeating the impropriety. This disapproval of the 'student of the Rabbis' is both ironic and ambiguous, so as not to wound the spiritual refinement of another scholar, Abaye. All this serves to attenuate the rigours of the *Mishnah*. Such rigours apply only to a high level of religious language, which a young colleague of the master may not have reached. The less refined religious feeling, which has recourse to a language which is spiritually less polished or less precise, must thus be treated cautiously. That is the first teaching.

The second intervention that is related concerns R. Hanina teaching a believer who, in his prayer, allows himself hyperbolical adjectives to praise the Lord. Here too, the master's attitude consists in teaching, not in interrupting – consequently, in having understanding for a naive religious feeling which has recourse to a natural and seductive, albeit improper, language. The highness of God is not expressed by the superlative of natural attributes.

But the second account is not the pure repetition of the first. It puts the exalting of God by moral attributes on the same plane as exalting him by attributes of power. They are all taken from the world. A royal treasury containing gold is converted into silver coins. R. Hanina's doctrine thus goes so far as to prohibit praises in religious language as such. But only that which is above all praise, the highness of the Most High, is implicitly thought here in order to prohibit these specific superlatives. Finally, beyond the tolerance granted to the spirituality which is less cultivated than that of the elite, the account seems to acknowledge the necessities peculiar to the institutional forms of the cult: the praises in a liturgy, those made known by Moses and written into the ritual by the Men of the Great Synagogue, must be allowed.[11] Were it not for the necessities of these institutions, for the small number of permitted hyperboles, for the authority of the masters, the praises of God as religious language would be intolerable.

6 The Fear of God

It is in the manner of the Talmudic text – which can be considered as a process of compilation – to quote, in evoking the adage of a rabbinical scholar, his other sayings, which may seem to bear no relation to the subject under discussion. But it must always be asked whether there is not, between these apparently disparate sayings, a profound link which revives the discussion, opens it up to new perspectives, throws new light on to it or discovers its true object. R. Hanina has just spoken. His new saying concerning the unique value of the fear of God in the 'divine treasury', to which man alone can contribute, for it is not within God's power to do so, in fact reveals the secret of the relation to God and of religious discourse, towards which the whole of the discussion we are commenting upon was moving.[12]

The unique treasure of the divine treasury is the fear of God. Despite everything that has been said about love! But perhaps because of everything that has been said about interested love. The love which is not a sense of 'gratitude motivated by satisfaction'[13] envelops the fear of God which determines its level. It is the unavoidable nerve-centre of the relation to God. A fear which is not simply a fear aroused by threat, which would be well within the power of an almighty! A fear which, consequently, answers essentially not to the almighty thought from the point of view of the world's forces, but to the absolutely Other. The only way this latter could reveal its alterity, without betraying it in the actual revelation, would be in the heteronomy acknowledged by obedience as a non-violent superiority, as unique, as a specifically divine superiority: that is the true height of heaven. Is not that what fear is? A free fear: acknowledgement in the form of obedience, but an obedience without servitude in the discovery of obligations without necessity beyond the laws which govern being. The terror felt before the evil inscribed in the disobedience to the most high. The fear of God which reveals itself concretely as the fear for the other man. But a sense of terror which would bear witness to God.[14] A testimony which would be his signification or his originary revelation. But the possibility of adhering to this total and unique alterity – that is, of bearing witness through this obedience to Highness – would define and justify the humanity of Man, and describe his freedom. The fear of heaven is not in the power of heaven, says R. Hanina, but he also says that this fear is the unique treasure of heaven. For his unique treasure, God is doing the asking. Man is in a position to respond. This response would be nothing if it were only the result of a threat – if it were a matter, as it were, of reciprocal acts being played out in the world. Our text seems to contrast what Ricœur speaks of as a dependence without heteronomy with an exalting of heteronomy and obedience which would signify precisely an independence.

Man capable of bearing witness to God is necessary to the divine economy. Curiously, the end of the verse in Isaiah (33: 6) which allows R. Hanina to assert that the fear of God is the unique treasure of the heavenly treasury permits an ambiguity, in its Hebraic version, to hang over the possessive of '*his* treasure'. The verse addresses man in the second person and ends in the third person of the possessive. Is it a question here of God's treasure or man's treasure? Unless the peculiarity of the syntax in the verse in Isaiah signifies for R. Hanina that the fear of God is God's treasure to the extent that this state of mind entirely belongs exclusively to man.[15]

7 The Fear of God and the Fear for Man

That the fear of God can be expressed other than by reference to the banal emotion of the fear felt before a threat, endangering our being or our well-being,[16] is perhaps what the rest of our text also suggests.

The Lord asks for 'nothing but the fear of God', and he asks it of his people and through the mouth of Moses. Does he ask for so little? Is he not asking for the value of the heavenly treasury itself? The *Gemara's* reply consists in emphasizing that the phrase 'nothing but the fear of God' belongs precisely to Moses. It expresses his point of view. The fear of God is within his power. Is he not 'Moses our Master' and 'the most humble of men'? The fear of God whose price, in fact, is priceless costs Moses little; both Moses and his disciples, the master of the Torah and the people of the Torah. The link is thus established between the fear of God on the one hand, and the acknowledgement – knowledge and study – of the Torah on the other.[17] We are now back to the fundamental role played by a text – that is, the birth of meaning in language. Whatever carries meaning, even if it were that of obedience, would be inseparable from it. The relation to transcendence is inseparable from the discourse. Admittedly, it is not impossible to invoke the presence of the poetic faculty, in the broadest meaning of the term, in the hermeneutics which guides its listening and reading. Nevertheless, the virtues and the authority of the master – that is, the 'acts of violence' of tradition and the community – delineate the heteronomous limits to the spontaneity of this 'poetry' which is essential to signification.

8 The Fear of God and Education

Man, therefore, learns the humanity of the fear of God through the Torah. The study of the Word of God thus establishes or constitutes the most direct relation to God, perhaps more direct than the liturgy. Hence the central place in Judaism of teaching in order to ensure the religiosity of religious discourse. But the education of the fear of God is not forgotten. Before closing, our text returns once more to the initial 'interdiction' of repeating the phrase 'We give thanks'. Why not liken the occurrence of this repetition to that of the repetition (authorized yet treated as reprehensible by R. Zera) of the prayer of the *Shema*? Here is an opportunity to point out that the interdict is not aimed at the simple repetition of words (as in the case of the *Shema*), verbal gestures which, by being repeated, lose the meaning they had in the proposition; the interdict is concerned only with the repetition of propositions which have a meaning.[18] The return to the 'interdict of repeating' is also an opportunity to insist, in concluding, on the idea of discipline, and consequently on the authoritative educational intervention of the community: to excuse the repetition of the formulations of prayer on the pretext of a possible first recitation being purely mechanical, and thus requiring a second recitation with more concentrated thought, is to give a bad excuse. A purely mechanical recitation is carelessness. The fear and the love of God exclude such 'familiar' behaviour. An education is needed, and that education can become a constraint. The constraint of the community or of tradition, which has been – or, more exactly, can be – the first word on which everything depends.

THEOLOGIES

7
On the Jewish Reading of Scriptures

It is not a question here of drawing up an inventory of the figures of Jewish hermeneutics of the Bible. This would require a vast amount of research, taking into account the diversity of epochs and tendencies. It would also mean determining the credibility of the interpreters measured less by any consensus than by the intelligence of each person and his familiarity with tradition. R. Ishmael's often-quoted 'Thirteen figures of the interpretation of the Torah', or the famous four levels of reading: *peshat* (plain meaning), *remez* (allusive meaning), *derash* (solicited meaning), *sod* (secret meaning), whose vocalized acronym gives the word *pardes* (orchard), call in their turn for exegesis, and constitute only aspects of rabbinism in its relation to the text. Only the modern formulation of this relation, which has yet to be done, might put an end to the improper teachings where traditional sources are quoted as if, beneath the Hebrew letters that conceal them, they all derived from the same depth.

Our more modest intention is to illustrate, by examples, certain ways of reading. We shall do this by presenting a Talmudic extract which produces, in the form of arguments, the exegesis of biblical verses. Nevertheless, in doing this we shall find ourselves being led to some propositions of a more general character, for the chosen extract, in its final section, concerns precisely the scope of exegesis. Exegesis of the exegesis, a privileged text, even if it does not exclude different insights into the same subject. This is in keeping with the characteristic pluralism of rabbinical thought, which paradoxically aspires to be compatible with the unity of the Revelation: the multiple stances of the scholars would constitute its very life, all of them being the 'words of the living God'.

The Talmudic passage that we shall comment upon will also introduce us in particular to the meaning that, for Jewish religious consciousness, commentary of the Scriptures can take on as the path towards transcendence. It is, perhaps, essential to the actual creation of this notion.

But a Talmudic text that comments on verses requires an interpretation in its turn. What it intends to do is not immediately apparent in terms which, for an inexperienced reader, may seem unusual, and which in fact allow for several levels and dimensions. Hence a third stage in the final section of our commentary: an interpretation of the Talmudic exegesis of the exegesis. This reading of the Talmud would not be possible for us without recourse to a modern language – in other words, without touching on the problems of today. Admittedly, it too is not the only possible reading, but it has the value of a testimony. It testifies to at least one of the ways in which contemporary Jews understand traditional Jewish hermeneutics, and above all to the way in which they understand it when they ask it for food for thought and teachings on the content.

1 Preliminary Remarks

The text we shall comment upon is taken from one of the last pages of the Tractate Makkoth in the Babylonian Talmud. This short Tractate of about fifty pages deals with judicial punishments of which one, in reference to Deuteronomy 25: 2–3, is flogging (*makkoth* = blows). The passage dealing with the exegesis of page 23b has as its immediate context a theologico-legal discussion: is it possible, through the penalty of flogging, inflicted by a human tribunal, to make atonement for the punishment known as being 'cut off from among their people', decided, according to the Talmud, by the 'celestial tribunal'? Being 'cut off from among their people', the most serious theological punishment, means being excluded from the 'world to come', which designates the eschatological order in its ultimate terms, whereas the 'Messianic epoch', still belonging to History, constitutes a penultimate stage of the 'end of times'. How can a human decision – in the case of flogging atoning for being 'cut off' – intervene in a domain which exceeds man? How can it be guaranteed to be in keeping with the divine will? These questions imply transcendence and a relation which passes through this absolute distance. They touch on the problem of the possibility of such a relation, which also arises in the exegesis examining divine thought.

Before tackling the text, it would be useful to make some general remarks which, for a reader coming from outside, are called for by the particular or outdated nature of being flogged or cut off. This whole evocation of 'blows', of the transgression and guilt it presupposes, may wound our liberal souls; just as the reference to a 'celestial tribunal' may go against our modern minds by the dated or questionable 'vision of the world' which it implies.

But in order to move towards a meaning which is retained despite an apparently antiquated language, it is necessary first of all to accept patiently – as one accepts the conventions of a fable or a stage setting – the particulars of the text in their specific universe. It is necessary to wait for them to set themselves in motion and free themselves from the anachronisms and local colour on which the curtain rises. In no way must this 'exotic' or 'outmoded' language stop thought by its picturesque elements, or by the immediate meaning of the things and deeds it names. This will change. Often from apparently incongruous or insignificant questions. Without fading before their concepts, things denoted in a concrete fashion are yet enriched with meanings by the multiplicity of their concrete aspects. This is what we call the paradigmatic modality of Talmudic reflection: notions remain constantly in contact with the examples or refer back to them, whereas they should have been content as springboards to rise to the level of generalization, or they clarify the thought which scrutinizes by the secret light of hidden or isolated worlds from which it bursts forth; and simultaneously this world inserted or lost in signs is illuminated by the thought which comes to it from outside or from the other end of the canon, revealing its possibilities which were awaiting the exegesis, immobilized, in some way, in the letters.

2 The Tribunal and the Love of One's Neighbour

Let us come back now to the principal points of a discussion on flogging, being 'cut off from among their people', and the punishments of the human and celestial tribunal. Let us accept these figures of speech and the legal formal nature of the words.

According to R. Hananiah b. Gamaliel, those who are guilty of certain transgressions that the Law of the Pentateuch punishes by cutting them off obtain remission from this damnation if they submit to the flogging imposed by the earthly tribunal. The human tribunal would thus have to be aware of sins which expel human beings from the human (the decision of God's tribunal would measure the seriousness of the sin), and would thereby have to repair the irreparable. Can the tribunal do as much as celestial compassion or mercy? Is mercy shown at the tribunal? Reference is made by R. Hananiah to Deuteronomy 25: 3: 'Forty stripes may be given him, but not more; lest, if one should go on to beat him with more stripes than these, your brother be degraded in your sight.' The word 'brother' would be essential here. It is a matter of punishing without degrading: would the tribunal and justice have the secret of the extreme measure of a difference which is a differential? In any case, R. Hananiah breaks with the dark mythological fatality whose eventuality would indicate a religious tyranny, in order to proclaim that no sin exists in relation to Heaven which cannot be expiated among men and in the light of day. The tribunal would thus also be the place where the divine regenerative will is revealed. Admittedly, there is violence. But it is an act without a spirit of violence, contempt or hatred. A fraternal act, without passion. It proceeds from a responsibility for others. To be the guardian of others, contrary to the vision of the world according to Cain, defines fraternity. For the tribunal which reasons and weighs up, the love of one's neighbour would be possible. Justice dispensed by the just becomes compassion – not in uncontrollable indulgence, but through a judgement. God speaks with a compassion that is born in the severity of the tribunal. Excessiveness? It certainly is. But pure indulgence, free forgiveness, is always at the expense of someone innocent who does not receive it. The judge is allowed such indulgence only if he personally assumes the costs.[1] But it is proper for the earthly judge, for man, for the brother of the guilty party, to restore to human fraternity those who have been excluded. To be responsible to the point of being answerable for the other's freedom. This heteronomy among the conditions of autonomy in human fraternity is acutely thought in Judaism with the category of divine paternity as its point of departure.[2] Divine justice arrays itself in fraternity by revealing itself in a human tribunal.

R. Hananiah b. Gamaliel's second argument is an '*a fortiori*'. If the transgression of certain interdicts 'cuts off a human being from his people', then all the more reason for his carrying out the Law to return him to them. Now, to suffer the flogging decided on by the tribunal is to obey the Law to which a guilty person is subject. But why 'all the more reason'?[3] Because divine compassion is still more certain than its severity. A theme that is present throughout rabbinical thought, and to which R. Hananiah implicitly refers. Is it not written (Exodus 34: 7):

[The Lord keeps] steadfast love for thousands [of generations], forgiving iniquity and transgression and sin, but who will by no means clear the guilty, visiting the iniquity of the fathers upon the children and the children's children, to the third and the fourth generation ...?

And the Rabbis gloss 'thousands' as at least two thousand! For at least two thousand generations steadfast love granted to merit is handed down; for four generations iniquity cries out for justice: compassion is thus five hundred times greater than divine severity. Behind this arithmetic of mercy there is moral optimism: the triumph of evil has one time only; nothing is ever lost from the triumph won over evil or from good.

From this point onwards, R. Simeon intervenes with the merit attached to the obedience to the interdicts. An intervention which, above and beyond the theological meaning of the terms, defines a certain conception of human life: 'One who desists from transgressing is granted reward like one who performs a precept'. The constraint imposed on the spontaneity of life, such as is provided for in the negative commandments of Leviticus 18 (whose sexual interdicts appear as the privileged example of negative commandments), is asserted by R. Simeon as the guarantee of 'rewards'. The negative commandment is the constraint *par excellence*, restraining the tendencies where life is lived in its spontaneity as an 'outgoing force', and in particular the blind abundance of sexual desire. It would be the promise of rewards, if we are to believe R. Simeon. Certainly one can expect from this promise what simple and unquestioning faith expects: longevity, eternal life or earthly happiness – just as one can denounce its spirit of repression which abuses that faith. But as a reward for a life accepting limitations, one can also understand the nature of this very life: the limitation of the wild vitality of life, through which this life wakes from its somnambulant spontaneity, sobers up from its nature and interrupts its centripetal movements, in order to be opened up to what is other than self. A life in which Judaism is recognized, limiting through the Law this wild, animal vitality, accepting this restriction as the best share – that is, as a 'reward'.[4] The plenitude of a sense of responsibility and justice is preferred to life intoxicated with its own essence, to the invasion of the unharnessed appetite of desire and domination where nothing, not even other people, can stand in its way.

R. Simeon b. Rabbi deduces the reward reserved for those who do not transgress the interdicts from the promise made in Deuteronomy 12: 23–5 to the person who refrains from eating blood: if the abstinence consonant with a natural. loathing is rewarded, how much more so is the resistance against what is desirable! Perhaps the horror of blood here has a meaning which is not only of a gastronomic nature. Resistance to sexual excesses and to the taste for plunder is, *a fortiori*, worthy of merit. And yet this is the 'true life', if we follow the literary writers of the great Metropoles! All this accounting of merits and rewards has a wider meaning. Life as it is lived, natural life, begins, perhaps, in naivety, in tendencies and tastes which are still in keeping with a code of ethics; but if it is allowed to run its course unhindered, it ends in loveless debauchery and plunder established as a social condition, and in exploitation. The human begins when this apparently innocent but virtually murderous vitality is brought under control by interdicts. Does not authentic civilization, however it may be marked by biological failures or political defeats, consist in holding back the breath of naive life and remaining fully awake in this way, 'for generations and generations to come, to the end of all generations'?[5]

We can now understand R. Hananiah b. 'Akashia's thought which closes the *Mishnah*: 'The Holy One, blessed be He, desired to make Israel worthy, therefore gave he them the law (to study) and many commandments (to do)'; and '[the Lord made] the law great and glorious' (Isaiah 42: 21). This is certainly not to create artificial merits or to put up hurdles deliberately. It is for the greatness of justice and for his glory that commandments are necessary against a life lived as an 'outgoing force'. Even in cases – such as the horror that may be felt in eating or shedding blood – where nature seems to protect us from evil! There is no natural tendency that is healthy enough not to be able to be inverted. Holiness is necessary for the healthiness of the healthy.[6]

But the greatness of justice evoked by R. Hananiah b. 'Akashia, which is conditioned by a life obeying the many commandments, is also the glory of the tribunal and the judges. To make the law glorious! Only the judges who themselves practise the many commandments can form the glorious council to which God's will aspires. The judge is not just a legal expert of laws; he obeys the Law he administers, and he is trained by this obedience; the study of the Law is itself the essential form of this obedience.[7] Such a situation is necessary in order for earthly punishment to reduce celestial punishment; for it to be rightfully thought, with the Psalmist, that 'God has taken his place in the divine council', and that 'in the midst of the gods [judges] he holds judgement' (Psalms 82: 1). It is necessary in order simply to justify man's judgement passed on man and the punishment inflicted by one on the other – that is to say, the responsibility of one person for the other. This is the strange ontological structure presupposed by this responsibility whereby one person assumes the destiny and the very existence of another, and is answerable for this other in a way, however, that is not characteristic of him. It is a responsibility that precedes freedom, which would mean precisely belonging to God, a unique belonging which, anterior to freedom, does not destroy freedom and thereby defines, if one may say so, the meaning of the exceptional word: God. God appearing *through* a council of the just, itself called divine; God as the actual possibility of such a council. And, conversely, a council of the just which is not only the ultimate source of his judgement: a different will wills within it, the judge's judgement is inspired and exceeds or overflows human spontaneity. This is what our text will say further on. Justice cannot be reduced to the order it institutes or restores, nor to a system whose rationality commands, without difference, men and gods, revealing itself in human legislation like the structures of space in the theorems of geometricians, a justice that a Montesquieu calls the 'logos of Jupiter', recuperating religion within this metaphor, but effacing precisely transcendence. In the justice of the Rabbis, difference retains its meaning. Ethics is not simply the corollary of the religious but is, of itself, the element in which religious transcendence receives its original meaning.

3 Transcendence and Exegesis

In the Talmudic extract we are commenting upon, the text relating to transcendence comes immediately after the one that discusses the powers a human tribunal would have in order to modify the decisions of Heaven in some way, and to be certain of agreeing with the absolute Tribunal. Here are the terms in which the problem is put: 'Said R. Joseph: Who has gone up (to Heaven) and come (back with this information)?'

The answer is supplied by another scholar, Abaye, in the name of a Tanna master, R. Joshua b. Levi:

'Three things were enacted by the (mundane) Tribunal below, and the Celestial Tribunal on high have given assent to their action'; (we might also exclaim,) who has gone up (to Heaven) and come (back with this information)? Only, we (obtain these points by) interpreting certain texts; and, in this instance too, we so interpret the texts.

R. Joshua b. Levi would thus entrust to the interpretation of texts, what the Rabbis call *Midrash* (exposition of meaning), the ability to force open the secret of transcendence.

Here are the three 'things' which are said to have been instituted by the earthly tribunals whose exegesis would prove to have the assent of the celestial will. First of all, the established custom, under the magistracy of Mordecai and Esther, of the liturgical reading of the 'Scroll of Esther' on the Feast of Purim. It would find its justification in a biblical verse (Esther 9: 27): 'They confirmed, and the Jews took upon them and their seed [The Jews acknowledged and accepted]'. Why two almost synonymous verbs in this verse? Because confirmation [acknowledgement] and taking upon themselves [acceptance] were two distinct acts: acceptance below, acknowledgement in Heaven.

Then the authorization of saluting another person with the Divine Name: in Ruth 2: 4, Boaz (whom the Rabbis class among the judges) greets the reapers: 'The Lord be with you!'; and in Judges 6: 12 the angel says to Gideon: 'The Lord bless thee, thou mighty man of valour'.

Finally, the prescription of bringing the tithe (due to the Levites) to the Temple-chamber, established as a custom by Ezra according to Nehemiah 10: 39. It is confirmed by the prophet Malachi (3: 10): 'Bring ye the whole tithe unto the store house that there may be food in My house, and try Me herewith, saith the Lord of Hosts, if I will not open you the windows of heaven and pour you out a blessing, until there be no enough'. And the Talmud adds: 'What means: "until there be no enough"? Said Rami b. Rab: (It means), until your lips weary of saying "Enough, enough"!'

Do not such 'proofs' imply the inspired origin of the whole biblical canon? Does it not present the notions of height and transcendence as established, and the very idea of God as clear and distinct?

Unless R. Joseph's question, in its apparent naivety, is an extremely audacious one, questioning the mythological meaning of transcendence and the revelation it seems to acknowledge. Unless, in questioning the idea of someone 'going up to Heaven', he goes so far as to concern the great man called upon in Exodus 24: 12: 'Come up to me on the mountain, and wait there; and I will give you the tables of stone, with the law and the commandment'. A calling upon whose reality in fact would be vouched for, ultimately, only by a text which itself already belongs to the statement of the truth which it ought to be able to establish: *petitio principii* which would hint at the whole of historical criticism today. But does not Abaye's reply indicate that he already understands his interlocutor on this higher level? Instead of establishing exegesis on some dogmatism of traditional metaphysics adopted as a truism, does not Abaye's reply consist in basing a new meaning for transcendence, and the old vocabulary, on the structure of the Book of books inasmuch as it allows for exegesis, and on its privileged status of containing more than it contains – in other words, of being, in this sense exactly, inspired?

The reading processes that we have just seen at work suggest, first, that the statement commented upon exceeds what it originally wants to say; that what it is capable of saying goes beyond what it wants to say; that it contains more than it contains; that perhaps an inexhaustible surplus of meaning remains locked in the syntactic structures of the sentence, in its word-groups, its actual words, phonemes and letters, in all this materiality of the saying which is potentially signifying all the time. Exegesis would come to free, in these signs, a bewitched significance that smoulders beneath the characters or coils up in all this literature of letters.[8]

Rabbinical hermeneutics is rashly considered as neglecting the spirit, whereas the aim of the signified by the signifier is not the only way to signify; whereas what is signified in the signifier, according to its other modes, answers only to the mind that solicits it and thereby belongs to the process of signification; and whereas interpretation essentially involves this act of soliciting without which what is not said, inherent in the texture of the statement, would be extinguished beneath the weight of the texts, and sink into the letters. An act of soliciting which issues from people whose eyes and ears are vigilant and who are mindful of the whole body of writing from which the extract comes, and equally attuned to life: the city, the street, other men. An act of soliciting which issues from people in their uniqueness, each person capable of extracting from the signs meanings which each time are inimitable. An act of soliciting issuing from people who would also belong to the process of the signification of what has meaning. This does not amount to identifying exegesis with the impressions and subjective reflections left by the word once it has been understood, nor to including them gratuitously in the 'outside' of meaning. It does, however, amount to understanding the very plurality of people as an unavoidable moment of the signification of meaning, and as in some way justified by the destiny of the inspired word, so that the infinite richness of what it does not say can be said or that the meaning of what it does say can be 'renewed', to use the technical expression of the Rabbis. As the people of the Book, for whom the demanding reading of the Scriptures belongs to the highest liturgy, would not Israel also be the people of continued revelation?

But in the light of this, the language that is capable of containing more than it contains would be the natural element of inspiration, despite or before its reduction to the instrument of the transmission of thoughts and information (if it can ever be entirely reduced to this). One may wonder whether man, an animal endowed with speech, is not, above all, an animal capable of inspiration, a prophetic animal. One may wonder whether the book, as a book, before becoming a document, is not the modality by which what is said lays itself open to exegesis, calls for it; and where meaning, immobilized in the characters, already tears the texture in which it is held. In propositions which are not yet – or which are already no longer – verses, and which are often verse or simply literature, another voice rings out among us, a second sonorous voice that drowns out or tears the first one. The infinite life of texts living through the life of the men who hear them; a primordial exegesis of the texts which are then called national literature and on to which the hermeneutics of universities and schools is grafted. Above and beyond the immediate meaning of what is said in these texts, the act of saying is inspired. The fact that meaning comes through the book testifies to its biblical essence. The comparison between the inspiration conferred on the Bible and the inspiration towards which the interpretation of literary texts tends is not intended to compromise the dignity of the Scriptures. On the contrary, it asserts the dignity of 'national literatures'. Yet how is it that a book is instituted as the Book of books? Why does a book become Bible? How is the divine origin of the Word indicated? How is it signed in Scripture? And does not this signature, which is more important for people living today than 'the thunderings and the lightnings' of Sinai, betray simple faith?

Inspiration: another meaning which breaks through from beneath the immediate meaning of what is meant to be said, another meaning which beckons to a way of hearing that listens beyond what is heard, beckons to extreme consciousness, a consciousness that has been awoken. This other voice resonating in the first takes control of the message as a result of this resonance coming from behind the first. In its purity of message, it is not just a certain form of saying; it organizes its content. The message as message awakens listening to what is indisputably intelligible, to the meaning of meanings, to the face of the other man.[9] Awakening is precisely this proximity of others.[10] The message as message in its method of awakening is the modality, the actual 'how' of the ethical code that disturbs the established order of being, unrepentantly leading its style of being.[11] With its referent as reading, as the book – yet no less wondrous for all that – do we not have here the original figure of the beyond freed from the mythology of ulterior worlds?[12]

That *ethics* is not determined in its elevation by the pure height of the starry sky; that all height takes on its transcendent meaning only through ethics and the message incessantly breaking (hermeneutically) the texture of the Book *par excellence*: these, undoubtedly, will constitute the teaching to be drawn – one of the teachings to be drawn – from the passage we are commenting upon.

Curiously, the biblical text first cited by R. Joshua b. Levi in consideration of the agreement between the earthly tribunal and the celestial tribunal is taken from the book of Esther from which, it might be said, God has gone so far as to withdraw his name, the word by which he is named. Yet in this book the message emerges from between the events recounted according to their 'natural' motivation, the necessities and the casting of lots. That these events, instituted as liturgy by Mordecai and Esther, could have been understood as belonging to holy History is the 'miraculous' surplus of their place in the divine plan. There arises the historical order of the facts (their established order), and consciences are awoken at the highest ethical moment in which Esther disturbs royal etiquette and consents to her ruin in order to save other men. The order upset by this awakening is paralleled by the king's insomnia. Does not a *Midrash* from the Tractate Megillah compare the insomnia of Ahasuerus to the very insomnia of God? As if, in the impossibility of sleeping, the ontological rest of being were to be torn and entirely sobered up. Is not the relation to transcendence this extreme consciousness?

No less remarkable is the second text in which the epiphany of God is invoked in the human face. The face of the other, irreducible difference, bursting into all that gives itself to me, all that is understood by me and belongs to my world; an appearance in the world which un-makes and dis-orders the world, worries me and keeps me awake. That is what is perceived by bringing together Ruth 2: 4 and Judges 6: 12. A transcendence both in the text in which exegesis finds more than the written seems to say, and in the ethical content, the message, which is thus revealed.

The third moment – in which the gift of the tithe is transformed by being brought to the Temple – would signify the transformation of the very act of giving into an absolutely free act of generosity where the person giving, not knowing the beneficiary, does not hear the expression of the latter's personal gratitude.[13] Is that not one of the meanings, the figure, as it were, of the cult itself? What 'strong minds' would be tempted to mock as duties towards an 'empty heaven' is enigmatically the absolute opening of the soul: the opening of dis-interestedness, of sacrifice without reward, of discourse without answer or echo, which 'confidence in God' and prayer must have the strength to reach. The opening of self to the infinite that no confirmation can equal, and that is proven only by its very excessiveness. That would be the abundance for which lips cannot be enough, drying out through saying 'enough', of which Rami b. Rab speaks in his strange hermeneutic of Malachi 3: 10. A beyond the discourse. This is probably what this sudden transformation is: in the dis-interested generosity of the act of giving, receiving becomes infinite, the opening on to the infinite.

4 The Ambiguity

In our reading of the Talmudic passage, inspiration and the exegesis that discovers it, we have discerned the spirituality of the spirit and the actual figure of transcendence. Have we been right to do so? Have we been right to recognize in the ethical code on the level of the tribunal, understood as a council of the just, the actual place in which the spirit blows and the Other penetrates the Same? Will a person today not resist such readings by reducing the transcendence of inspiration, exegesis and the moral message to man's interiority, to his creativity or his subconscious? Is not ethics basically autonomous? In order to dispute such modern-day resistance, would it not have been necessary to interpret as inspiration the reasons of reasoning, reason in which philosophy, in its logic, recognizes the reign of Identity which nothing that is *other* could disrupt or guide?

Now this is precisely what the final section of the Talmudic extract that concerns us wishes to suggest. R. Eleazar intervenes to confirm in his own way the general argument of Makkoth 23b on the possible agreement between earthly courts of law and celestial justice. He refers to Genesis 38: 26, where Judah, the son of Jacob, recognizes the injustice of the accusation he had brought against his daughter-in-law Tamar (this 'is said to have taken place', according to our text, at the Tribunal of Shem, Noah's son, who was still alive). R. Eleazar refers to I Samuel 12: 3–5, where all of Israel testifies at the Tribunal of Samuel to the disinterestedness of the judge Samuel; and he refers to I Kings 3: 27, where King Solomon, in his own Tribunal, recognizes the mother among the two women arguing over a child. Confession of the guilty party, testimony of the people, sentence of the king: to each of these human speeches (unquestionably human in the verses quoted), R. Eleazar – in the name of a supremely audacious exegesis, but probably also in the name of a daring thought – lifts out, under various pretexts, the ends of verses which he attributes to the echo of a heavenly voice. Will the holy spirit thus have been present at men's tribunals?

One interlocutor, Raba, questions such extravagance: there is no need to have voices intervening in discourses where reason is sufficient. But it is R. Eleazar's lesson that the Talmudic text retains. It retains it without discussion, in the name of tradition. Inspiration is thus said to be in the exercise of reason itself! The logos would already be prophetic! Through the uncertainties and presumptions of reasoning thought, the light of evidence would come as if under the trauma of the Revelation. A message would be declared in all evidence.

This is true, but it should be emphasized that despite tradition, the red actors of the Talmudic text recorded the opinion that was rejected: Raba's scepticism. It is still written down. As if an ambiguity had to remain in the conclusions of the lofty debate that has just taken place according to the style of the Talmud, with remarks that are apparently without relief and made 'without appearing to be made'.

Would not the man of today recognize in this ambiguity the alternating movements of his own thought?

To say that the ideas on transcendence and the very idea of transcendence come to us through the interpretation of writings is, admittedly, not to express a subversive opinion. Yet it is less dogmatic to people today. It suggests on the one hand that language, at the hour of its ethical truth – that is, of its full significance – is inspired, that it can therefore say more than it says, and that prophecy is thus not an act of genius, but the spirituality of the spirit expressing itself, the ability of human speech to extend beyond the primary intentions that carry it. This is perhaps possession by God, through which the idea of God comes to us. But this language offered to transcendence is also the object of philology; thus the transcendence that is expressed through it would be just an illusion, the prestige of influences to be demystified by History. Let us prefer, then, the genesis of every text to its exegesis, the certainties of given signs to the hazards of mysterious messages, the combinations of the shadows in the Cave to the uncertain calls from outside! This is also a science, at times an admirable one, to destroy false prophecies.

Alternative or alternation. And even an alternation of alternations before the letters of Scripture. These letters, for those who respect them as for those who mock them, may still support the dogmatic principles of a God, a power stronger than others, who interrupts – like a monstrous force or a heroic person – the necessities of nature. Then, through a science that they nurture with their presence as relics, these letters strike their readers, one and all, and rescue them from the level of asserted or denied mythologies. But in this start that readers receive there is a new alternation of movements: they go from the traumatic experience of the unknown and strange meaning to the grammar which, already operating on another level, restores order, coherence and chronology. And then there is a movement back: from history and philology to the understanding of meaning coming from behind the literature of letters and anachronisms, an understanding that again affects and awakes, forcing us out of the bed of the preformed and customary ideas that protect and reassure.

An alternation which, admittedly, testifies to the hesitation of our little faith, but from which also stems the transcendence that does not impose itself with denials through its actual coming and which, in inspired Scripture, awaits a hermeneutic – in other words, reveals itself only in dissimulation.

8
The Name of God according to a few Talmudic Texts

1 The Limits of the Talk

Professor Enrico Castelli has asked me to talk about the 'Name of God in the Talmud'. Did the book I had published with Editions de Minuit under the title *Quatre lectures talmudiques* [*Four Talmudic Readings*] have anything to do with it? I had pointed out in the preface, however, that I was not a Talmud specialist. Like an amateur practising on a violin, this small volume was just an attempt. But in the case in point, the violin, as it were, is an orchestra, even several orchestras. To hold the conductor's baton as one holds a bow is certainly to betray the work being interpreted. The Talmud, which represents the oral tradition of Israel – written down between the second and the end of the sixth century after Christ – is, with its sixty-eight Tractates, an immense text: more than three thousand pages in-folio, covered with commentaries and commentaries on commentaries. This covering was built up over a period of almost fifteen hundred years in the intellectual life of the Jewish communities dispersed throughout the world. The text is a living dialectic sustaining the discussions of Israel's scholars. It airs more problems than it imposes solutions, despite the apparent or real concern that guides it, which is to determine the ritual, legal and moral life of the faithful. There is nothing folkloric in this text: in its very train of thought it remains scholarly, a hidden science, but reserved for extreme requirements. It will be readily understood that this science has a particular style that distinguishes it from philosophical discourse. A style that is in no way contingent in relation to its subject matter and truth, but a style that is entirely different from our methods of exposition.

A whole lifetime is needed to master this science. What I might give today – having spent my life in other exercises and coming late, though under the firm rule of a prestigious master, to these difficult readings, unfortunately reserving them just for my spare time – what I might give, as an 'amateur Talmudist', will be but partial and approximative.

At least I will not give way to the temptation to speak about this science as if it were an ethnographical or archaeological curiosity. Nor will I make homiletic or apologetic use of it (whatever the inevitable element of apologia in any discourse may be). Indeed, I think that on the specific point that interests us today, a philosophical option can be distinguished in the Talmudic positions. I shall try to extract it from a thought that moves in multiple dimensions. We need not go into it any further today – fortunately for my incompetence – nor even delineate the metaphysical space figured by these dimensions. I think, too, that in order to seek out this option it would be a good idea to confine ourselves to a few particular texts rather than vacuously skimming over those three thousand pages in-folio.

2 To Know And To Obey

The names of the revealed God are known from Scripture. This platitude – which needs to be fully understood – means that these names are letters traced on parchment, and that a living oral tradition is necessary to learn how to read them. These names are pronounced whenever the Bible is read aloud, in prayers, when an oath is taken, and in various circumstances of Jewish ritual life. They are said to be holy. I shall come back to the meaning of this expression, for it is essential to the whole of our talk. But it is not the relation with these Names that, by itself, would constitute the greatest intimacy with God, according to traditional – that is, Talmudic – Judaism. Nor the knowledge which, by some miracle, would seek the essence behind the Names. Intimacy is of a different order. This must be said right from the beginning.

All relation of the believer to the revealed God admittedly begins in his relation to the Scriptures: reading and also the transcription by the scribe which perpetuates them by protecting them from all corruption. But writing and reading, tracing and uttering, protecting and studying, are observances. They come and take their place among all those other observances – ritual, ethical and liturgical – that Scripture commands and determines in the *Name* of this very God that it reveals. The relation to God, at the time of writing and reading the Name, admittedly depends on the intention and fervour of the reader or scribe. It depends above all on the faithfulness of this act to the commandment (the *mitzvah*) that the reader and the exegete will have drawn out from the actual text. And this is the characteristic method for Judaism. A different relation altogether with Him who is named is superimposed on the honesty of the intention towards the Name: the obedience to his commandments. All other relation is dominated by the relation with God through the ritual act that has been commanded. This relation is not measured by the uprightness of knowledge, as if it were only its approximation. It is thought and lived in Judaism as the greatest proximity, as a total adherence, prior, in some way, to all initial act of adhesion; yet as distinct from identification. The adjectives *tam* or *tamim* express this totality, which is also said of the lambs intended for sacrifice.[1] The Talmud can proclaim that the person who practises according to the commandment that has been received is greater than the person who practises without having received any commandment at all.

The rabbinical reflection on God is never separated from the reflection on practice. To reflect on God by reflecting on his commandments is, admittedly, an intellectual act of a different order to the philosophical thematization of God. It would be a mistake, however, to consider it as a simple stage towards philosophy, as its infancy. But, this being understood, the mode of Talmudic thinking tolerates philosophical contact. The specific truth of Talmudic reflection, at the expense of some oversimplification, can be reflected in the philosopher's mirror.[2]

3 Neither Efface Nor Pronounce: The Name and the Beyond

Let us now take a text, in the Tractate Shebu'oth (35a), which refers directly to the names of God. Its practical character may no longer surprise us. It teaches us first that in copying the names of God one must on no account efface them.[3] It lists those names that are proper names; there arc nine of them in our text,[4] among which figure names like *El* or *Eloha*, which are usually translated, however, as 'God'. It lists the names that may be effaced, such as the names made up of substantival attributes: the Great, the Mighty, the Revered, the Majestic, the Strong, the Powerful, the Merciful and Gracious, the Long-Suffering, the One

Abounding in Kindness. It refuses to raise to the position of a name the invocation of heaven and earth, even though heaven and earth refer to their Creator. In the final section of the extract that concerns us, the text wonders whether all the names of God mentioned in Scripture fall under the rules that have just been expressed, and which ones are the exceptions.

It is obvious that behind the practical problem of 'which names may be erased?' the text deals with the question of the dignity of the various names and, ultimately, the very meaning of the relation to God. What the text sets forth – which we have listed, and which appears at first sight to be unimportant – corresponds to problems that we shall try to draw out.

The first point is that the Hebrew terms of the Old Testament that we are led to translate by God, or *Deus*, or *Theos*, are proper names according to the wishes of the Talmud. The name of God is always said to be a proper name in the Scriptures. The word God would be absent from the Hebrew language! A fine consequence of monotheism in which there exists neither a divine species nor a generic word to designate it. The first book of the famous Tractate in which Maimonides, in the twelfth century, summarizes and systematizes the Talmud, begins in fact as follows: 'The foundation of the foundation and the pillar of wisdom consists in knowing that the Name exists and that it is the first being'. The word designating the divinity is precisely the word Name, a generic term in relation to which the different names of God are individuals. To say 'Dieu' [God] as we say it in French, or *Gott* like the Germans, or *Bog* like the Russians, is in the Talmud to say 'the Holy One, blessed be He' (the naming of an attribute, Holiness, by means of an article). In rabbinical thought holiness evokes above all separation (like our word 'absolute'). The term thus names – and this is quite remarkable – a mode of being or a beyond of being rather than a quiddity. It is the same for the word *Shekhinah*, equally used for God. The term *Shekhinah* means the dwelling of God in the world or, more exactly, his dwelling in the midst of Israel, which still indicates a modality, a way of being. In the Talmudic texts God is commonly found as: 'Master of the World' or 'King of the World' or 'our Father in Heaven'. Here again the terms express relations, not essence.

But revelation by the proper Name is not solely the corollary of the unicity of a being; it leads us further. Perhaps beyond being. Our text teaches us a gradation: the names not to be effaced, and the substantival attributes that can be effaced. These latter names refer immediately to

Him who bears them. They give Him a meaning that the substantive Names can receive but not confer. Only they thematize Him too. In so doing they get nearer to God as though to an essence which then distances them from the unrepresentable and holy, that is, absolute God, who is beyond all thematization and all essence. But as we have said, our text disputes the dignity as a name of the invocation of Heaven and Earth, unique beings like the Creator they evoke, for 'they belong to him'. One must not adjure someone by Heaven and Earth! They are excluded from among the holy appellations. The God who is revealed by his Name is not originally a cosmological principle. To refuse substances the dignity of the Name, even if they are unique and consequently suggestive of divine unity, is to exclude from the paths which lead to God the ascent to the Unconditional. It is also to refuse God all analogy with beings which are admittedly unique but which make up a world or a structure with other beings. Approaching through a proper name is to assert an irreducible relation to the knowledge which thematizes, defines or synthesizes and which, through these very acts, understands what this knowledge correlates as being, as finite and as immanent. It is to understand revelation both as a modality which paradoxically preserves transcendence from what is revealed, and consequently as something that goes beyond the capacity of an intuition, and even of a concept.

Would the interdiction to efface mean that these letters of the Name have the capability of a God that 'heaven and the highest heaven cannot contain' (I Kings 8: 27)? Would it not sketch out another religion? Whatever our mistrust towards the letter and our thirst for the Spirit may be, monotheistic humanity is a humanity of the Book. Scriptural tradition provides the trace, of a beyond of this very tradition. Monotheistic humanity, despite its philosophical claim to be posited at the very origin of its self and the non-self, recognizes in the Written the trace of a past that precedes all historical past capable of being remembered. It is not surprising, therefore, that the Talmudic text I am commenting upon should forbid the effacement not only of the written Name as a whole but also of its first syllable. But it is in this way, precisely, that there appears the ambiguity – or the enigma – of this manifestation, by which it contrasts strongly with the 'objectivity' of the perceived and the historical and, through this, with the world where this objectivity would enclose it. It is thus outlined as a modality of transcendence. The square letters are a precarious dwelling from which the revealed Name is already withdrawn; erasable letters at the mercy of the man who traces or copies out. A writing that is quite ready to merge with the writings subjected to history and textual criticism, a writing that opens itself up to the search for its origin and, in doing so, becomes contemporaneous with the history which can be remembered and in which transcendence is cancelled out, an epiphany bordering on atheism.

But this uncertain epiphany, on the boundary of evanescence, is precisely the one which man alone can retain. This is why he is the essential moment both of this transcendence and of its manifestation. And why, through this ineffaceable revelation, he is called upon with unparalleled rectitude.

But is this revelation precarious enough? Is the Name free enough in respect of the context in which it is lodged? Is it protected in its written form from all contamination by being or culture? Is it protected from man whose vocation is certainly to retain it, but who is capable of every abuse?

Added to the obligation not to efface is the obligation in Judaism not to 'utter for no purpose'. This is how a passage from the Tractate Temurah (4a) interprets the verse in Deuteronomy 6: 13: 'Thou shalt fear the Lord thy God and serve him'. As if this presence of the Name in Scripture must not be rendered present in saying it for no reason and at any time at all. Is not the notion of holiness best translated by the separation from whatever from time immemorial is (and perhaps from whatever, quite simply, is)?

A new gradation is established; this time, among the names not to be effaced. The Tetragrammaton – the 'explicit' Name, *Shem Hamephorash* – is privileged. This privilege consists in this strange condition for a name of having never to be pronounced (except at the moment in which the high priest enters the Holy of Holies, on the so-called Day of Atonement – that is to say, for post-exilic Judaism, never). The name *Adonai* – which, in its turn, must not be pronounced in vain – is the name of the Tetragrammaton. The name has a name! The name is revealed and is hidden.[5] Whatever comes in the context of meaning must also always be anchoretic or holy; the voice which resounds in speech must also be the voice which softens or falls silent. The proper name can have this modality. It is a name which 'sticks' to what it names, in a quite different manner to the common name which, clarified by the language system, designates a species but does not stick to the individual and embraces him, so to speak, in indifference. But the proper name, close to what is named, is not connected logically with it; consequently, despite this proximity, it is an empty shell like a permanent revocation of what it evokes, a disembodiment of what is embodied through it. Through being forbidden to be uttered, it is held between the two: a Tetragrammaton that is never pronounced in the way it is written.

But is not this withdrawal, contemporaneous with presence, maintained in the proximity of prayer? Throughout this talk we have avoided conceptions taken from the Kabbalah.[6] Let us make an exception here, for it is an illuminating one.

According to the Kabbalists, here is the intention of Israel's ancient scholars who had instituted the blessings. The role of these expressions is considerable in Jewish liturgy. The blessing begins by invoking God in the form of Thou. But the second-person personal pronoun is followed by the Tetragrammaton. There is no blessing that does not invoke the Tetragrammaton as the Lord (Tractate Berakoth 12a). The expression for the blessing, in the second person up until the Name, is in the third person in the words that are placed on the other side of the Name. The Thou becomes He in the Name, as if the Name belonged simultaneously to the correctness of being addressed as Thou and to the absolute of holiness. And it is without doubt this essential ambiguity – or enigma – of transcendence that is preserved in the standard expression in the Talmud for designating God: 'The Holy One, blessed be He'.

4 The Name and its Meanings

Does not this enigma or ambiguity of presence and withdrawal, a modality that in some way is formal, receive any signification, any content? Is this anchoretic nature of God when he reveals himself – where the *Klingen* [sounding] is already *Abklingen* [fading away] – only negative theology? What is it positively?

The text I am commenting upon, in its final and longest section, asks whether the Names mentioned in the various books and episodes of the Bible are all holy. From the reply that lists some of the episodes in which the 'Names are holy', we understand that the God revealed in his Names is given a meaning from out of the human situations, of misery or happiness, in which he is invoked. 'The Lord is near to all who call upon him' (Psalms 145: 18).[7] Ritual, invocations and – as we shall see forthwith in trying to determine the meaning of the anchoretism and effacement – the responsibility for the other man: according to the Rabbis of the Talmud, these constitute a proximity that is closer than that of thematization, which, if we are to believe the philosophers or Spinozism, is said to be intimacy itself.

But what is the positive meaning of the withdrawal of this God who says only his names and his orders? This withdrawal does not cancel out revelation. It is not purely and simply a non-knowledge. It is precisely man's obligation towards all other men. According to the words of the prophet (Jeremiah 22: 16), to judge the cause of the poor and needy, 'Is not this to know me? says the Lord'. Knowledge of the unknowable: transcendence becomes ethics. This is why, in the terms of a discussion mentioned in the text we have commented upon, the objection disputing the holiness of the Name *Zebaoth* is rejected. Does not this name, meaning multitudes, refer to the multitudes of Israel? Does it not name the Absolute through his relation to men? Now the Law is not in accordance with this objection, and the scholars wish to ignore it. Let us comment on this: the reference to Israel is essential to the Name. Its holiness and the holiness it suggests, 'beyond all objectivization and all thematization', mean precisely the constitution of a human society which is under obligation. The notion of Israel in the Talmud, as my master had taught me, must be separated from all particularism, except for that of election. But election means a surplus of duties, in accordance with the phrase from Amos (3: 2): 'You only have I known of all the families of the earth; therefore I will punish you for all your iniquities'.

The transcendence of the named God could not be expounded thematically. Hence the extreme precariousness of this revelation of the Name for which the interdiction to efface provides some help. But here is a case where the Name is traced only with a view to its own effacement. It is discussed at length in the Tractate Sotah (7a–7b).[8] The woman suspected by her husband, without proof, of adultery must, according to Numbers 5, be brought by the jealous husband to the priest at the Temple and submit to a test (which sociologists will recognize as an ordeal but which, all things considered, is a good way to take the heat out of the conflict by the very appearance of a third party, in the form of the priest). At a certain moment, according to the rite described in the Bible, the priest entreats the woman: 'If some man (other than your husband) has lain with you, then ... "the Lord [written as the Tetragrammaton] make you an execration". ... And the woman shall say, "Amen, Amen"'. The priest will write these words (mentioning the Tetragrammaton) in a book, and efface them in the water of bitterness. This effacement also effaces the Tetragrammaton written with a view to this effacement. The Talmudic text, going beyond the particulars of a very ancient rite, asserts a new idea: the effacement of the Name is the reconciliation of men. Beyond this specific case, the phrase figures as purely paradigmatic. Here is another parable that echoes it (Tractate Sukkah 53b): King David digs the Pits in order to discover, in the place where one day his son will build the Temple, the source of the running water necessary for the future libations of the altar. The water suddenly rises up and threatens to submerge the universe. How can the cataclysm be stopped? David then receives advice: 'If, for the purpose of establishing harmony between man and wife, the Torah said, Let My name that was written in sanctity be blotted out by the water, how much more so may it be done in order to establish peace in the world!'

Does not the transcendence of the Name of God, in comparison to all thematization, become effacement, and is not this effacement the very commandment that obligates me to the other man? We believe that this is the meaning of one of the apologues of the text we have been pondering over from the beginning. It is grafted on to a verse in Genesis and is introduced, as is proper in the Talmud, in connection with a practical question: must all the names of God mentioned in the Bible be treated as holy names? The reply is affirmative in particular for all the verses relating the story of Abraham. The obvious and first meaning of this reply is that humanity according to Abraham invokes the true Name. But is not the name 'Adonai', which Abraham pronounces in Genesis 18: 3, addressed to one of the three angels who visit him? 'Adonai (Lord), if I have found favour in your sight, do not pass by your servant.' Is saying Adonai to an angel who, in human form, is an unknown passer-by for Abraham, really to pronounce the Name of God? To get out of the difficulty, there is an apologue. God is said to have appeared to Abraham at the same time as the three passers-by. It is to him that Abraham said: 'Adonai, do not pass by your servant'. He said to him: 'Wait for me to receive the three travellers', because since the passers-by were overcome with the heat and thirst, this comes before the Lord our God. The transcendence of God is his actual effacement, but this obligates us to men. Humility is higher than greatness. This is the meaning of monotheism according to Abraham. I said a short while ago that the Talmud grafts an apologue on to a verse. Yet is it a graft? Is not the meaning suggested already in the very fact of saying Lord, Adonai, to an anonymous passer-by lost in the wilderness? Is not the apologue merely paying extreme attention to the letter of the text?

But the Revelation that becomes ethics signifies a new vision of man. The human soul here is not the origin of self, a subject aware of self and the universe, nor is it an existence concerned in its existence with this very existence. It is obligated before all commitment. It is not only practical reason, the source of its obligations for others, but responsibility in the forgetting of self. Here is a text[9] that tells us of those who are worthy to pronounce the Name – that is, of those who, alone, can accede to the Name. It concerns names other than the Tetragrammaton, names of twelve and forty-two letters, Kabbalistic themes about which I am saying nothing. 'Our Rabbis taught: At first (God's) twelve-lettered Name used to be entrusted to all people [priests]. When unruly men increased, it was confided to the pious of the priesthood, and these "swallowed it" during the chanting of their brother priests.' This is followed by: 'Rab Judah said in Rab's name: The forty-two lettered Name is entrusted only to him who is pious, meek, middle-aged, free from bad temper, sober, and not insistent on his rights'. Humility, discretion, forgiving of offences, which must not be taken solely as virtues; they 'turn inside out' the ontological notion of subjectivity in order to see it in renunciation, effacement and a total passivity.

5 Philosophy

It remains for me to show that the possibility of a transcendence staying absolute despite the relation it enters through revelation – a possibility suggested to us by the texts relating to the Name of God that we have just analysed – can be thought philosophically, that is, independently of the authority of Scripture and its exegesis. But I will be able to move forward here only by leaps and bounds.

The first hypothesis of Plato's *Parmenides* ends up in the impossibility of the One separated from Being which should be 'neither named nor described nor thought of nor known' (142a), whereas it is named, described and known in the words and the thought that ensure it this absolute transcendence.

We wonder whether this contradiction is not based on a postulate that dominates Western philosophy, a postulate that is even taken for the definition of this philosophy. It posits the relation of the soul with the Absolute as knowledge, consciousness and discourse. Knowledge, consciousness, discourse, thematizing an object or something that is said; but in a movement that is as one with freedom – which is admittedly expressed in the old (or new) term of 'intentionality', where the idea of noetic purpose does not succeed in cancelling out the idea of intention, that is, of free spontaneity.

In fact, thematization, whether actual or virtual, by which consciousness is described is the modality in which the relation with the Other separated from it – with the Absolute – is achieved as freedom. Thematization is the fact that the soul is affected so as *not to be subject to*: what affects it, reveals itself to it, 'presents' itself. Nothing enters it by being smuggled in, without being declared. Nothing that concerns it escapes from truth. All clandestine entry is confessed or recuperated in memory or History. No past that is not present is conceivable. Being, the fact of revealing itself, has an origin in a present – that is, it begins with my freedom, miraculously removed from the depths of the past that seems, however, to carry it. Being has an origin; it is *arkhe.* In Western philosophy, rationality is identified with the search for the origin. It is essentially archaeology.

In the light of this it is understandable that the Transcendent, or the Absolute, or the One, cannot enter into relation with the soul without beginning within it; but by doing so it ceases to justify its transcendence. The One can do nothing but resist knowledge. Not only sensory intuition, but all forms of thematization: concept, idea, symbol.

But is thematization the only event of the soul? And is the Absolute's only modality the act of entering into the present, becoming origin, revealing itself, becoming being?

Admittedly, the modalities of the Absolute are unthinkable. They can be retreat and anchoretism only when thought is applied: a passing beyond all past that can be remembered, a total diachrony, in other words, no longer forming a structure with consciousness. But is there nothing in the soul that comes before the originary? Has nothing entered it surreptitiously, without suggesting itself to freedom as a theme and without opening out into the present and without offering itself to reminiscence?

This abstract idea of something that precedes the originary which we seem to be constructing is provided for us in a concrete way by the responsibility prior to all commitment, by the responsibility that obligates us to others, by my responsibility for the deeds, the fortune and the misfortune that are due to the freedom belonging to others and not to myself. Or, more simply, by human fraternity. A configuration of purely ontological notions turns here into ethical relations. As in the Talmud: the absolution of the Ab-solute, the effacement of God, is positively the obligation to make peace in the world.

A responsibility preceding freedom, a responsibility preceding intentionality! Do we not end up in a determinism where the soul is passive like an effect, even losing its ipseity? But in the responsibility for others – the subject, the self – I am summoned to appear rather than simply appearing, replying to a subpoena that cannot be declined and seizes me precisely in my non-interchangeable identity by calling to me.

How can such a subpoena affect me? Anarchically, without beginning in a present, without beginning at all. This situation of non-beginning must not be understood as a weakness or a primitive state of being where a self is still a slave to the unknown forces that one day it will discover – to assume them, convert them to its design, or break them. This anteriority of responsibility must be understood in relation to freedom as the very authority of the Absolute which is 'too great' for the measure or finitude of presence, revelation, order and being, and which consequently, as neither being nor non-being, is the 'excluded third party' of the beyond of being and non-being, a third person that we have called 'illeity'[10] and that is perhaps also expressed by the word God. A beyond being, resistant to thematization and origin – something preceding the originary: beyond non-being – an authority that orders my neighbour for me as a face.

The illeity of the excluded third party is not some kind of power of obliqueness refusing the straightforwardness of thematization and causality, and thus perhaps causing the eye to squint. Illeity, in an extremely specific way, is excluded from being, but orders it in relation to a responsibility, in relation to its pure passivity, a pure' susceptibility': an obligation to answer preceding any questioning which would recall a prior commitment, extending beyond any question, any problem and any representation, and where obedience precedes the order that has furtively infiltrated the soul that obeys. Neither expected nor welcomed: the contrary would still be a near activity, an assumption; a 'traumatizing' order coming from a past that was never present, since my responsibility is answerable for the freedom of others.

A responsibility which, before the discourse revolving around what is said, is probably the essence of language.

There will certainly be an objection to this: if, between the soul and the Absolute, there can exist a relation different to thematization, does not the fact of speaking and thinking about it at this very moment, the fact of wrapping it up in our dialectic, mean that thought, language and dialectic have sovereign power over this Relation?

But the language of thematization that we are using at the moment has perhaps been made possible only by this Relation, and is subservient to it.

9
Revelation in the Jewish Tradition

I The Content and its Structure

1 The Problem

I think that our fundamental question in these lectures concerns less the content ascribed to revelation than the actual fact – a metaphysical one – called the Revelation. This fact is also the first and most important content revealed in any revelation. From the outset this revelation is alleged to be unusual, extra-ordinary, linking the world in which we live to what would no longer be of this world. How is it thinkable? What model do we use? Suddenly, by opening a few books, there would enter into a positive world, open in its consistency and steadfastness to perception, to enjoyment and to thought, a world given over in its reflections, metaphors and signs to reading and science, truths that come from elsewhere – but from where? – and dated according to a 'chronology' called holy History! And, as in the case of the Jews, a holy History against which stands, without a break in continuity, a 'History for historians', a profane History! That the holy History of the Christian West is, in its greater part, the ancient history of a people of today, retaining a still mysterious unity, despite its dispersion among the nations – or despite its integration into these nations – is undoubtedly what constitutes the originality of Israel and its relation to the Revelation: of its reading of the Bible, or its forgetting of the Bible, or of the memories or the remorse that remain from this very act of forgetting. Against the transfiguration into myth that threatens, with degradation or sublimation, this 'far and distant past' of the Revelation, is the surprising present existence of Judaism, a human collectivity, albeit small and continuously sapped by persecution, weakened by half-heartedness, temptations and apostasy, yet capable, in its very irreligiosity, of founding its political life on the truths and rights taken from the Bible. And indeed, chapters of holy History are reproduced in the course of profane History by trials that constitute a Passion, the Passion of Israel. For many Jews who have long since forgotten or never learnt the narratives and the message of the Scriptures, the signs of the Revelation that was received – and the muted calls of this exalting Revelation – are reduced to the trauma of lived events long after the completion of the biblical canon, long after the Talmud was written down. (The Talmud is the other form of the Revelation, distinct from the Old Testament which Christians and Jews have in common.) For many Jews, holy History and the Revelation it entails are reduced to the memories of being burnt at the stake, the gas chambers, and even the public affronts received in international assemblies or heard in the refusal to allow them to emigrate. They experience the Revelation in the form of persecution!

These are the 'history-making events' of which Paul Ricœur spoke in taking up Emil Fackenheim's expression. Do they not refer us to the Bible that remains their living space? Does not the reference materialize in reading, and is not reading a way of inhabiting? The volume of the book as a form of living space! It is in this sense, too, that Israel is a people of the Book, and that its relation to the Revelation is unique of its kind. Its actual land is based on the Revelation. Its nostalgia for the land is fed on texts. It derives nothing from belonging in some organic way to a particular piece of soil. There is certainly in this a presence to the world where the paradox of transcendence is less unusual.

For many Jews today, communities and individuals alike, the Revelation is still in keeping with the conception of a communication between Heaven and Earth, such as the plain meaning of biblical narratives would have it. It is accepted by many excellent minds that cross the deserts of the religious crisis of our time by finding fresh water in the literal expression of Sinaitic Epiphany, of the Word of God calling to the prophets, and in the confidence in an uninterrupted tradition of a prodigious History that testifies to it. Both orthodox people and communities, untouched by the uncertainties of modernity, even when they sometimes take part professionally in the fever of the industrial world, remain, despite the simplicity of this metaphysics, spiritually attuned to the noble virtues and most mysterious secrets of divine proximity. Men and communities thus live, in the literal sense of the term, outside History where, for them, events neither come to pass nor relate to those that have already passed. It is nevertheless true that for modern Jews – and they are the majority – to whom the intellectual destiny of the West, with its victories and its crises, is not borrowed clothing, the problem of the Revelation insistently arises and demands new conceptions. How are we to understand the 'exteriority' particular to truths and revealed signs striking the human mind which, despite its 'interiority', is a match for the world and is called reason? How, without being of the world, can they strike reason?

Indeed, these questions arise acutely for us, for anyone among men today still sensitive to these truths and signs, but who, living in modern times, is more or less troubled by the news of the end of metaphysics, by the victories of psychoanalysis, sociology and political economy; to whom linguistics has taught the significance of signs without signifieds and who, in the light of this, confronted with all these intellectual splendours – or shadows – sometimes wonders if he is not present at a magnificent funeral for a dead god. The ontological status or regime of the Revelation is thus worrying essentially for Jewish thought, and its problem should come before any presentation of the content of this Revelation.

2 The Structure of a Revelation: The Call to Exegesis

However, we shall devote this first section to explaining the structure presented by the content of the Revelation in Judaism. Certain inflections in this structure will already, in fact, suggest the sense in which the transcendence of the message can be understood. I think that this explanation will also be useful because the forms of the Revelation as they appear to Jews are not well known to the general public. Ricœur has given a brilliant account of the organization of the Old Testament which Judaism and Christianity have in common. This will certainly save me having to go back over the various literary genres of the Bible: prophetic texts, the narration of founding historical events, prescriptive and sapiential texts, hymns and thanksgiving. Each genre is said to have a revelatory function and power.

But for the Jewish reading of the Bible these distinctions are perhaps not established with the same steadfastness as in the lucid classification proposed to us. Prescriptive lessons that are above all to be found in the

Pentateuch, in the Torah – the 'Torah of Moses', as it is called – are privileged in Jewish consciousness for the relation they establish with God. They are required in every text; certain psalms would allude to figures and events, but also to commandments: 'I am a sojourner on earth; hide not thy commandments from me!' says Psalms 119: 19 in particular. The sapiential texts are prophetic and prescriptive. Between the 'genres', then, allusions and references visible to the naked eye circulate in multiple directions.

One further remark: there is a vital search, throughout, to go beyond the plain meaning. This meaning is, of course, known and acknowledged as plain and as wholly valid at its level. But this meaning is perhaps less easy to establish than the translations of the Old Testament lead one to suppose. It is by going back to the Hebrew text from the translations, venerable as they may be, that the strange or mysterious ambiguity or polysemy authorized by the Hebrew syntax is revealed: words coexist rather than immediately being co-ordinated or subordinated with and to one another, contrary to what is predominant in the languages that are said to be developed or functional. Returning to the Hebrew text certainly and legitimately makes it more difficult than one thinks to decide on the ultimate intention of a verse, and even more so on a book of the Old Testament. Indeed, the distinction between the plain meaning and the meaning to be deciphered, the search for this meaning buried away and for a meaning even deeper than it contains, all gives emphasis to the specifically Jewish exegesis of Scripture. There is not one verse, not one word of the Old Testament – read as a religious reading, read by way of Revelation – that does not half-open on to an entire world, unsuspected at first, which envelops what was easily read. 'R. Akiba went as far as to interpret the ornamentation of the letters of the sacred text', says the Talmud. The scribes and scholars who are said to be slaves of the letter attempted to extract from the letters, as if they were the folded-back wings of the Spirit, all the horizons that the flight of the Spirit can embrace, the whole meaning that these letters carry or to which they awake. 'Once God has spoken; twice have I heard this': this part of Psalms 62: 11 proclaims that innumerable meanings dwell in the Word of God. At least if we are to believe the Rabbi who, already in the name of this pluralism, scrutinizes the very verse that teaches him this right to scrutinize! This is the exegesis of the Old Testament called *Midrash*, or search, or interrogation. It is at work well before grammatical research, which came late, although it was well received, and was added to the decipherment of enigmas locked away in a quite different mode to the grammatical in the gramma of Scripture.

The diversity of styles and the contradictions of the text of the Old Testament did not escape this awakening attention. They became the pretexts for new and more penetrating readings, for renewing meanings that measure the acuteness of the reading. Such is the breadth of Scripture. A Revelation that can also be called a mystery; not a mystery that dispels clarity, but one that demands greater intensity.[1]

But this invitation to seek and decipher, to *Midrash*, already constitutes the reader's participation in the Revelation, in Scripture. The reader, in his own fashion, is a scribe. This provides us with a first indication of what we might call the 'status' of the Revelation: its word coming from elsewhere, from outside, and simultaneously dwelling in the person who receives it. More than just a listener, is not the human being the unique 'terrain' in which exteriority can appear? Is not the personal – that is, the unique 'of itself' – necessary to the breach and the revelation taking place from outside? Is the human as a break in substantial identity not, 'of itself', the possibility for a message coming from outside not to strike 'free reason', but to take on the unique figure that cannot be reduced to the contingency of a 'subjective impression'? The Revelation as calling to the unique within me is the significance particular to the signifying of the Revelation. It is as if the multiplicity of persons – is not this the very meaning of the personal? – were the condition for the plenitude of 'absolute truth'; as if every person, through his uniqueness, were the guarantee of the revelation of a unique aspect of truth, and some of its points would never have been revealed if some people had been absent from mankind. This is not to say that truth is acquired anonymously in History, and that it finds 'supporters' in it! On the contrary, it is to suggest that the totality of the true. is constituted from the contribution of multiple people: the uniqueness of each act of listening carrying the secret of the text; the voice of the Revelation, as inflected, precisely, by each person's ear, would be necessary to the 'Whole' of the truth. That the Word of the living God may be heard in diverse ways does not mean only that the Revelation measures up to those listening to it, but that this measuring up measures up the Revelation: the multiplicity of irreducible people is necessary to the dimensions of meaning; the multiple meanings are multiple people. We can thus see the whole impact of the reference made by the Revelation to exegesis, to the freedom of this exegesis, the participation of the person listening to the Word making itself heard, but also the possibility for the Word to travel down the ages to announce the same truth in different times.

A text from Exodus (25: 15), prescribing the making of the holy Ark of the Tabernacle, makes provision for poles to be used in transporting the Ark: 'The poles shall remain in the rings of the Ark; they shall not be taken from it'. The Law carried by the Ark is always ready to be moved. It is not attached to a point in space and time, but is continuously transportable and ready to be transported. This is also indicated by the famous Talmudic apologue relating the return of Moses on earth at the time of R. Akiba. He enters the Talmudic scholar's school, understands nothing of the master's lesson, but learns from a celestial voice that the teaching he has not understood at all comes, however, from himself. It was given 'to Moses at Sinai'. This contribution of readers, listeners and pupils to the open-ended work of the Revelation is so essential to it that I was able to read recently, in a quite remarkable book by a rabbinical scholar from the end of the eighteenth century, that the slightest question put by a novice pupil to his schoolmaster constitutes an ineluctable articulation of the Revelation which was heard at Sinai.

However, how is such a call to the person in his historical uniqueness – and this means that the Revelation requires History (which means, outside all theosophical 'wisdom', a personal God: is a God not personal, before all other characteristics, inasmuch as he appeals to persons?) – how is such a call to the diversity of people insured against the arbitrary nature of subjectivism? But perhaps there are crucial reasons why a certain risk of subjectivism, in the pejorative sense of the term, must be run by the truth ...

This in no way means that in Jewish spirituality the Revelation is left to the arbitrariness of subjective fantasies, that it desires to be without authority and that it is not highly characterized. Fantasy is not the essence of the subjective, even if it is its by-product. Without recourse to any doctrinal authority, the 'subjective' interpretations of the Jewish Revelation have managed to maintain the awareness of unity in a people in spite of its geographical dispersion. But, what is more, a distinction is allowed to be made between the personal originality brought to the reading of the Book and the pure play of the fantasies of amateurs (or even of charlatans); this is made both by a necessary reference of the subjective to the historical continuity of the reading, and by the tradition of commentaries that cannot be ignored under the pretext that inspirations come to you directly from the text. A 'renewal' worthy of the name cannot avoid these references, any more than it can avoid reference to what is known as the oral Law.

3 Oral Law and Written Law

The allusion to the oral Law leads us to point out another essential feature of the Revelation according to Judaism: the role of the oral tradition as recorded in the Talmud. It is presented in the form of discussions between rabbinical scholars that took place in the period between the first centuries before the Christian era and the sixth century after Christ. From the point of view of historians, these discussions continue more ancient traditions and reflect a whole process in which the centre of Jewish spirituality was transferred from the Temple to the house of study, from cult to study. These discussions and teachings are principally concerned with the prescriptive part of the Revelation: rituals, morality and law. But they are also concerned in their fashion, and by way of apologues, with the whole spiritual universe of men: philosophy and religion. Everything is bound up around the prescriptive. Outside Judaism, or within de-Judaized Judaism, the picture that one has of the prescriptive – which is reduced to the pettiness of rules to be respected, or to the 'yoke of the law' – is not a true picture.

Contrary to what is often thought, the oral Law is not just a matter, moreover, of commentary on the Scriptures, whatever the eminent role incumbent upon it on this level may be. It is religiously thought as deriving from its own specific source of Sinaitic Revelation. Here, then, is an oral Torah, next to the written Torah and of at least equal authority.[2] This authority is claimed by the Torah itself. It is accepted by religious tradition and agreed upon by the philosophers of the Middle Ages, including Maimonides. For Jews it is a Revelation that complements the Old Testament. It is able to enunciate principles and to give information lacking in the written text or passed over in silence. The Tannaim, the oldest scholars of the Talmud, whose generation comes to a close towards the end of the second century after Christ, speak with sovereign authority.

Clearly, the oral teaching of the Talmud remains inseparable from the Old Testament. It orientates its interpretation. This reading – scrutinizing the text in the literal mode described above, to which the Hebrew of the original of the Bible miraculously lends itself – is precisely the way the Talmud works. The entire prescriptive part of the Torah is 'reworked' by the rabbinical scholars, and the entire narrative part is expanded and clarified in a specific way. In such a way that it is the Talmud that allows the Jewish reading of the Bible to be distinguished from the Christian reading or the 'scientific' reading of the historians and philosophers. Judaism is definitely the Old Testament, but through the Talmud.

The spirit guiding this reading, which is said to be naively 'literal', perhaps consists, in actual fact, in maintaining each specific text in the context of the Whole. The connections that may appear verbal or attached to the letter represent, in fact, an effort to let the 'harmonics' of one verse resound within other verses. It is also a question of keeping the passages that appeal only to our taste for spiritualization and interiorization in contact with tougher texts, in order to extract from these, too, their real truth. Yet it is a question too, in extending the remarks that may seem severe, of bringing together the generous vital forces of harsh realities. The language of the Old Testament is so suspicious of the rhetoric which does not stutter that its chief prophet was 'slow of speech and of tongue'. There is undoubtedly more to this than just the avowal of being limited in this defect: there is the awareness of a kerygma which does not forget the weight of the world, the inertia of men, and the deafness of understandings.

The freedom of exegesis is upheld at this Talmudic school. Tradition, running through history, does not impose its conclusions, but the contact with what it sweeps along. Does this constitute an authority on doctrinal matters? Tradition is perhaps the expression of a way of life thousands of years old which conferred unity on the texts, however disparate the historians claim their origins may have been. The miracle of confluence, which is as great as the miracle of the common origin attributed to these texts, is the miracle of that way of life. The text is pulled tight over what tradition expands, like the strings on a violin's wood. The Scriptures thus have a mode of being that is quite different from the exercise material for grammarians, entirely subject to philologists; a mode of being whereby the history of each piece of writing counts less than the lessons it contains, and where its inspiration is measured by what it inspires. These are a few of the features of the 'ontology' of the Scriptures.

We have said that the oral Torah was written down in the Talmud. This oral Torah is thus itself written. But its writing down came late. It is explained by contingent and dramatic circumstances of Jewish History, external to the nature and specific modality of its message. Even written down, however, the oral Torah preserves in its style its reference to oral teaching; the liveliness provided by a master addressing disciples who listen as they question. In written form, it reproduces the diversity of opinions expressed, with extreme care taken to name the person providing them or commenting upon them. It records the multiplicity of opinions and the disagreement between the scholars. The great disagreement running all through the Talmud between the school of Hillel and the school of Shammai (in the first century before Christ) is called the discussion or disagreement 'for the glory of Heaven'. Despite all the care it takes to reach an agreement, the Talmud never ceases to apply to the differences of opinion between Hillel and Shammai – and to the flow of divergent ideas which proceed from them through the successive generations of scholars – the well-known phrase: 'These and those alike, are the words of the living God'. A discussion or dialectic which remains open to readers, who are worthy of this name only if they enter into it on their own account. Consequently, the Talmudic texts, even in the physiognomical aspects that their typography takes on, are accompanied by commentaries, and by commentaries on and discussions of these commentaries. The page is continuously overlaid and prolongs the life of the text which, whether it is weakened or reinforced, remains 'oral'. The religious act of listening to the revealed word is thus identified with the discussion whose open-endedness is desired with all the audacity of its problematics. To the extent that Messianic times are often designated as the epoch of conclusions. Not that this prevents discussion, even on this point! One text from Berakoth (64a) says: 'R. Hiyya b. Ashi said in the name of Rab: The disciples of the wise have no rest either in this world or in the world to come, as it says, *They go from strength to strength, every one of them appeareth before God in Zion* (Psalms 84: 7)'. This going from strength to strength is attributed pre-eminently by R. Hiyya to the scholars of the Law. And it is the eleventh-century French commentator, Rashi, whose explanations guide every reader, even the modern one, through the sea of the Talmud, who adds by way of commentary: 'They go from one house of study to another, from one problem to another'. The Revelation is a constant hermeneutics of the Word, whether written or oral, discovering new landscapes, and problems and truths fitted into one another. It reveals itself not only as the source of wisdom, the path of deliverance and elevation, but also as the nourishment of this life and the object of the particular enjoyment that goes with acquiring knowledge. To the extent that Maimonides, in the twelfth century, was able to attach to the hermeneutics of the Revelation the pleasure or happiness that Aristotle attached to the contemplation of pure essences in Book 10 of the *Nicomachean Ethics*.

As the 'people of the Book' through its land which extends the volume of in-folios and scrolls, Israel is also the people of the Book in another sense: it has fed itself, almost in the physical sense of the term, on books, like the prophet who swallows a scroll in Ezekiel Chapter 3. The remarkable digestion of celestial food! As we have said, this excludes the idea of a doctrinal authority. The strict formulas which, in the shape of dogmatic principles, would bring the multiple and sometimes disparate traces left in Scripture by the Revelation back to unity, are absent from the spirit of Judaism. No Credo brings together or orientates the reading of texts, according to the method in which even the renewal of the reading and of the meanings given to the verses would still be like a new wine poured into old goatskins and preserving the old forms and even the bouquet of the past. In Judaism, the formulation of articles of faith is a late philosophical or theological genre. It does not appear until the Middle Ages – that is, after an already well-ordered religious life of two thousand years (to go by historical criticism, which is always making the spiritualization of texts more recent while looking much further back for their genealogy anchored in the mythical). Between the first formulations of the Jewish Credo – which is to vary as to the actual number of essential points – and the opening out of the prophetic message of Israel situated in the eighth century before Christ (the period in which many of the Mosaic elements of the Pentateuch are said to have been composed), two thousand years have already passed; more than a thousand years separated these formulations from the completion of the biblical canon, and several centuries from the writing down of the Talmudic teachings.

4 Halakhah *and* Aggadah

But if there is no dogmatism in the Credo to summarize the content of the Revelation, the unity of this Revelation is concretely expressed for Jews in another form. Indeed, crossing the distinction between written Revelation and oral Revelation which is particular to Judaism is the distinction, to which we have already alluded, between the texts and teachings relating to conduct and formulating practical laws, the *Halakhah* – the actual Torah in which can be recognized what Ricœur qualified as prescriptive – and, on the other hand, the texts and teachings of homiletic origin which, in the form of apologues, parables and the development of biblical narratives, represent the theologico-philosophical part of tradition and are collected together under the concept of *Aggadah*. The first gives to the Jewish Revelation, both written and oral, its own physiognomy, and has maintained as an orthopraxis the unity of the very body of the Jewish people throughout dispersion and History. From the outset Jewish revelation is commandment, and piety is obedience to it. But an obedience which, while accepting practical decrees, does not stop the dialectic called upon to determine them. This dialectic continues and is valid by itself in its style of open-ended discussion.

The distinction between oral Law and written Law on the one hand, and *Aggadah* and *Halakhah* on the other, constitute, as it were, the four cardinal points of the Jewish Revelation. The motivations of the *Halakhah* remain, let me repeat, under discussion. This is because, through the discussion of the rules of conduct, the whole order of thought is present and living. It gives access to the exercise of the intellect from the obedience and the casuistry it entails. This is very significant: the thought that issues from the prescriptive goes beyond the problem of the material gesture to be accomplished; although, right in the heart of the dialectic, it also enunciates what conduct is to be kept, what the *Halakhah* is. A decision which is not, therefore, strictly speaking, a conclusion. It is as if it were based on a tradition of its own, although it would have been impossible without the discussion which it in no way cancels out. The antinomies of the dialectic that are the waves of the 'sea of the Talmud' are accompanied by 'decisions' or 'decrees'. And very soon after the completion of the Talmud, 'decision manuals' appeared which fixed the form of the *Halakhah*. A work of several centuries which culminated in a definitive code entitled *Shulchan 'Arukh*, 'Prepared Table', in which the life of the faithful Jew was fixed down to the smallest details.

Jewish revelation is based on prescription, the *mitzvah*, whose strict accomplishment was taken, in the eyes of Saint Paul, to be the yoke of the Law. It is in any case through the Law, which is in no way felt as a stigma attached to being enslaved, that the unity of Judaism comes about. On the religious plane, this unity is clearly distinct from any doctrinal unity which, in any case, is the root of all doctrinal formulation. Rashi's first rabbinical commentary, which opens the 'Jewish editions' of the Pentateuch, expresses the surprise caused by the first verse of the Torah: why begin with the account of Creation, when the prescriptions begin in Exodus 12: 2: 'This month shall be for you the beginning of months'? The commentator thus endeavours to explain the religious value of the account of Creation. It is observance which gives unity to the Jewish people. In contemporary Judaism this unity is still alive through the awareness of its ancient status and is still accorded respect even when the

137

Law, in the strict sense, is poorly observed. It would not be wrong to claim that it is this unity, conferred upon the Jews by the Law – observed in the past by everyone – which nourishes, without them actually knowing, those Jews who no longer practise, yet still feel a sense of solidarity with Jewish destiny. Finally, it is worth noting that the study of the commandments – the study of the Torah, that is, the resumption of the rabbinical dialectic – is equal in religious value to actually carrying them out. It is as if, in this study, man were in mystical contact with the divine will itself. The highest action of the practice of prescriptions, the prescription of prescriptions which equals them all, is the actual study of the (written or oral) Law.

Besides these halakhic texts we have just discussed, which unite the prescriptions of the Law, and where strictly ethical laws are placed side by side with ritual prescriptions, immediately positing Judaism as an ethical monotheism, there are the apologues and parables called *Aggadah* which constitute the metaphysics and philosophical anthropology of Judaism. In the Talmudic texts they alternate with the *Halakhah*. The *Aggadah* also contains special collections, of diverse antiquity and quality, which have given life to Judaism and which, without being aware of historical perspective, are treated as if their wisdom were of the same order as the *Halakhah* which unifies the religion. In order to know the system of thought on which Judaism has lived as a unity throughout the centuries of its religious integrity (which is not the same as knowing its historical development), it is necessary to consider these texts from various epochs as contemporaneous. The lucid work of historians and Jewish and non-Jewish critics – who can reduce the Jewish miracle of the Revelation *or* that of national spirit to a multiplicity of influences that they have undergone – loses its spiritual importance at the critical hours which have frequently struck in the course of two thousand years for post-exilic Judaism. What we called earlier the miracle of confluence takes on a voice that is immediately recognizable, and reverberates in a sensibility and a thought which hear it as if they were already expecting it.

5 *The Content of the Revelation*

But up until now we have spoken about the form or the structure of the Revelation in Judaism, without saying anything of its content. It is not a matter of attempting to give a body of dogma, a task that resisted the Jewish philosophers of the Middle Ages. What we wish to do, in an empirical way, is to list some of the relations that are established between, on the one hand, Him whose message the Bible carries, and, on the other, the reader, when he agrees to take as the context of the verse being examined the whole of the biblical text – that is, when he takes the oral tradition as the point of departure for his reading of the Bible.

This will undoubtedly be an invitation to follow at all times the highest path, to keep faith only with the Unique, and to distrust myth which dictates to us the *fait accompli*, the constraint of custom and land, and the Machiavellian State with its reasons of State. But to follow the Most-High is also to know that nothing is greater than to approach one's neighbour, than the concern for the lot of the 'widow and orphan, the stranger and poor'; and that to approach with empty hands is not to approach at all. The adventure of the Spirit also takes place on earth among men. The trauma I experienced as a slave in the land of Egypt constitutes my humanity itself. This immediately brings me closer to all the problems of the damned on earth, of all those who are persecuted, as if in my suffering as a slave I prayed in a prayer that was not yet oration, and as if this love of the stranger were already the reply given to me through my heart of flesh. My very uniqueness lies in the responsibility for the other man; I could never pass it off on to another person, just as I could never have anyone take my place in death: obedience to the Most-High means precisely this impossibility of shying away; through it, my 'self' is unique. To be free is to do only what no one else can do in my place. To obey the Most-High is to be free.

But man is also the irruption of God into being, or the explosion of being towards God: man is the rupture of being which produces the act of giving, only giving with one's hands full rather than bringing struggle and plunder. Hence the idea of election which can deteriorate into pride, but which originally expresses the awareness of an indisputable summons which gives life to ethics and through which the indisputability of the summons isolates the person responsible. 'You only have I known of all the families of the earth; therefore I will punish you for all your iniquities' (Amos 3: 2). Man is called upon in the judgement of justice which recognizes this responsibility. Mercy – the *rachamim* (the trembling of the womb[3] where the Other is in gestation in the Same, maternity within God, so to speak) – attenuates the rigours of the Law (without suspending it in principle; yet it can go so far as to suspend it in reality). Man can do what he must do. He will be capable of mastering the hostile forces of History and realizing a Messianic reign foretold by the prophets. Waiting

139

for the Messiah is the actual duration of time. Or waiting for God. But now waiting no longer testifies to an absence of Godot who will never come. It testifies, rather, to the relation with something that cannot enter into the present, because the present is too small for the Infinite.

But the most characteristic aspect of Jewish difficult freedom lies perhaps in the ritual that governs all the acts of daily life, in the famous 'yoke of the Law'. In ritual, nothing is numinous. There is no idolatry. In ritual a distance is taken up *within* nature *in respect of* nature, and perhaps therefore it is precisely the waiting for the Most-High which is a relation to Him – or, if one prefers, a deference, a deference to the beyond which creates here the very concept of a beyond or a towards-God.

II The Fact of the Revelation and Human Understanding

I come now to the main question: how might a Jew 'explain' to himself the very fact of the Revelation in all its extraordinariness, which, if the Scriptures are taken literally, tradition presents to him as coming from outside the order of the world? It will not have escaped the reader that the exposition of the content and above all of the structure of the Revelation presented so far has allowed us to take a few steps towards this question.

1 A Few Particulars

Let us confine ourselves for a moment to the literal meaning. Here are a few significant remarks. The Bible itself tells us of the supernatural quality of its origin. There were men who heard the celestial voice. The Bible also warns us against false prophets. So much so that prophecy is suspicious of prophecy, and a risk is run by the person associated with the Revelation. In this there lies a call to vigilance which undoubtedly belongs to the essence of the Revelation: it cannot be separated from anxiety. A further important point is when Moses recalls the Sinaitic Epiphany in Deuteronomy 4: 15: 'Therefore take good heed to yourselves. Since you saw no form on the day that the Lord spoke to you at Horeb out of the midst of the fire'. The Revelation is a saying which outlines, without mediation, the uprightness of the relation between God and man. In Deuteronomy 5: 4 we read: 'The Lord spoke with you face to face'. These expressions will authorize the rabbinical scholars to confer prophetic dignity on all the Israelites present at the foot of Sinai, and therefore to suggest that in principle the human spirit as such is open to inspiration, that man as such is potentially a prophet! Let us look, too, at Amos 3: 8: 'The Lord God has spoken; who can but prophesy?' Prophetic receptivity already lies in the human soul. Is not subjectivity, through its potential for listening – that is, obeying – the very rupture of immanence? But in the text quoted from Deuteronomy, the Master of the Revelation insists on the fact that the Revelation is word, not a visible image. And if the words in Scripture designating the Revelation are borrowed from visual perception, God's appearance is reduced to a verbal message *(devar elohim)* which, more often than not, is a command. Commandment rather than narration constitutes the first movement in the direction of human understanding; and, of itself, is the beginning of language.

The Old Testament confers upon Moses the dignity of being the greatest of prophets. Moses has the most direct contact with God, called a 'face to face' (Exodus 33: 11). And yet he is not allowed to look at the divine face; according to Exodus 33: 23, only the 'back' of God is shown to Moses. In order to understand the very spirit of Judaism, it is perhaps of some interest to mention the way in which the rabbinical scholars interpret this text on the Epiphany: the 'back' that Moses saw from the cleft of the rock from which he followed the passing of divine Glory was nothing other than the knot formed by the straps of the phylacteries on the back of God's neck! A prescriptive teaching even here! Which demonstrates how thoroughly the entire Revelation is bound up around daily ritual conduct. This ritualism suspends the immediacy of the relations with Nature's given and determines, against the blinding spontaneity of Desires, the ethical relation with the other man. To the extent that this ritualism does this, it confirms the conception of God in which He is welcomed in the face-to-face with the other and in the obligation towards the other.

The Talmud upholds the prophetic and verbal origin of the Revelation, but it already lays more stress on the voice of the listener. As if the Revelation were a system of signs to be interpreted by the listener and, in this sense, already revealed to him. The Torah is no longer in heaven, but is given: henceforth it is at men's disposal. A famous apologue from the Tractate Baba Mezia (59b) is significant on this point: R. Eliezer, disagreeing with his colleagues on a problem of *Halakhah*, is supported in his opinion by miracles, and finally by a voice or an echo of a heavenly voice. His colleagues reject all these signs and the echo of a voice, on the irrefutable pretext that the heavenly Torah has been on Earth since Sinai and appeals to man's exegesis, against which the echoes of heavenly voices can no longer do anything. Man is not, therefore, a 'being' among 'beings', a simple receiver of sublime information. He is simultaneously him to whom the word is said, but also him through whom there is Revelation. Man is the place through which transcendence passes, even if he can be described as 'being-there', or *Dasein*. In the light of this situation the whole status of subjectivity and reason must perhaps be revised. In the event of the Revelation, the prophets are succeeded by the *chakham*: the sage, or scholar, or man of reason. In his own way he is inspired, since he bears the oral teaching. He is taught and he teaches, and he is sometimes suggestively called *talmid chakham*: the disciple of a Sage or disciple-sage who receives, but scrutinizes what he receives. The Jewish philosophers of the Middle Ages, in particular Maimonides, admittedly trace the Revelation back to prophetic gifts. But instead of thinking of them in the heteronomy of inspiration, they assimilate them, to varying degrees, to the intellectual faculties described by Aristotle. Like Aristotelian man, Maimonidean man is a 'being' situated *in his place* in the cosmos. He is a part of being which does not go outside being and in which there never occurs the rupture of the same, the radical transcendence that the idea of inspiration and the whole trauma of prophecy seem to entail in the biblical texts.

2 Revelation and Obedience

Let us now come to the main problem. It is certainly not a problem of an apologetic nature requiring the authentication of the various revealed contents, confessed by the religions described as revealed. The problem lies in the possibility of a rupture or a breach in the closed order of totality, of the world, or of the self-sufficiency of its correlative, reason. A rupture which would be caused by a movement coming from outside, but a rupture which, paradoxically, would not alienate this rational self-sufficiency. If the possibility of such a fissure in the hard core of reason could be thought, the most important part of the problem would be resolved. But does not the difficulty come from our habit of under-standing reason as the correlative of the possibility of the world: a thought which is equal to its stability and identity? Can it be otherwise? Can a model of intelligibility be sought in some traumatic experience in which intelligence is broken, affected by something that overflows its capacity? Certainly not. Unless, however, it were a question of a 'Thou shalt' which takes no account of what 'Thou canst'. The act of overflowing here is not insane. In other words, is not the rationality of the rupture practical reason? Is not the model of revelation an ethical one?

In the light of this, I wonder whether there are not aspects in Judaism which indicate the 'rationality' of a reason less turned in upon itself than the reason of philosophical tradition. For example, there is the primordial importance in Judaism of the prescriptive, in which the entire Revelation (even the narrative) is formed according to both the written teaching (the Pentateuch) and the oral teaching. Or the fact that the revealed is welcomed in the form of obedience, which Exodus 24: 7 expresses in the phrase: 'All that the Lord has spoken we will do, and we will be obedient [we will listen to it]'. The term evoking obedience here ['we will do'] is anterior to that which expresses understanding ['we will listen'], and in the eyes of the Talmudic scholars is taken to be the supreme merit of Israel, the 'wisdom of an angel'. The rationality here would not appear as that of a reason 'in decline', but would be understood precisely in its plenitude from out of the irreducible 'intrigue' of obedience. This obedience cannot be reduced to a categorical imperative in which a universality is suddenly able to direct a will. It is an obedience, rather, which can be traced back to the love of one's neighbour: a love without eros, without self-complacency and, in this sense, a love that is obeyed, the responsibility for one's neighbour, the taking upon oneself of the other's destiny, or fraternity. The relation with the other person is placed at the beginning! Moreover, Kant himself, in the statement of the second phrase of the categorical imperative, hastens towards this relation through a regular or irregular deduction from the universality of the maxim. Obedience, which finds concrete form in the relation with the other, indicates a reason that is less centred than Greek reason, the latter having as its immediate correlative something stable, the law of the Same.

The rational subjectivity which we have inherited from Greek philosophy – and not to begin with this inheritance does not mean that we are rejecting it, or that we shall not have recourse to it later, or that we are 'sinking into mysticism' – does not entail the passivity which, in other philosophical essays, I have been able to identify with the responsibility for the other. A responsibility which is not a debt limited by the extent of a commitment that has been actively made, for such a debt can be settled; whereas, without compromising my thought, we can never pay our debt to the other. This is an infinite responsibility, a responsibility against my will, one that I have not chosen: the responsibility of the hostage.[4]

Admittedly, it is not a matter of deducing from this responsibility the actual content of the Bible: Moses and the prophets. We are concerned, rather, with formulating the possibility of a heteronomy which excludes subservience, an ear retaining its reason, an obedience which does not alienate the listener; and with recognizing, in the ethical model of the Bible, the transcendence of understanding. This opening on to an irreducible transcendence cannot occur within the conception of reason that prevails in our philosophical profession today. Here, reason is solid and positive; it begins with all meaning to which all meaning must return in order to be assimilated to the Same, in spite of the whole appearance it may give of having come from outside. Nothing in this reason can cause the fission in the nuclear solidity of a thought which thinks in correlation with the world's positivity, which thinks from its starting point of the vast repose of the cosmos; a thought which freezes its object in the theme, which always thinks to its measure, which thinks *knowingly*. I have always wondered whether this reason that remains closed to the excessiveness of transcendence is capable of expressing the irruption of man into being or the interruption of being by man or, more exactly, the interruption of the alleged correlation of man and being in *essance*[5] in which the figure of the Same appears. I have wondered, too, whether the anxiety that the Other causes the Same is not the meaning of reason, its very rationality: the anxiety of man caused by the Infinite of God which he could never contain, but which inspires him. This inspiration is the originary mode of anxiety, the inspiration of man by God which is man's humanity. Here the 'in' of the 'excessiveness in the finite' is made possible only by the 'Here I am' of man welcoming his neighbour. Inspiration's original mode is not in listening to a Muse dictating songs, but in obedience to the Most-High as an ethical relation with the other.

This is what we have said right from the outset: the subject of our enquiry is the fact of the Revelation, and a relation with exteriority which, unlike the exteriority with which man surrounds himself whenever he seeks knowledge, does not become simply the content of interiority, but remains 'uncontainable', infinite and yet still maintaining a relation. The path I would be inclined to take in order to solve the paradox of the Revelation is one which claims that this relation, at first glance a paradoxical one, may find a model in the non-indifference towards the other, in a responsibility towards him, and that it is precisely within this relation that man becomes his 'self': designated without any possibility of escape, chosen, unique, non-interchangeable and, in this sense, free.[6] Ethics is the model worthy of transcendence, and it is as an ethical kerygma that the Bible is Revelation.

3 The Rationality of Transcendence

What we would also like to suggest and – albeit very briefly – to justify is that the openness to transcendence, as it appears in ethics, does not mean the loss of rationality, that which gives significance to meaning. Rational theology is a theology of being where the rational is equated with the identity of the Same, suggested by the firmness or positivity of the firm ground beneath the sun. It belongs to the ontological adventure which led the biblical God and man, understood from the standpoint of the positivity of a world, towards the 'death' of God and the end of the humanism, or the humanity, of man. The notion of subjectivity coinciding with the identity of the Same and its rationality meant the connection of the world's diversity and the unity of an order which left nothing outside; an order produced or reproduced by the supreme act of Synthesis. The idea of a passive subject and one which, in the heteronomy of its responsibility for the other, differs from all other subjects, is a difficult one. The Subject which does not return to itself, which does not join up again in order to settle, triumphantly, into the absolute repose of the earth beneath the vault of heaven, is unfavourably treated as a product of Romantic subjectivism. The opposite of repose – anxiety, questioning, seeking, Desire – is taken to be a repose that has been lost, an absence of response, a privation – a pure insufficiency of identity, a mark of self-inequality. We have wondered whether the Revelation does not precisely restore the thought of inequality, difference, and irreducible alterity which is 'uncontainable' in gnoseological intentionality; the thought which is not knowledge but which, overflowing knowledge, is in relation with the Infinite or God. We have wondered too whether intentionality, which in its noetic and noematic correlation thinks 'to its measure', is not, on the contrary, an insufficient psyche, one that is more impoverished than the question which, in its purity, is directed towards the other, and is thus a relation with something that can never offer an investment. And finally, we have wondered whether seeking, desire and questioning, far from carrying within themselves the emptiness of need, are not the explosion of the 'more in the less' that Descartes called the idea of the Infinite, a psyche that is more awake than the psyche of intentionality and the knowledge adequate to its object.

The Revelation, as it is described from the standpoint of the ethical relation and where the ethical relation with the other is a modality of the relation with God, denounces the figure of the Same and of knowledge in their claim to be the only place of signification. This figure of the Same and this knowledge are only a certain level of intelligence where it is dulled, becomes middle-class in the satisfied presence of its place, and where reason, always being brought back to the search for repose, calm and conciliation – which imply the ultimateness or priority of the Same – is already absent from living reason. Not that the lack of plenitude, or self-inadequacy, is worth more than coincidence. If it were just a matter of the self in its substantiality, then equality would be better than lack. It is not a question of making the Romantic ideal of dissatisfaction preferable to full self-possession. But does the Spirit end in self-possession? Is there not good cause to think of a relation with an Other which would be 'better' than self-possession? Does not a certain way of 'losing one's soul' signify a deference to what is more, or better, or 'higher' than the soul? It is perhaps in this deference that the very notions of 'better' or 'high' are uttered only as a sense, and that seeking, desire and questioning are thus better than possession, satisfaction and response.

Should we not go beyond the awareness which is equal to itself, or which seeks this equality through assimilating the Other, in order to emphasize the act of deference to the other in his alterity, an alterity which can occur only by way of an awakening by the Other of the Same sleeping in his identity? And, as we have suggested, is not obedience the modality of this awakening? And is it not possible to think of this awareness, in its self-adequacy, as a modality or modification of this awakening, this disturbance that can never be absorbed, of the Same by the Other, in his difference? Rather than being seen in terms of received knowledge, should not the Revelation be thought of as this awakening?

These questions concern the nature of the ultimate, and bring into question the rationality of reason and even the possibility of the ultimate. Should not stupor and fossilization be feared in the identity of the Same to which thought aspires as if to a repose? The other is thought of only quite improperly as an enemy of the Same, his alterity leading not to a dialectic play but to an incessant questioning, without the ultimateness, the priority and the tranquillity of the Same, like an inextinguishable flame which burns yet consumes nothing. Is not the prescriptive of Jewish revelation, in its unfulfillable obligation, its very modality? An unfulfillable obligation, a burning that does not even leave any ash, which would still be, in some respect, a substance based on itself. There is always this explosion of the 'less', incapable of containing the 'more' that it contains, in the form of 'the one for the other'. 'Always' signifies here in its native force: the sense of great patience, of its dia-chrony and temporal transcendence. A sobering up that is 'always' deeper and, in this sense, the spirituality of the spirit in obedience. We may well ask questions about the manifestation of these things in what is said. But can transcendence as such be converted into answers without being lost in the process? And is not the question, which is also a calling into question, the distinctive feature of the voice commanding from beyond?[7]

10

'In the Image of God', according to Rabbi Hayyim Volozhiner
To Herman Heering, Professor of Theology at the University of Leyden

---

1 Who is Rabbi Hayyim Volozhiner?

Rabbi Hayyim Volozhiner, or Rabbi Hayyim of Volozhin (1749–1821), was the disciple and admirer of the famous Gaon of Vilna. The small town of Volozhin to which his name refers is situated in Lithuania. It was here in 1802 that Rabbi Hayyim founded a *yeshivah* which was to exercise a considerable influence on the life of Judaism in Eastern Europe, and more especially in the regions described as Lithuanian. It determined a particular style of study which was to inspire the *yeshivot* throughout the world right up to the present day.

Rabbi Elijah, the Gaon of Vilna (1720–97), the master of Rabbi Hayyim Volozhiner, was one of the last great Talmudists of genius. With his strong personality, the extent and precision of his Talmudic and Kabbalistic knowledge, and the originality and depth of his interpretation, he marked both rabbinical science and the very life of the Jews of his time. In a certain sense, he is still marking it today. He played, among others, a key role in the resistance put up by a whole section of Judaism to the spread of Hasidism. The Gaon of Vilna considered that this popular movement, demanding more fervour than knowledge, denied Talmudic science and dialectic their primary place in Jewish religious life, and that by grouping the communities around spiritual personalities with charismatic power – the *Tsadikim* or the 'miraculous Rabbis' who did not refuse the adoration of the faithful – it changed the true relations between disciple and master, and undermined the fundamental principles of Jewish monotheism. The Gaon was the soul and the leader of these opponents – these *Mitnagedim,* as they continue to be called today, when the antagonisms between them and the *Hasidim* have died down. The *Mitnagedim* were suspicious of the sentimental mysticism of the new doctrine. The Talmudic study whose spiritual primacy they asserted was not limited for them to any acquisition of knowledge: it was the life of the Torah itself, the principle of creation, the object of the contemplative life, the participation in the highest form of life. When Rabbi Hayyim Volozhiner founded a *yeshivah* at Volozhin, this meant a practical confirmation of that primacy.

But Rabbi Hayyim, while fighting the excesses of the Hasidic movement, had a less intransigent attitude towards it than the Gaon. The doors of the *yeshivah* were not closed to those among the *Hasidim* who sought to enter them. Rabbi Hayyim Volozhiner and his school of advanced Talmudic studies thus played their part in restoring Talmudic studies to the heart of Hasidism and, in a general way, helped to prevent this religious movement, in spite of its novelties, from becoming schismatic.

The influence of Rabbi Hayyim Volozhiner and the Talmudic studies that were renewed by the *yeshivah* of Volozhin, and the houses of study that were created after its example, perhaps also shows through in the way that the 'Age of Enlightenment', the rationalism of the *Haskalah,* had been assumed by the Jewish communities of Eastern Europe. From the nineteenth century onwards they in fact found themselves progressively led towards studies that were different to those of the Torah, and towards forms of what are known as Western thought and life; a process into which Western European Jewry had voluntarily been entering since the eighteenth century. This movement towards so-called modern life really became apparent with the Russian, Polish and Lithuanian Jews almost concurrently with the influence that can be attributed to the *yeshivah* of Volozhin. But while undergoing the seduction of the West and its rationalist culture, Eastern Judaism, for the greater part, remained immunized against the temptations of pure and simple assimilation to the surrounding world. It refused to treat as secondary the spiritual world of its origins, and to doubt the complete maturity of traditional Jewish culture, even when it gradually distanced itself in its way of life and intellectual preoccupations from the strict rules handed down by tradition. This faithfulness to the Torah as culture, and a national consciousness determined by this culture, remained the distinctive feature of the Eastern Jew at the heart of a Western style of life. There were, admittedly, many demographic, social and political reasons for this. But among the causes of this steadfastness, it is also necessary to include the education received in the *yeshivot* like that in Volozhin by the elite of these Eastern Jews. The Judaism of the Talmudic schools – or the memory of this Judaism as it persisted in families – was to protect the Jewish masses from assimilation, as it had protected the Hasidic movement from schism. In any case, it had a lot do with it.

But this priority of the Torah that Rabbi Hayyim of Volozhin asserted through pedagogy is also the theme of a theoretical exposition which he left in the form of a small posthumous book which appeared in 1824 in Vilna under the title *Nefesh ha'Hayyim* ('The Soul of Life'). It is a quite remarkable work in which the glorification of the Torah, to which in particular the fourth and last part ('Gate 4') is devoted, is presented as an essential moment of a vast synthesis of Jewish spirituality, and as its crowning achievement. Written during the last years of his life for the students of the *yeshivah,* the work is a learned exposition of the system of Judaism and of Judaism as a system. This is relatively rare in what is known as rabbinical literature, where doctrinal insights are either dispersed among the studies concerning the rules of conduct, the *Halakhah,* or implicit and implicitly understood as if they did not require, among people of learned good company, to be made explicit. It is a rare privilege for a modern reader to possess a text on Judaism like the *Nefesh ha'Hayyim* which, while presenting a general survey (one of the possible general surveys) of Jewish spirituality in the form of a system, is the work of a Talmudic authority who was an expert in *Halakhah* and had to compile the traditional 'questions and answers' on practical problems.

In the pages that follow, we would like to present an aspect of this work which is an attempt to establish the meaning of the humanity of man in the general economy of Creation. But the undertaking is not free of difficulties.

The form in which the problems are posed and treated in *Nefesh ha'Hayyim* might disconcert an uninformed modern reader. He will be surprised by the dogmatic and religious character of the book, and by the way it proves its statements that might be taken as mysticism, which our author rejects – or, at least, rejects in its Hasidic excesses. But this metaphysical or doctrinal essay, which appeals to the intellect for its meaning, proves only by referring to texts. It is exclusively based on the exegesis of writings from the Bible and the Talmud (*Halakhah* and *Midrash*) and the Kabbalah (the *Zohar* and the Tractate *Ets Hayyim* by Rabbi Hayyim Vital, recording the Kabbalah from Safed by Luria, the famous Ari). There is no direct influence in it from the modern West. Not even an explicit allusion to Jewish medieval philosophy inspired by Aristotle and Neo-Platonism, despite the gnostic cosmology offered to the reader; there are few references to Maimonides, whom the Gaon of Vilna disputed. But there is nothing, absolutely nothing, of the philosophy or the science of the new times. No Descartes, no Leibniz, no Spinoza and – although only a few hundred kilometres away from Königsberg, Jena and Berlin – no sign of Kant, Fichte or Hegel. But if the proof remains exegetic from beginning to end, it is, moreover, a question of an exegesis conducted according to the rabbinical mode, the mode of the *Midrash* which solicits the letter of the text in order to seek out, above and beyond the plain meaning, the hidden and allusive meaning. One needs to be used to this hermeneutic in order to understand that for the Bible, for example, even when exegesis appears to be ignoring or neglecting the immediate signification of the text, it is in fact restoring the spirit of the whole to a purely 'local' meaning, deepening and reinforcing it. At times, this hermeneutic, with its rules and tradition, separates the verse from its context and even isolates from the rest of the verse a short sequence of words, like a piece of broken glass conveying meaning. In doing so, all the dimensions of the 'Word of God' are explored. That the Word of God – and indeed even language, which would surely be naturally religious? – should have more dimensions of meaning than its logical structure lets show will perhaps not surprise a reader today. Presented under rabbinical cover, this ultra-modern wisdom is regarded as outdated. Yet in fidelity to tradition it is not impossible to allow oneself to be convinced and edified by a work resting on the authority of venerable quotations. One may even, at least when the method is familiar to you, appreciate the felicitous use that *Nefesh ha'Hayyim* makes of the well-tried processes of rabbinical exegesis, and admire the subtle art of the 'renewal of the meaning of verses' and of quoted sayings, the famous *chidushim*. One may even, therefore, tell oneself that a little of this art takes us away from the plain meaning, but that a lot of this art raises it solely to thought. All of this, however, may surprise and even irritate an impatient reader coming from outside and naturally inclined to take this virtuosity as a means of falsifying the texts. At the very most, he will conceive for it some historical project to draw out the influences which would explain these opinions, aberrations, or 'childish pursuits', and would help to classify them.

We shall try to find in them a vision of the human which is still meaningful today and, in some way, freed from its language of the time. But this is precisely what is difficult, even to explain a single aspect of the work: the inimitable resonances of this language would be lost with the ousting of originary formulations which consequently could not be declared outdated. The latent birth of this thought in the light of its ancient religious expression, the link of notions with certain words, remains in its way essential to the contents and their wealth of thought. It becomes indispensable, at least at times, to evoke them, and not in purely archaeological terms. It is not sufficient, but it is necessary. Even the pre-Copernican universe to which our author refers has a symbolic suggestive power which does not merely belong to a bygone intellectual era. Thus, for example, the 'worlds', 'forces' and 'souls' mentioned in the pages that we shall try to present give an ontological seriousness to elements which are not to be taken solely in their astronomical sense. It is a matter, rather, of designating being in its pluralism and in the relations which govern the terms of this plurality. It concerns the various orders of the real in their coherence or in the ruptures which separate them. It may even concern the diversity of human beings where each person constitutes a world. The way that the notions used are referred back to Scripture, to the texts from the Bible, Talmud or Kabbalah, invites us to search behind the outdated cosmology they express for a spiritual meaning, and thus to get back to permanent problems, to return to a concrete experience and to questions that are still alive. Interpretation here is inevitable, and must be granted certain liberties.

2 Man, The Soul of the Universe

The humanity of man in *Nefesh ha'Hayyim* is understood not in the light of the rational animality of the Greeks but in the light of the biblical notion of man created in the image of God. More precisely, the biblical expression set out in Genesis 1: 27: 'in the image of Elohim' and in Genesis 5: 1: 'in the likeness of Elohim'. That God is designated by the word Elohim is not immaterial to the definition of man, but it also signifies the existence of the problem of God's divinity and of the absolute meaning he may have behind the names he receives. We shall return to this important point in the second part of our exposition.

But what does *Elohim* mean? And what does 'in the likeness of Elohim' or 'being in his image' mean? In this likeness *Nefesh ha'Hayyim* seeks 'the depth of interiority' (I. 1),[1] its secret, beyond the trivial distinction of the world's exteriority and the interiority of the psychological.

The term *Elohim* which names God in the two passages which express the likeness of man and God would designate the divinity in terms of 'mastery of all forces' (I. 2). All the specific forces return to *Elohim,* but they can by extension bear this name: such as the driving forces or the spirits of the stars, the national spirits, the political forces, and the judicial powers.[2] Idolatry consists in forgetting the fact that all these relative forces are due to *Elohim* in the originary meaning of the term.[3] To be master of all forces is equivalent to the power to create *ex nihilo* 'countless worlds and forces'. The existence of the creature pulled from nothingness – countless worlds and forces – depends on its association with the creative energy of Elohim: 'At every moment, the whole energy of their being, their order and subsistence depends on the fact that His will spreads into them a new power and a new wealth of light: if this influence were to cease, the worlds would return to nothingness and chaos' (I. 1). The very mode of being of creature would thus be what we call 'continued creation': the being of creature is its 'association' with *Elohim.*[4]

Is the being of creature guaranteed this association? Is it unconditional? This is a fundamental question. It leads precisely to the notion of interiority.

But let us clarify the notion of *Elohim* a little more. It also indicates a certain hierarchy which commands the worlds and its forces, through which energy is spread from top to bottom:

Every force, from the lowest to the highest, is but the extension of the existence and life of *Elohim*, an extension which reaches the force below it through the intermediary of the force above it, which is the soul poured forth in its interiority. And as we know from Ari's Kabbalah, the light and interiority of every world and force is the external being of the force and the world which are above it. And it is according to this order that one rises from the high to the highest. (III. 10)

Every world is governed 'according to the movements of the force of the world which is above it and which governs it like a soul governs its body. Such is the order from the high to the highest right up to Him who is the soul of everyone' (I. 5). The various worlds, then, are arranged in such a way that each one is the body, or – as *Nefesh ha'Hayyim* again puts it – the clothing that dresses the one which is above it and the soul or the force of the one which is below. That which is higher is always internal in relation to that which is lower: height and interiority coincide. Superiority is life and inspiration. The soul is also called the root: the upper worlds are the roots of the roots of the lower worlds.

> For every soul, its root or the principle of its life conforms to the soul of the world that is above it and that becomes and is thus called the soul of the soul. And he (*Elohim*) is the Master of all forces, for he is the soul and the life and the root of the roots of all forces. As it is written: 'Thou givest life to all beings [Thou preservest all of them]' (Nehemiah 9: 6). Which taken literally means: Thou givest it all the time. This is why He, blessed be He, is called the soul of all souls and the principle and the root of all worlds. (III. 10)

God is the soul of the universe.

In this initial study we cannot emphasize the various orders into which the Kabbalist – whose language our author adopts quite naturally, even though he is suspicious of Hasidic mysticism – subdivides the incatenation of worlds. It would be justified to find out its code in order to express its truth in a less specific way. A symbolic classification of the worlds, taken from the 'vision of the chariot' (the *Merkavah*) in the first chapter of Ezekiel, in which four planes are distinguished. We should note, in particular, that of the celestial Throne, above the creatures that are carrying it, yet a Throne that carries its carriers (I. 5). A symbol that is suggestive of a relation that commands the whole of this hierarchy: the highest rests on the lowest, but it is the life or the soul or the interiority of the lowest.

The creature, however, is not limited to this hierarchy whose structure, deriving from Kabbalistic sources, still remains consonant with a Hellenic model. If the idea is thought through, interiority is not limited to height. In the incatenation of worlds, man occupies an exceptional place. Everything depends on him who is at the bottom, in contact with the matter on which his actions are carried out. Man has an affinity with all levels of the real. He does not count just in terms of foundation. The 'roots of his soul' reach the top of the hierarchy. He is 'above the Throne', where souls take root, where the tips of the 'roots' of all Israel[5] do or do not merge (the texts are not explicit, perhaps deliberately) with *Elohim*, with the human face that is above the Throne in Ezekiel's vision. Human souls come from the divine breath: is it not written in Genesis 2: 7 that God 'breathed into [man's] nostrils the breath of life'? Their relationship with the divinity of *Elohim* is a privileged one that is certainly not a pure and simple identification, but is not a pure distinction either.

Various images and symbols that are also taken from the Kabbalistic tradition express the privileged character of the relation between man and the world on the one hand, and man and *Elohim* on the other, without it being immediately possible to bring together in a unique plastic form the images used. On the one hand, what is visible throughout is a connatural element between man and the whole of the worlds, and a special intimacy between man and *Elohim* – an intimacy that asserts both the superiority of *Elohim* in relation to man and a certain dependence of *Elohim*, or, more exactly, the dependence of his association with the worlds concerning man. Man 'feeds' presence or the divine 'association' with the worlds (11. 7). On the other hand, man is made up of the residues or the 'samples' of each of these countless worlds: his substance is a mixture of the worlds' substances (I. 6). Or the worlds are connected with the various organs of the human body, each one subject to the norms of the Torah's commandments,[6] in such a way that the whole of the worlds constitutes a human stature (I. 6). In another respect, a relation is established between the human body and the Temple of Jerusalem, which for its part is an exact replica of the heavenly Temple, the order of absolute holiness. Within the body, the heart is the foundation stone of the heavenly Temple. When the Talmudic scholars, therefore, recommend turning one's heart towards the Holy of Holies when praying, they do not just mean turning in a certain direction but are indicating an act of identification or an intention to identify: one must become the sanctuary itself, the place of all holiness, and responsible for all holiness. Hence, finally, the divine chariot, the *Merkavah*, is likened to the men who have reached this identification, the Patriarchs: 'The Patriarchs are the *Merkavah* itself' (I. 6; III. 13).

This privileged relation is one of analogy, yet it produces the basic desired effect: man's deeds, situated at the bottom, ring out to the top and guarantee or compromise the presence of *Elohim* to the creature (or his

155

departure from it), and the degree of his proximity or distance; that is, the confirmation in being or the reduction to the nothingness of the myriads of worlds. Man, then, plays a primordial role in the being of creature. The presence of God to the world, in the form of its soul, and in the light of this, the coherence of the whole system and the presence of the soul to each world, all depends on man.[7]

Hence the likeness between *Elohim* and man: man is the soul of the world like *Elohim* himself. In the hierarchy of creature, many worlds, many perfect and incorporeal (angelic) beings, are superior to man; yet they are all given over to him because of the unique structure of the human, simultaneously at the bottom of the ladder and rooted 'above the Throne'. Man's deeds, words and thoughts – his three ways of being, originating in his three souls: vital principle (*nefesh*), spirit (*ru'ach*) and divine breath (*neshamah*), which are so many knots in the thread linking the human being to the top of the hierarchy – act on the worlds and forces of creature. Depending on whether he conforms to the Torah's commandments, the worlds and forces that surpass him in elevation and perfection are reinforced 'in their being, their light and their holiness' (I. 6). Or, on the contrary, he helps to diminish them and to lead these forces and worlds to their ruin and destruction. There is here an ethical significance to religious commandments: they amount to letting those who are other than self either live or, in the case of transgression, die. Does not the being of man amount to being-for-the-other? Man exercises his mastery and responsibility as mediator between *Elohim* and the worlds by ensuring the presence or absence of *Elohim* to the incatenation of beings which never ceases to need its living force in order to be.[8] And Volozhiner expressly says:

> His will, blessed be He, confers upon man the power to free or to stop ('to open and close') thousands of myriads of forces and worlds, on account of all the detail and all the levels of his conduct and all his perpetual concerns, thanks to the superior root of his deeds, words and thoughts, as if man too were the master of the forces that command these worlds. (I. 3)

This mastery is interpreted without hesitation as responsibility:

> Let no one in Israel – God forbid! – say to himself: 'What am I and what can I accomplish through my humble deeds in the world?' Let him understand, rather, let him know and let him fix in his

thought that not one detail, from any moment at all, is lost of his deeds, words and thoughts. Each one goes right back to its root in order to carry on in the height of heights, in the worlds and among the pure superior lights. The intelligent man who understands this according to the truth will fear and tremble in his heart in thinking of the points reached by his bad deeds, of the corruption and destruction that even a slight misdeed may cause, well beyond what was destroyed by Nebuchadnezzar and Titus (the destroyers of the Temple of Jerusalem). They did no harm or destruction in the heights, for they have no share in the superior worlds nor roots in those worlds. These worlds are out of their reach, whereas, through our sins, the force of the superior power is diminished and worn out. (I. 4)

As simple pagans, Nebuchadnezzar and Titus do not have the responsibility reserved in the economy of Creation for the children of Israel. The harm they do does not have the same repercussion as that which is attached to the deeds, words and thought of the holy people. Nebuchadnezzar and Titus were able to destroy or profane only the earthly Temple: 'They ground already ground grain' (I. 4), whereas the man of the holy people is in a position to undermine the very holiness which, precisely, is what is always above.

> Let the heart of the holy people tremble, for it includes in its stature all the forces and all the worlds. . . ., for these are the holiness and the sanctuary of above. . . . Thus, when man has an impure thought in his heart, a concupiscent thought, it is as if he were to introduce a prostitute into the Holy of Holies of above. (I. 4)

In the light of this, we would understand the interpretation given by *Nefesh ha'Hayyim* of Genesis 2: 7: 'Then the Lord God formed man of dust from the ground, and breathed into his nostrils the breath of life; and man became a living being'. This is the plain meaning. *Nefesh ha'Hayyim* first evokes it by quoting the ancient translation of the *Targum Onkelos*. It adds:

> But the verse, literally, does not say that the breath became a living soul *in* man; it says that man became a living soul for the countless worlds. . . . Just as the body's behaviour and movements are due to the soul that is inside man, man as a whole is the power and living

soul of the upper and lower countless worlds which are allied by him. (I. 4)

And it is also in a literal sense (a more literal but also more speculative one than the plain sense) that our author reads the ancient blessing pronounced by the Israelite after reading the Torah: 'Thou hast planted an eternal life within us' (*chayei 'olam*), which becomes: 'Thou hast planted the life of the world within us'.

The remarkable 'materialism' of this theory of inspiration should perhaps be emphasized in passing. The whole course of the universe is decided at the bottom, in man. The spirit is not thought of in rhetorical terms, in the splendour of its elevation. It becomes effective in the higher levels through the control it exerts on its bodily life which is subject to the Torah. Consequently, the system of the *mitzvot* acquires a cosmic import and, in its universality, confirms its ethical significance: to practise the commandments is to endure the being of the world. It is not through substantiality – through an in-itself and a for-itself – that man and his interiority are defined, but through the 'for the other': for that which is above self,[9] for the worlds (but also, by interpreting 'world' broadly, for spiritual collectivities, people and structures). In spite of his humility as a creature, man is in the process of damaging them (or protecting them). For all that, by existing, he *is*. This is a fundamental non-narcissism.

This idea of a non-narcissistic interiority is an ethical one. It is the truth of this language or of this cosmological symbolism, and probably the profound experience of Jewish ritual. Why is man inserted between the God who creates and governs the world if it is not to subordinate a purely cosmological vision of being to an ethical understanding? The simple idea of conscience, or even freedom, is still the possibility for an element of creature to posit itself for itself, like another God to whom all is permitted. In subordinating God's action on the world to the possibility for the least powerful creature to be *for* the whole of creature, the (one-way) cosmological hierarchy is broken, without being replaced by any other new hierarchy, or the reverse of this hierarchy, or anarchy. Man is interiority through his responsibility for the universe. The power of God subordinated to responsibility becomes a moral force. Man does not sin against God when he disobeys commandments; he destroys worlds. He 'pleases God' when he does obey because he reinforces and illuminates the being of the 'worlds'. The text from the Talmudic Tractate Aboth II.1: 'Know what there is above thee [and] thou wilt not come into the power of sin', which literally invites the faithful to think of God before acting, is interpreted as: 'Know what upheaval thy action determines in the worlds that are above thee'. Man's deeds count before God because they engage others. The fear of God is the fear for others.

3 Man and the Absoute

But there is yet another aspect to man's role before God. Associated with the world, God would not exhaust his religious significance, for he would thus represent only God from the human viewpoint – God 'on our side', as *Nefesh ha'Hayyim* expresses it. But God also has a meaning in the Tetragrammaton, signifying something that man cannot define, formulate, think, or even name. The creation of the worlds does not in fact introduce any difference into God which would have made a definition possible. In its invariance, the order of Creation does not affect the hierarchy which thus reigns among the 'myriads of worlds' or beings (II. 4,5,8 and *passim*). The Talmudic expression 'God has no place in the world, it is the world which has a place in God', is read in a radical way: God, like the spatial dimension of place, is the condition of all being and is not, moreover, in his geometrical essence, affected by that which fills him (III. 2). It is 'God on his own side'. Like the Kabbalists, our author designates him by the term of *En-Sof*: the In-finite. A contradiction sets the God 'on our side', towards which we return in the light of the hierarchy of the incatenation of beings, against the God 'on his own side', which is not affected by the distinctions that the Torah presupposes between things (III. 6). The phrase 'The Holy One, blessed be He', by which God is designated in pious terms, brings together the idea of separation included in the term 'Holy One' and that of the union to the worlds implied by the notion of blessing (III. 5).

What does the human mean in relation to this new notion? Is there a relation here? Is there a notion? Admittedly, it will be said precisely when speaking of the Infinite, or when thinking of the unpronounceable Tetragrammaton, that man is already creating for himself a certain idea of God in his absolute, and giving him a name. But is it an idea, and is it a name? Does it not bring us down to a negative theology?

Here we are coming up against a domain that would require a special study. But the ideas that express it can be found, as it were, in the background to the whole of the *Nefesh ha'Hayyim*. The general nature of these ideas cannot but be mentioned, albeit very briefly, and however highly suggestive it remains.

The notion of God 'on his own side', whose origin might be suspected of being philosophical rather than biblical (and which modern readers risk taking as the 'God of metaphysics'), is a religious notion in our author's thought. The soul in prayer must be 'orientated' towards the Infinite in his absolute, and not towards his hypostases. This is continuously asserted (III. 8, 14 and *passim*), and would thus be possible despite the fact that the terms of prayer, as discourse, refer to the world and to God's association with the world. An orientation of the soul which, according to *Nefesh ha'Hayyim*, is translated into the text of the ancient blessings of the liturgy of Israel, which possess the authority attached to the prestige of the men of the Great Synagogue who are said to have instituted them. An orientation that is reflected not in the vocabulary but in a syntactic peculiarity: these blessings begin by calling upon God in the second person and end by designating him in the third (II. 3).[10] According to our author's hermeneutic, this God is to be understood behind the plain meaning of the central expression of the daily liturgy of Israel, from the famous 'Hear, O Israel' – in other words, from Deuteronomy 6: 4 (III. 2, 11 and *passim*). This verse would esoterically assert that 'God expressed as our God' in the first part of the verse by the word *Elohenu* (that is, as united to the worlds) is the very one that the Tetragrammaton in the second part of the verse asserts as absolutely one – that is, as unaffected by the multiplicity and hierarchy of the worlds with which he is 'associated'. He is one to the point of being unique and, speaking in absolute terms, there is nothing beside him (III. 2). This is a meaning that should also be found in Deuteronomy 4: 39: 'Know therefore this day, and lay it to your heart, that the Lord is God in heaven above and on the earth beneath; there is no other [there is nothing outside him]'. 'There is nothing outside him' is the literal translation of what is usually rendered as 'and there is no other'.[11] Monotheism would thus be asserted in its absolute vigour without it being from the onto-theological perspective, and despite the resemblance between the One of Deuteronomy and the One of the Enneads. This is an absolute unity which would not be external to Jewish religious life and in which, beyond all thematizing theory and all questioning dialogue, prayer, and, eminently, the study of the Torah studied for itself (prayer and Torah 'in their total purity' (IV and I. 26)), would precisely be the originary 'place'. But it is necessary to clarify what is meant by this near-reference.

The Tetragrammaton, the unpronounceable Name, but a Name nevertheless, already betrays, as a name, the unnameable *En-Sof*. The following text is fundamental on this point: 'The essence of *En-Sof* is hidden away more than any secret, and no name must name it, not even the Tetragrammaton, not even the end of the smallest letter' (III. 2). And by opening a parenthesis the author adds the most important point:

And even if the *Zohar* designates this essence by the name of *En-Sof* (Infinite), this is not a name. For this concerns only the way in which we reach it from out of the forces that have emanated from It, when It desires to associate itself with the worlds. This is why it is called *En-Sof* (endless) and not beginningless. For in reality, *on its own side*, it has neither end nor beginning, but our means of understanding its forces, our understanding, is only a beginning; there is no end for the understanding that goes out to reach the forces emanated from it. (III. 2)

And having closed the parenthesis, he says: 'And the little that we do reach is what we name and qualify with names, surnames and attributes' (III. 2). Strictly speaking, then, that which is infinite and never-ending is not the absolute of God which nothing can determine, but the *act of thinking of the Absolute which never reaches the Absolute*, and this has its own way – which is quite something – of missing the Absolute. Is the word 'thinking' out of place here? Does not this word conjure up, if not vision, then at least aim, which in its way posits another end or sets it as a target? The text we have just quoted suggests a beginning that does not move towards an end, but traces, as it were, a relation without a correlate. And yet it is from this remarkable possibility of the human psyche (or perhaps from the source of all psyche) that *En-Sof* takes its meaning in order to appear in discourse, as if man were its very means of signifying. The human, therefore, would not be just a creature to whom revelation is made, but something through which the absolute of God reveals its meaning. This human impossibility of conceiving of the Infinite is also a new possibility of signifying. We have to come back to the contradiction between 'God on our side' and 'God on his own side'.

In this radical contradiction, neither of the two notions could efface itself before the other. But it is, moreover, paradoxical. *En-Sof*, indifferent to the hierarchy of worlds and beings, indifferent to the relative of rules, expresses a universal, omnipresent God. Is it not him whom we inwardly adore, beyond the differences' which could not act as a shield and make distinctions within him? And yet this 'modality' of the divine is also the perfection of the moral intention that animates religious life as it is lived from the world and its differences, from the top and the bottom, from the pure and the impure. A spiritualization that dismisses the forms whose elevation it perfects, but which it transcends as being incompatible with the Absolute. Is not this transcendence ambiguous? Our author seems to suggest this affinity as much as this transcendence when he recalls the 'incomparable' prophetic dignity that the end of Deuteronomy acknowledges for Moses: the man of the Torah is exceptionally intimate with *En-Sof* (III. 13, 14). God is omnipresent for Moses. He speaks to him from a simple bush. Before his Infinite, Moses is literally annihilated. Abraham still said: 'I who am but dust and ashes' (Genesis 18: 27). Moses says: 'What are we?' (Exodus 16: 7) (III. 13). From then on, God speaks in the first person through the mouth of Moses (III. 13, 14). This intimacy around which prayer, in its purity, appeared to us as the effort of exceptional transcendence (and this is perhaps the originary meaning of purity) is asserted as the distinctive feature of the study of the Torah in its purity, of which Moses would have had complete mastery. The notion of *En-Sof* is thus the perfection of the Torah, freed from the worlds whose incatenation and hierarchy its legalism presupposes through the plain meaning of the text. Is everything pure for the person who has reached that far? Must we go as far as this liberation, as to the height of the religious? Must we lay stress on the elevation above the Law and ethics from out of the Law, as on the very dynamism of the Torah? *Nefesh ha'Hayyim* is aware of this temptation to go above the ethical. At least, it perceives it in the excesses of Hasidism. But its criticism goes further. A step that is not to be taken. The spiritualism beyond all difference that would come from creature means, for man, the indifference of nihilism. All is equal in the omnipresence of God. All is divine. All is permitted. But God who is everywhere, excluding differences from creature, is also God who is nowhere. On its own, the thought of *En-Sof*, of the Infinite, the height of religiosity, is also its abyss. The thought of *En-Sof*, when it is fully understood, leading outside and beyond the Torah which suggests it (III. 3), is the impossibility of the religious idea of God. We must therefore make space for the religion of *Elohim*, for the Law of the Torah, 'for the God associated with the worlds in their differences' and for our access to God in the light of the incatenation of worlds (III. 6, 7).

It is here that *Nefesh ha'Hayyim* has recourse to the ancient idea of

Kabbalistic speculation: the idea of the 'originary contraction' of the Divine, the idea of the *Tsimtsum*. Through this idea the Kabbalah resolved the antinomy between God's omnipresence and the being of creature outside God. God first contracts himself from Creation in order to make space, next to self, for something other than self. In an original way, *Nefesh ha'Hayyim* understands this *Tsimtsum* as a gnoseological event by deducing the notion of the *Tsimtsum* from the texts or analogous terms which suggest concealment (III. 7). The Infinite is enveloped in obscurity. It is forbidden to examine him in order to leave space for the truth of the association of the Infinite and the worlds. This is where the meaning of the hidden God in Isaiah 45 lies (III. 7). It is not, therefore, a question of purely and simply asserting human finitude: the *Tsimtsum* is not a weakness of man, but an originary event. The human finitude that it determines is not a simple psychological powerlessness, but a new possibility: the possibility of thinking of the Infinite and the Law together, the very possibility of their conjunction. Man would not simply be the admission of an antinomy of reason. Beyond the antinomy, he would signify a new image of the Absolute.

11
Spinoza's Background

1 The works published in Dutch over the course of the last ten years by Van Dias and Van der Tak give a less dramatic vision of Spinoza's excommunication than the one that was current up until now, which would have remained definitive only because of Spinoza's probable desire to leave the structure of a denominational community. They give rise to a certain doubt about many points that belong to the traditionally accepted biography of Spinoza, such as the studies he is said to have pursued with a view to entering the Rabbinate. In fact he is not mentioned on the list of pupils from the upper section of Amsterdam's Jewish school devoted to Talmudic studies, and he would not have been the pupil of Rabbi Morteira, a teacher of the Talmud. The works I am talking about are based on documentation from local archives and works published at the time on the school. They allow us to reconstruct the courses and administrative structure of this institution of Amsterdam's Jewish community.

But proving the legend wrong certainly does not mean compromising Spinoza's reputation as a Hebrew scholar and as someone familiar with holy Scriptures. It would aim to bring into question only the extent and depth of his practice of the Talmud. But if particular notice should be taken of the conclusions of these investigations, which involve the risk of their hypotheses and deductions, it is perhaps above all because of certain aspects of Spinoza's writings themselves. In reading the *Theologico-Political Treatise* – in rereading it again quite recently on the occasion of the fine book devoted to it by my friend Sylvain Zac – I had the impression that even though he knew medieval Jewish philosophy and certain Kabbalistic writings perfectly, Spinoza had had no direct contact with the pre-medieval work of the Talmud. This contact, moreover, could already have been broken in the community itself in which he was born, where the ideas, customs and preoccupations of Marranism were still very vivid memories, and interest in the Kabbalah and eschatological waiting were prevailing over the attraction that the advanced dialectic of the Talmud and rabbinical discussion must have exercised. It would be a mistake to think that Jewish communities – and even their Rabbis – are at all times and in all places the authentic interpreters of Talmudic tradition which most often already appears in aspects that are decadent, frozen or dead. Nothing in the historical studies we are speaking about measures the Talmudic potential of Jewish life in Amsterdam at Spinoza's time.

It is not at all certain, then, that Spinoza's environment was favourable in the domain of Talmudic science. This is significant beyond its biographical importance. In the critique that the *Theologico-Political Treatise* makes of it, rabbinical exegesis of Scripture is, as it were, separated from its Talmudic soul, and consequently appears as a blind and dogmatic apologetic of the 'Pharisees' who are attached to the letter (but who are quick to give it an arbitrary meaning) and as a forced reconciliation of obviously disparate texts. *Rabini plane delirant* (Chapter IX), *rem plane fingunt* (Chapter II) ['The Rabbis evidently let their fancy run wild . . . this theory is plainly an invention'].[1] It is here, more than by consulting documents, that the suspicion of a lack of knowledge is born. As far as a Spinoza is concerned, it is more likely to be this than any misappreciation or lack of understanding.

This is neither the moment nor the place to present the Talmud for itself. I shall recall only its structure, which is unique of its kind. The problems it deals with are constantly under discussion. Its arguments conflict with one another, yet they remain, these and those alike, to use its own expression, 'the words of the living God'. It substantiates the idea of a single spirit, despite the contradictions of dialogues which have no conclusion. An open-ended dialectic which cannot be separated from the living study whose theme it becomes. This study echoes and extends the disturbing dynamism of the text. The master's word is required here, and everything depends on the way that he 'talmudizes', if one may put it like that. The name and the essence of the Talmud is the oral Law, even if, at least since the end of the sixth century, it is written down. Did Spinoza ever understand the correct way to 'talmudize'? No one is foolish enough to think that very great minds can be understood by what nourished them in their studies and surroundings. But background involves its own specific causality.

2 Let it suffice for me to mention a few possibilities of the exegesis that the Talmud inspires and which, if we are to believe Spinoza's criticism and the philological method he puts forward against it, would be confined to doing violence to the texts.

What is sought after, and often achieved, in the incessant return to verses by the Talmudic scholars – about whom Spinoza says: *Verba Scripturae extorquere conantur ut id quod plane non vult dicat* (Chapter II) ['They try to wrest the Scriptural words away from their evident meaning'] – which indeed does end up in multiple interpretations that apparently move away from the plain meaning, is a reading where the passage commented upon clarifies for the reader its present preoccupation (which may be either out of the ordinary or common to its generation), and where the verse, in its turn, is renewed in the light of this clarification. This is what I shall call the 'homiletic' essence of the text. Before being the edification of a community, homily is this intimate relation with the text, this renewal and constant updating of meaning. Hermeneutics – which Ricœur, in his preface to Bultmann, designates as 'the very decoding of life in the mirror of the *text*' – is, in its fashion, practised and even instituted here.

For those whom Spinoza calls Pharisees, a model was perhaps laid down for exegesis that the religions issuing from the Bible followed. Scripture as writing involves a call to posterity. Exegesis would be the possibility for one epoch to have a meaning for another epoch. In this sense, history is not something that relativizes the truth of meaning. The distance that separates the text from the reader is the space in which the very evolution of the spirit is lodged. Only this distance allows meaning to mean fully, and to be renewed. In the light of exegesis, then, one may speak of continuous Revelation, as one speaks in theology and philosophy of continuous Creation. According to a Talmudic apologue (Tractate Menahoth 29b), what is taught at the school of R. Akiba is said to be incomprehensible to Moses, but is yet the very teaching of Moses. According to another apologue (Tractate Baba Mezia 59b), the Torah is no longer in Heaven but in the discussions that men have; to persist obstinately in seeking its original meaning (its celestial meaning) is, paradoxically, as if one were to uproot trees or reverse the flow of rivers. When exegesis goes beyond the letter, it is also going beyond the psychological intention of the writer. A pluralism is thus accepted for the interpretation of the same verse, the same biblical character, the same 'history-making event', in the acknowledgement of the various levels, or various depths of meaning. In this polysemy of meaning the word is like 'the hammer striking the rock and causing countless sparks to fly'. The various epochs and the various personalities of the exegetes are the very modality in which this polysemy exists. Something would remain unrevealed in the Revelation if a single soul in its singularity were to be missing from the exegesis. That this process of renewal may be taken as alterations of the text is not ignored by the Talmudic scholars. Hence the obvious irony of exclamations such as: 'Akiba, do not falsify the verses any more, return to the themes of Scripture in which you excel, to those concerning impurity and tents!'

But this coming and going from text to reader and from reader to text, and this renewal of meaning, are perhaps the distinctive feature of all written work, of all literature, even when it does not claim to be Holy Scriptures. The meaning that arises in an authentic expression of the human exceeds the psychological content of the writer's intention, whether he is a prophet, philosopher or poet. In expressing itself, intention cuts through currents of meaning objectively carried by language and the experience of a people. These currents ensure the balance, success and echoes of what is said. The act of saying causes a vibration of something that precedes whatever is thought within it. Interpretation draws it out and is not just perception, but the formation of meaning. From this point of view, every text is inspired: it contains more than it contains. The exegesis of all literature stems from the way in which the plain meaning suggested by the letters is already situated in the unthought. The Holy Scriptures, admittedly, have another secret, an additional essence that purely literary texts have perhaps lost. But they are literary texts nevertheless. And it is because all literature is inspired that religious revelation can become text and reveal itself to hermeneutics.

3 Spinoza's critique makes no mention at all of this 'ontology' of meaning. If Spinoza, the inspired Spinoza, had intimately known the life of the Talmud, he would not have been able to reduce this ontology to insincerity on the part of the Pharisees, nor explain it away by the fact that 'many more ideas can be constructed from words and figures than from the principles and notions on which the whole fabric of reasoned knowledge is reared' (*nam ex verbis et imaginibus longe plures ideae componi possunt quam ex solis principiis et notionibus, quibus tota nostra natrualis cognitio superstruitur*) (Chapter I).

In Spinoza there is no other dimension added to the rules of philology advocated by the *Theologico-Political Treatise*, which unquestioningly designate the field of the modern reading of texts. Now, in our opinion, the way we read today is not confined to the field advocated by the Spinozist method. For Spinoza, all knowledge that sums up a temporal experience, everything that assumes a poetic style, bears the mark of the imaginary. The Bible, conditioned by time, is outside appropriate ideas. Its coherence is made only from the *figmenta* of commentaries. Only its subjective reality, with its subjective intentions, is real. To find the reality of the acts of thought and their subjective intentions written down in the text is all that a method of knowledge concerned with reality can seek in Scripture. *Mentem authorum Scripturae concludere* ['To infer the intention of the authors of Scripture']: subjective intention and its causes, not its imaginary capacity! To establish the genesis of the text rather than carrying out its exegesis! Meaning is, admittedly, referred to the circumstances of its formulation, but from the outset it is already wholly itself, reified in the text and almost fitted within it before all historical development and all hermeneutics: the absolute of the origin, not of the result. Consequently, Spinoza not only reduces the Bible to the level of any text, he also assimilates the exploration of all writing to the exploration of Nature: *Dico methodum interpretandi Seripturam haud differre a methodo interpretandi naturam, sed cum ea prorsus convenire* (Chapter VII) ['I am saying that the method of interpreting Scripture does not widely differ from the method of interpreting nature – in fact, it is almost the same'].

Spinoza will certainly have freed modernity from the obsession with the unique source of the Scriptures. The divine is whatever in the Scriptures is in accordance with the practical consequences of his Ethics. *Quare scripturae divinitas ex hoc solo constare debet quod ipsa veram virtutem doceat* (III. 173) ['So that the divine inspiration of Scripture must consist in this alone, that it teaches true virtue']. Henceforth, the fragments that come from various origins are in a position to bear the good news. But Spinoza will not have conferred a role in the production of meaning on the reader of the text, and – if one may put it this way – he will not have given a gift of prophecy to the act of hearing. Whereas for man today, the attention paid to the message, the religious moment of any reading of books and of all poetic pleasure, is linked to meaning coming from behind the signs that are immediately given: a coming that seeks out a hermeneutic. This, moreover, permits us to understand that while there may be numerous interpretations of Spinozism itself, they do not exclude its truth but testify to it.

ZIONISMS

12
The State of Caesar and the State of David

---

1 Yes to the State

In the Judaism of the Rabbis, in the centuries immediately preceding the birth of Christianity, as in post-Christian rabbinical doctrine, the distinction between the political order and the spiritual order (between the earthly City and the City of God) does not possess the clear-cut character suggested by the evangelical expression 'Render to Caesar the things that are Caesar's, and to God the things that are God's'. In Christianity, the kingdom of God and the earthly kingdom are separated yet placed side by side without touching and, in principle, without contesting each other. They divide the human between themselves, and do not give rise to conflicts. It is perhaps because of this political spirit of indifference that Christianity has so often been a State religion.

It would certainly not be true to say that, for Israel, political power and the divine order are one and the same. And it is not for having been incapable of expecting from God anything other than the salvation of their nation and the deliverance of Judea oppressed by the Romans that the Jews remained untouched by the Christian message. Being beyond the State was an era that Judaism could foresee without accepting, in an age of States, a State that was removed from the Law, and without thinking that the State was not a necessary path, even for going beyond the State. The doctrine of the prophets was perhaps only this anti-Machiavellianism anticipated in the refusal of anarchy.

It is the idea of kingship which expresses the principle of state control in biblical texts. Deuteronomy 17: 14–20 and I Samuel 8 involve a charter of political power. The institution is claimed to be common to Israel and the Gentiles. The prophet consents to it rather than recommending it, and with more good grace in Deuteronomy than in I Samuel. Deuteronomy wants a king who is chosen by God and faithful to the Torah, in which he must 'read all the days of his life' so as not to boast in respect of his brothers. He must have little money; only a few wives, so that his heart does not wander and turn away from the Law; and only a few horses, so as not to return to Egypt. This is the idea of a power that does not abuse its powers, of a power that safeguards Israel's moral principles and particularism, which an institution common to Israel and the nations risks compromising. An idea to which the image of Saul at the beginning of his reign, 'hiding himself among the baggage' and continuing to plough his field, seems to conform.

The text from I Samuel, on the other hand, is an impassioned indictment. The prophet foresees the ruler's enslavement of his subjects, the attack on their property, their persons and their family. Power eventually becomes tyranny. 'And in that day you will cry out because of your king, whom you have chosen for yourselves; but the Lord will not answer you in that day.' It is impossible to escape the State.

The Talmud goes on to present as royal prerogatives what in the text of I Samuel 8 are exactions.[1] And the commentary on Deuteronomy 17: 14–20 tones down the firmness of the biblical remarks.[2] The king shall not have too many horses (Deuteronomy 17: 16), but only as many as are required for the needs of his horsemen; nor shall he have silver and gold in excess (Deuteronomy 17: 17), but only as much as is required to pay the salary of his troops. Would the excesses of power be justified when it is a question of assuming the task of the survival of a people among the nations, or of a person among his fellow men? It would seem so.

But can an absolute law be suspended? Can it appear in Judaism purely and simply as a yoke that all life's necessities justify shaking off? Would a decision for the State be equivalent to choosing life over the Law, while this Law aspires to be the Law of life? Unless the divinity of the Law consists in entering the world other than as 'a great and strong wind (rending) the mountains and (breaking) in pieces the rocks', other than as an 'earthquake', other than as a 'fire';[3] unless its sovereignty or actual spirituality consists in extreme humility, calling from a 'still small silence [voice of fine silence]' for entry to the hearts of the just;[4] unless the just are a minority; unless the minority is constantly about to give way; unless the spirit-to-the-world is fragility itself;[5] unless the Law entering the world requires an education, protection, and consequently a history and a State; unless politics is the path of this long patience and these great precautions. We have tried here to go back, very carefully, to the philosophical presuppositions of the 'concession' granted by religion to political necessities, and of the 'provisional abdication' pronounced by the 'spirit of the absolute' before the spirit heedful of the diversity of circumstances and the necessities of place and time to which politics belongs – a 'provisional abdication' which is thinkable only if the temporal order in which it arises itself receives some justification in the absolute. The ultimate elevation of the Revelation would be due to its need for a response, its quest for interiority. It is precisely in this sense that it is a teaching or Torah. But it thus needs time. The weakness of something that needs time in order to develop must not be regarded abstractly: it points positively here to an order that is greater than the eternity of Platonic Ideas or Aristotelian forms – an order in which a spirit is in relation with the Other which brings to the spirit more than it is capable of alone. An order in which limits are surpassed, but an order which, by this very fact, exposes itself to risks. What is taught can be forgotten, to the point of total oblivion. Considering this, the security of times, favourable to pedagogical continuity, and the politics capable of ensuring it, must of course measure up to a metaphysical scale, but they are principles of 'concessions' and 'provisional abdications' which do not proceed from any dubious opportunism. The 'necessities of the hour' to which they desire to respond are those of the entry of eternity into the hour – that is, those of the essence of the Revelation. It is in this very precise sense that the Tractate Temurah states: 'It is better that one letter of the Torah should be uprooted than that the whole Torah should be forgotten [by Israel]'.[6] Is not the political act to be seen in the empty space left by such a sacrifice of the letter? It does not conceive of itself as belonging to an autonomous order freed from its original finality. According to the ideal doctrine, the Sanhedrin installs and controls the king.[7] Placed above the order involving war, taxes and expropriation is the Law of the Absolute which does not disappear after giving rise to political authority in order henceforth to leave Caesar unconditionally with what it entrusted to Caesar.

Taking up the text from Deuteronomy, the Talmud says:

And the king shall write in his own name a Sefer Torah [Book of the Law]. When he goes forth to war he must take it with him; on

173

returning, he brings it back with him; when he sits in judgement it shall be with him, and when he sits down to eat, before him, as it is written: *And it shall be with him and he shall read therein all the days of his life* (Deuteronomy 17: 19).[8]

And, to show the intimacy of the relationship which exists between the prince and the Book, here is the commentary:

And he must not take credit for a [Sefer Torah] belonging to his ancestors. Rabbah said: Even if one's parents have left him a Sefer Torah, yet it is proper that he should write one of his own, as it is written: *Now therefore write ye this song for you* (Deuteronomy 31: 19). [...] The [Sefer Torah] which is to go in and out with [the king], he shall write in the form of an amulet and fasten it to his arm, as it is written [of David], *I have set God always before me, surely He is at my right hand, I shall not be moved* (Psalms 16: 8).[9]

These precise ritual prescriptions, these minute recommendations, are also means of expression: the State, in accordance with its pure essence, is possible only if the divine word enters into it; the prince is educated in this knowledge; this knowledge is taken up by each person on his own account; tradition is renewal.

What is most important is the idea that not only does the essence of the State not contradict the absolute order, but it is called by it. Consequently, the Talmud thinks in a radical way what in fact takes place in I and II Samuel and I and II Kings: in the midst of troubles, wars and political assassinations the House of David asserts itself, in keeping with the will of God, as an eternal dynasty, the bearer of promises. Through the books of the prophets, it gradually goes so far as to enter eschatology. The Messiah institutes a just society and sets humanity free after setting Israel free. These Messianic times are the times of a reign. The Messiah is king. The divine invests History and State rather than doing away with them. The end of History retains a political form.[10] But the Messiah is a descendant of David. Yet what does a family tree of the line of David matter to the Messiah who is justified by his justice? It is of the utmost importance to David himself, and to the political structure that his name signifies. The State of David remains in the final stage of Deliverance. The epoch of the Messiah can and must result from the political order that is allegedly indifferent to eschatology and preoccupied solely with the problems of the hour. This political world must, therefore, remain related to the ideal world. The Talmudic apologue becomes remarkably suggestive here: King David wages war and rules during the day, and at night, when men are resting, he devotes himself to the Law:[11] a double life in order to remake the unity of life. The political action of each passing day begins in an eternal midnight and derives from a nocturnal contact with the Absolute.

In a famous passage from his *Yad Ha-Hazakah* concerning the State, Maimonides characterizes the Messianic age in a way which omits the supernatural element that haunts the imagination. As a non-apocalyptic Messianism in which philosophical and rabbinical thought meet once more, it certainly does not absorb all that waiting for the Messiah means for Jewish sensibility. Yet it does allow us to measure the importance that Jewish thought attaches to going beyond beautiful dreams in order to fulfil the ideal in events promised by a State. The extracts we shall read point to a distinction between Messianism and the ultimate religious promises ('the world to come'), but also to the very Platonic confidence in the possibility that the rational political order would have in ensuring the end of all exile and all violence and, in peacetime, bringing about the happiness of contemplation. Here are a few elements of this text, which is notable for its rationalist sobriety:

King Messiah will arise and restore the kingdom of David to its former state and original sovereignty. He will rebuild the sanctuary and gather the dispersed of Israel. . . . Do not think that King Messiah will have to perform signs and wonders, bring anything new into being, revive the dead, or do similar things. . . . The general principle is: this Law of ours with its statutes and ordinances is not subject to change. It is for ever and all eternity; it is not to be added to or to be taken away from. . . . If there arise a king from the House of David who meditates on the Torah, occupies himself with the command-ments, as did his ancestor David, observes the precepts prescribed in the Written and the Oral Law, prevails upon Israel to walk in the way of the Torah and to repair its breaches, and fights the battles of the Lord, it may be assumed that he is the Messiah. If he does these things and succeeds, rebuilds the sanctuary on its site, and gathers the dispersed of Israel, he is beyond all doubt the Messiah. He will prepare the whole world to serve the Lord with one accord, as it is written: *For then will I turn to the peoples a pure language, that they may all call upon the name of the Lord to serve Him with one consent* (Zephaniah 3: 9).[12]

Then Maimonides interprets the prophecies on the cohabitation of the wolf and the lamb as the reconciliation of peoples, Israel enjoying peace through contact with peoples who are like wild animals.

> Said the Rabbis: *The sole difference between the present and the Messianic days is delivery from servitude to foreign powers.* Taking the words of the Prophets in their literal sense, it appears that the inauguration of the Messianic era will be marked by the war of Gog and Magog; that prior to that war, a prophet will arise to guide Israel and set their hearts aright, as it is written: *Behold, I will send you Elijah the prophet* (Malachi 4: 5). He (Elijah) will come neither to declare the clean unclean, nor the unclean clean ..., but to bring peace in the world, as it is said: *And he shall turn the hearts of the fathers to the children* (Malachi 4: 6). ... But no one is in a position to know the details of this and similar things until they have come to pass. ... No one should ever occupy himself with the legendary themes or spend much time on midrashic statements bearing on this and like subjects. He should not deem them of prime importance, since they lead neither to the fear of God nor to the love of Him. Nor should one calculate the end. ... In the days of King Messiah, when his kingdom will be established and all Israel will gather around him, their pedigrees will be determined by him through the Holy Spirit which will rest upon him. ... The Sages and Prophets did not long for the days of the Messiah that Israel might exercise dominion over the world, or rule over the heathens, or be exalted by the nations, or that it might eat and drink and rejoice. Their aspiration was that Israel be free to devote itself to the Law and its wisdom, with no one to oppress or disturb it, and thus be worthy of life in the world to come. In that era there will be neither famine nor war, neither jealousy nor strife. Blessings will be abundant, comforts within the reach of all. The one preoccupation of the whole world will be to know the Lord. Hence Israelites will be very wise, they will know the things that are now concealed and will attain an understanding of their Creator to the utmost capacity of the human mind, as it is written: *For the earth shall be full of the knowledge of the Lord, as the waters cover the sea* (Isaiah 11: 9).

But if the Messianic City is not beyond politics, the City in its simplest sense is never this side of the religious. 'Pray for the welfare of the government', teaches the *Tractate of Principles* (Pirqe Aboth), 'since but for the fear thereof men would swallow each other alive'.[13] A passage from Bereshith Rabbah[14] paradoxically states:

> R. Simeon b. Lakish said: 'And God saw everything that he had made, and behold, it was very good' (Genesis 1: 31) alludes to the kingdom of God; 'And behold, it was very good', to the kingdom of the Romans. Is then the kingdom of the Romans very good? How strange! The kingdom of the Romans earns that title because it exacts Law and justice for men (*dyokan shel briyot*).

This hyperbole expresses the importance attached to the grasp on the real and the mistrust of finding satisfaction in dreams. And the Tractate Shabbath 11a puts it thus:

> It was said in Rab's name: *If all seas were ink, reeds pens, the heavens parchment, and all men writers, they would not suffice to write down the intricacies of government* [the glory of Power]. [. . .] What verse teaches this? *The heaven for height, and the earth for depth, and the heart of kings is unsearchable* (Proverbs 25: 3).

Homage is thus paid here to the State represented by Rome, one of the four powers (along with Babylonia, the Parthians and the Seleucid Empire) which, according to Jewish historical wisdom, incarnate the alienation or paganization of History, political or imperial oppression, *shi'bud malkuyot*. The Rabbis cannot forget the organizing principle of Rome and its law! They therefore anticipate, with remarkable independence of spirit, modern political philosophy. Whatever its order, the City already ensures the rights of human beings against their fellow men, taken to be still in a state of nature, men as wolves for other men, as Hobbes would have it. Although Israel would see itself as descended from an irreducible fraternity, it is aware of the temptation, within itself and around it, of the war which pits everyone against everyone else.

2 Beyond the State

But the State of Caesar, despite its participation in the pure essence of the

State, is also the place of corruption *par excellence* and, perhaps, the ultimate refuge of idolatry.

According to certain Talmudic scholars, the oppression of great States, the *shi'bud malkuyot*, constitutes the unique difference between the Messianic epoch and our own. The State of Caesar separates humanity from its deliverance by developing without hindrance and reaching the plenitude (or hypertrophy – natural, as it were) of the form it received from the Graeco-Roman world, the pagan State, jealous of its sovereignty, the State in search of hegemony, the conquering, imperialist, totalitarian, oppressive State, attached to realist egoism. Incapable of being without self-adoration, it is idolatry itself. A striking and essential vision independent of any text: in a world of scruples and respect for the man who issues from monotheism, the Chancellery, with its *Realpolitik*, comes to us from another universe and is protected against any infiltration of sensibility, any protestation from 'beautiful souls', any tear from the 'unhappy consciousness'.

Talmudic wisdom is entirely aware of the internal contradiction of the State subordinating some men to others in order to liberate them, whatever the principles embodied by those who hold power. It is a contradiction against which the very person who refuses the political order is not protected, since in abstaining from all collaboration with the ruling power, he makes himself party to the obscure powers that the State represses. A subtle page from the Talmud relates the way in which R. Eleazar took part in Rome's struggle against thieves.[15] The narrative derives its sense of the dramatic from the fact that R. Eleazar was the son of R. Simeon b. Yohai, to whom Israel's mystical tradition attributes the authorship of the Zohar, and who is said to have spent fourteen years in a cave (with his son, precisely) hiding from the Romans. A mystic in the service of the oppressive State! 'How long will you deliver up the people of our God for slaughter?' R. Joshua b. Karhah calls out to him. This people, of course, is Israel, but it is understood as humanity conscious of its original likeness with God. By serving the State, one serves repression; by serving repression, one becomes a member of the police force. Unless one should read: 'In the service of the State yourself, O son of our God, you lose your soul'. R. Eleazar, who is undoubtedly a just person, replies: 'I weed out thorns from the vineyard'. So there are thorns in the vineyard of the good Lord! R. Joshua b. Karhah's reply: 'Let the owner of the vineyard himself come and weed out the thorns!' It is not in terms of political action that the contradiction opposing monotheism and State can be resolved.

The owner of the vineyard, not his vicar! From behind the State of David, safeguarded from the corruption which already alienates the State of Caesar, the beyond of the State announces itself. In certain texts, Israel is thought of as a human society having gone beyond Messianism, one which is still political and historical. In others, the future world or the 'world to come' is announced – Messianism and this 'world to come' being radically distinguished. The Messianic State which seems to be entirely incorporated into Israel's destiny (though it could have been avoided, if we confine ourselves to the letter of I Samuel 8) would thus mark only a stage, a transition. Indeed, numerous Talmudic passages ascribe a finite duration to the Messianic era.[16] The true end of eschatology is the future world. It involves possibilities that cannot be structured according to a political schema. In the interpretation that Jewish mysticism gives of the spiritual life – the Kabbalah – kingship is the lowest among the ten *sefiroth* or categories of the presence of God in a creature. Yet there is no proof that elevation allows us to jump over the intermediaries!

'All the prophets prophesied only in respect of the Messianic era; but as for the world to come, *the eye hath not seen, O Lord, beside thee, what he hath prepared for him that waiteth for him* (Isaiah 64: 4).'[17] These texts can, admittedly, be taken as rigorously religious, separating salvation from all earthly reference; but they can also be read as announcing new possibilities of the human Spirit, a new distribution of its centres, a new meaning of life, and new relations with the other.[18] Messianism is surpassed; this is asserted in an even more precise manner: 'R. Hillel said: There shall be no Messiah for Israel, because they have already enjoyed him in the days of Hezekiah'.[19] A saying that the Talmud reports in order to condemn it: 'May God forgive him for saying so'. But the redactors of the Talmud did not consider it useful to exclude this saying in order thereby to condemn it to oblivion. For Israel, Messianism might be an outmoded stage. It was suitable for a very archaic Israel! How do the commentators interpret these daring words? If the Messiah has already come for Israel, it is because Israel is waiting for the deliverance that will come from God himself. Deliverance does not enter into the idea of kingship. We have here the highest hope, forever separated from political structures! Let the Messiah still be a King, and Messianism a political form of existence, and we have salvation through the Messiah as salvation through another – as if, having reached complete maturity, I could be saved by another; or as if, on the other hand, the salvation of all others were not incumbent upon me, depending on the most precise significance of my personal existence! As if the ultimate end of a person were not the possibility of listening only to my own conscience, and of rejecting reasons of State! A degree which modern man thinks he has reached and which is probably the best definition of modernity, but one which is perhaps more difficult than the 'spontaneism' with which it is confused. A dangerous and tempting confusion which is undoubtedly the reason why the scholars condemned R. Hillel's daring argument.

3 Towards a Monotheistic Politics

The culmination of the State of David in the Messianic State, and the going beyond of the State implied in the notion of the 'world to come', may appear utopian and, in any case, premature. Would the political philosophy of monotheism be a summary one, even if the utopia, as is evident, has rights over a thought worthy of this name? This indiscreet question is raised, paradoxically, in certain religious circles of the State which has been revived in the Holy Land, and to which Israel's tradition is the source of all meaning. The question is not raised in order to claim the idolatrous politics of the world, which in actual fact is the only one to exist, and which Christian monotheism has been unable to destroy. It is raised in order to expect from Zion the formulation of the political monotheism that nobody would have formulated yet. Not even the Talmudic scholars. Only the responsibility of a modern State, exercised on the land promised to Abraham's descendants, should allow his heirs to elaborate patiently, by comparing formulas to facts, a political doctrine suitable for monotheists.

Recently, in Paris, I attended a lecture given by Dan Avni-Segré,[20] an Israeli of Italian origin and Professor at the Faculty of Law in Haifa, where he runs a seminar on the new politics with the participation, in particular, of several Arab students. Let the testimony given there serve as a conclusion to the present comments. Professor Avni-Segré sees the whole return to Zion in a perspective which restores it to holy History. He lays stress not on the accomplishments of the young State but on the possibilities of political invention that it opens up. At the heart of daily conflicts, the living experience of the government – and even the painful necessities of the occupation – allow lessons as yet untaught to be detected in the ancient Revelation. Is a monotheistic politics a contradiction in terms? Or, on the contrary, is this the very culmination of

Zionism? Beyond the concern to ensure a refuge for those who are persecuted, is this not the main task? Is there, then, no alternative between recourse to the methods of Caesar, the idolatry scornful of scruples whose model is furnished by the 'imperial oppression', the *shi'bud malkuyot*, and the facile eloquence of a careless moralism, blinded by its dreams and words, and dooming the dispersed gathered back together to rapid destruction and a new dispersion? For two thousand years, Israel was uninvolved in History. Innocent of all political crime, as pure as the purity of the victim, a purity whose sole merit was perhaps its long patience, Israel had become incapable of thinking a politics which would bring to perfection its monotheistic message. Henceforth, the commitment has been made. Since 1948. But all has just begun. Israel is no less isolated in its struggle to complete its extraordinary task than was Abraham, who began it four thousand years ago. But this return to the land of our ancestors – beyond solving any specific problem, whether national or domestic – would thus mark one of the greatest events of internal history and, indeed, of all History.

13
Politics After!

1 The origin of the conflict between Jews and Arabs dates back to Zionism. It has been acute since the creation of the State of Israel on a piece of arid land which had belonged to the children of Israel more than thirty centuries ago – which, despite the destruction of Judea in AD 70, the Jewish communities never deserted; which in the Diaspora they never ceased to claim and which, since the beginning of the [twentieth] century, they have made flourish through their work. But this piece of land had also been lived on for centuries by those who call themselves Palestinians, who are surrounded on all parts and over vast expanses by the great Arab people of which they are a part. This conflict – which, for the moment, dominates all other Jewish–Arab questions – has always been treated in political terms by men of State, public opinion and even intellectuals. It has been a question for everyone of collectivities worthy of or usurping the designation of nations, the extent of the powers exerted on the territories, their confrontation in war, and their position within the climate of the great world powers. No one has explained or considered with sufficient attention the dimensions these political problems could owe to their spatio-temporal, psychological and moral particulars which, perhaps, explode the prefabricated categories of sociology and political science. Consequently, there has been no regard for the extraordinary nature of these particulars and the remarkable human adventure running through them. There has been only the unshakeable conviction that nature is never without order, that the extraordinary is a religious notion, the source of mystification and the refuge of ideologies, that the human is never remarkable and that man's

invocation is but a call for the pity conceded, possibly, to the camp victims. But the reasonable course of action, as the postulate goes, would first be political, even if the events in which it is engaged accommodate various and incompatible analyses.

We believe that 'for men purely as men', independently of all religious consideration issuing from a denomination and a set of beliefs, the meaning of the human, between peoples as between persons, is exhausted neither in the political necessities which hold it bound nor in the sentiments which release that hold. We believe that what escapes the order of things may impose itself upon the general picture without recourse to any supernatural or miraculous factor and, in demanding a behaviour that is irreducible to established precedents, may authorize its own projects and models to which, however, every mind – that is, every reason – can gain access.

2 A Jew does not need to be a 'prophet or the son of a prophet' to wish and hope for a reconciliation between Jews and Arabs; to foresee it, above and beyond becoming peaceful neighbours, as a fraternal community. The peace concluded between Israel and Egypt, the unusual conditions in which it had been brought about by President Sadat's trip to Jerusalem on 19 November 1977 and which, on the small screen, must have seemed like man's first steps on the moon (though no more irrational), represents in our eyes – despite all the ups and downs which in the reality of things almost ruined the agreement, and despite the pitfalls which perhaps await it and risk reducing it to nothing, the very path on which reconciliation had a chance to occur. Not because of the partial character of the solution and the alleged excellence that 'progression through short steps' would entail, but because peace had come by a path which led higher and came from further away than political roads, whatever their part may have been in the itinerary of this peace.

The place (or the diaspora or migrations) of the Jewish people among the nations, its ancientness as *one people* throughout the various and contradictory eras of History, ought already to bring into question the exclusive nature of political conceptualization. This, perhaps, is what interiority is. An interiority which would no longer be the imaginary dimension of 'beautiful souls' is no doubt gauged by such ancientness, even if it is faithfulness to memories or a book. A prophetic book in the case in point – that is, made up of subversive discourses defying kings and great people without fleeing into clandestinity. A book which carries the disputed land within it more deeply than do the geological strata of its depths. A faithfulness which is admittedly protective, but, more assuredly, indicates an impassivity in the face of the noises and commotions of the world, its wars, glories and hegemonies. In the hustle and bustle of events and men, this prevents the hypothetical imperatives from concealing their conditioning, imposing themselves and weighing categorically. This is an ethical destiny, without anchoretism or isolation, the distance necessary for judgement. It is the difficult freedom of Israel, which is to be treated not as an ethnographical curiosity but as an extreme form of human potential. This potential disturbs and irritates the awareness of sovereignty that nations which are well established among nations have of themselves. These nations are firmly settled on their land, and their self-affirmation is supported by this confidence in their land, this certainty, and this original experience of the unshakeable.

This ability to irritate and disturb constitutes an allergy that is more unpardonable, whatever the sociologists may say, than any alterity of simple quantitative or qualitative difference. Anti-Semitism is not simply the hostility felt by a majority towards a minority, nor just a xenophobia or some form of racism, even if it is the ultimate reason for these phenomena which are derived from it.[1] For anti-Semitism is the repugnance felt towards the unknown of the other's psyche, the mystery of his interiority or, beyond any conglomeration into a whole or organization into an organism, the pure proximity of the other man – in other words, social living itself.

The dramatic events of the twentieth century and the National Socialism which caused a complete upheaval in the liberal world on which Jewish existence, more or less successfully, was built and was reliant, have torn the apocalyptic secret from anti-Semitism and allowed us to see the extreme, demanding and dangerous destiny of humankind which, ironically, anti-Semitism denotes. Through the aftermath that Hitlerism left in people's minds anti-Semitism is still an issue today, on the right and on the left, even if it hides under other names. There are no more privileged Jews in the way that those from Western Europe still were in the eyes of the Jewish masses exterminated in Eastern Europe, the national minorities of the past who often unconsciously envied and hoped for this exceptional fate.

But there are no more Jews who are not noticed – or noted – as such in the so-called Socialist countries. 'Internationalism is when the Russian, the Georgian, the Ukrainian, the Chuvash, the Uzbek and others get together to strike at the Jews', notes Alexander Zinoviev in *The Radiant Future*.[2] And that is the ultimate test. Stalinism and post-Stalinist anti-Semitism – or, if you prefer, what sixty years of applied Marxism have not uprooted from the Slavic soul, whose influence on the Third World is echoed in the anti-Israeli votes of the progressive peoples at the UN – certainly constitute one of the greatest traumatic experiences that has ever struck the modern Jewish consciousness. Such trauma condemns in this consciousness all hope of a new and freed humanity that it could have imagined in the 'forgetting of Jerusalem'. In the last quarter-century, Zionism has been lived as a reminder of Psalm 137.

This inverted experience of universality in the latent state of a universal renunciation is lived as a second form of self-consciousness. But it is an experience which affects the inmost depths of the human at least as gravely as it is affected by the condition of the proletarian. An experience which is inverted into a choice of life, into a will-to-be, and even into political initiatives. But one with its back to the wall, or the sea, and one which already takes upon itself the whole ethical heritage of Israel, for the love of life *to that end*, for resurrection *to that end*. This is what the first syllable of 'Zionism' means: a message, first and foremost. 'Out of Zion shall go forth the Torah', according to Micah 4: 2, a verse which everyone knows from Jewish liturgy. The reference to the Bible, the doctrine of justice, counts as much as and more than the documentation of imprescriptible rights. From the outset, self-assertion is responsibility for everyone. It is both politics and already non-politics, epic and Passion, irrepressible energy and extreme vulnerability. After the realism of its political formulations at the beginning, Zionism is finally revealing itself, on the scale of substantial Judaism, as a great ambition of the Spirit.

3 This, moreover, is the way Zionism was very much understood, ever since its first message, by the vast strata of the Jewish population of Eastern Europe who had not yet entered nineteenth-century liberal society and were still exposed to persecutions and pogroms. For what was most important behind Herzl's political idea, which appeared to be so Western, was the identification between *Judenstaat* and the Promised Land and the reopening of the eschatological, forever planetary perspectives of holy History.

Paradoxically, it was this universalist finality of the Jew that also came into play in the Jewish refusal of the Zionist call in pre-Hitlerite Europe. The rehabilitation of Captain Dreyfus became the symbol in the West of the triumph of justice expressed in the ideas of 1789 and 1848. Zionism seemed inadequate to the prophetic ideal whose achievements the Western Jew thought he could perceive at the heart of the great democratic nations, and in all the splendour of their science and arts.

In Eastern Europe itself, the spreading of Marxist ideas which took place with the prolongation of the revolutions whose final struggles they seemed to herald was soon to subordinate the fate of the Jews to the fate of all the disinherited on earth. The vision of this disinheritance, these hopes and the mission which ensued from them, seemed to answer the human vocation as heard on the scale of the Bible, even if it divested itself of denominational, scriptural and geographical memories. Zionism in search of a Jewish State, developing out of the colonies in Palestine, was for a long time interpreted in terms of nationalism, despite the new forms of collective life which were springing up in the *kibbutzim*. A nationalism for poor people, perhaps, regarded by some as an almost philanthropic humanitarian work, and by others as a secular survival of an outdated religious particularism, parading folklore like a petty-bourgeois, self-interested ideology.

Yet some men of an elite nature experienced the true essence of the movement, without awaiting Hitlerism and Soviet anti-Semitism. To this effect I would like to cite the autobiographical narratives of the admirable and great Israeli scholar Gershom Scholem, who recounts his journey as a Westerner from Germany (Weimar) to Jerusalem, and analyses quite remarkably the spiritual dimension (which is not just a religious dimension) of Zionism, as he has understood it since the end of the First World War.

4 Zionism, supposedly a purely political doctrine, thus carries in the depths of its being the inverted image of a certain universality, while also correcting that image. This splinter in the flesh is not a right to pity. It is the measure and strange steadfastness of an interiority – that is, of a lack of support in the world, the absence of all 'position of withdrawal prepared in advance' and all solution. The steadfastness of a final place in which to entrench itself. Such is the actual land that Israel possesses in its State. The effort to build and defend it becomes strained under the dispute and the permanent and growing threat from all its neighbours. A State whose existence remains in question in all that constitutes its essence; while the land of political nations is forever the famous 'depth which lacks least' and remains when all is lost. A land which is at stake, or an impasse for Israel. It is to this position in the impasse that the words

heard in Israel refer: *En bererah,* 'no choice'! An armed and dominating State, one of the great military powers of the Mediterranean basin, against the unarmed Palestinian people whose existence Israel does not recognize! Is that the real state of affairs? In its very real strength, is not Israel also the most fragile, the most vulnerable thing in the world, in the midst of its neighbours, undisputed nations, rich in natural allies, and surrounded by their lands? Lands, lands and lands, as far as the eye can see.

Hence Sadat's grandeur and importance. His trip has probably been the exceptional transhistorical event that one neither makes nor is contemporaneous with twice in a lifetime. For a moment, political standards and clichés were forgotten, along with all the deceitful motives that a certain wisdom attributes even to the gesture of a man who transcends himself and raises himself above his cautiousness and precautions. Cautiousness and precautions were forgotten, but for how long? A few days, a few hours? A moment? Perhaps. But who can say how long true events last, or when the true has come? Who has gauged the ephemeral secretly at work in the years of History? Has Sadat understood the human perfectly human which unfolds in historical events in the form of Judaism, patience and a Passion that are forever beginning afresh right until they revert to action in order to rescue the human? Politics and a precarious state of being from which the despair beyond which one must go is never absent. Did Sadat sense all this in Zionism, which is taken to be an imperialist endeavour, whereas it still carries pain and dereliction in its depths and, outside its truth, still has no reserved and inalienable patrimony which gives support to those who govern States elsewhere? In one respect, this struggle will always have been the struggle of the Warsaw ghetto up in arms but with no ground to which to withdraw, where each step taken in retreat counts and costs. as if it were everything. Oh, what bad negotiators the Israelis are! Whereas they are leading a struggle from which the memory of Massada is never absent, and which one dares to denounce as dependent on Western ideologies. Will one go so far in criticizing Israeli mistrust as to take the weapons from the defenders of the last ramparts? On the other hand, did not Sadat understand the opportunities opened up through friendship with Israel – or simply through already recognizing its existence and entering into talks – and all the prophetic promises that are hidden behind the Zionist claim to historical rights and its contortions under the political yoke? All injustices, capable of being put right. All the impossible becoming possible. Which less lofty minds among Sadat's enemies in the Near East, or his friends in our proud West, have never sensed, plunged as they are in their political bookkeeping. 'A State like any other' and a lot of eloquence? Oh really! So there would be no alternative between recourse to unscrupulous methods whose model is furnished by *Realpolitik* and the irritating rhetoric of a careless idealism, lost in utopian dreams but crumbling into dust on contact with reality or turning into a dangerous, impudent and facile frenzy which professes to be taking up the prophetic discourse? Beyond the State of Israel's concern to provide a refuge for men without a homeland and its sometimes surprising, sometimes uncertain achievements, has it not, above all, been a question of creating on its land the concrete conditions for political invention? That is the ultimate culmination of Zionism, and thereby probably one of the great events in human history. For two thousand years the Jewish people was only the object of history, in a state of political innocence which it owed to its role as victim. That role is not enough for its vocation. But since 1948 this people has been surrounded by enemies and is still being called into question, yet engaged too in real events, in order to think – and to make and remake – a State which will have to incarnate the prophetic moral code and the idea of its peace. That this idea has already managed to be handed down and caught in full flight, as it were, is the wonder of wonders. As we have already said, Sadat's trip has opened up the unique path for peace in the Near East, if this peace is to be possible at all. For what is 'politically' weak about it is probably the expression both of its audacity and, ultimately, of its strength. It is also, perhaps, what it brings, for everyone everywhere, to the very idea of peace: the suggestion that peace is a concept which goes beyond purely political thought.

14
Assimilation and New Culture

In good sociology assimilation appears as an objective process, controlled by rigorous laws, and even as the social process *par excellence.* Among its factors there figure both the attraction exerted by a homogeneous majority over the minority and the different kinds of difficulties which await those who obstinately persist in being the exception to the rule – and even to custom and the economic necessities which, in modern society at least, break down those differences. The individual needs courage and strength in order to resist the natural current that sweeps him along.

But despite the obvious constraint governing such movement, assimilation is denounced as a betrayal or decadence. Its supposed intentions are put on trial. The defendants are still suspected of selfish thoughts, opportunism, a petty aspiration for a trouble-free life, and the fear of living dangerously.

I would not think of contesting this judgement when assimilation means de-Judaization. But I would like to recall, or at least emphasize, the fact that as far as assimilation to Western culture is concerned, it cannot be thought to result only from causes. It involves spiritual reasons and requirements which are imposed on active consciences. Hence there is a serious problem for those who, whether as educators or as men of action, care about the future of Judaism. The solution supposes much more than a simple 'reorganization of community services', a reform of school curriculums, and a new pedagogical politics. It requires an effort to create a culture – that is, as it were, a new Jewish life.

The forms of European life have conquered the Israelites to the extent that these forms reflect the spiritual excellence of universality, the norm of feeling and thinking, and the source of science, art and modern technology, but also the thought of democracy and the foundation of the institutions linked to the ideal of freedom and the rights of man. Certainly no one could forget the events of the twentieth century: two world wars, Fascism and the Holocaust. The doctrines and institutions of Europe emerge from these events as highly compromised. Nevertheless, we still refer to them in order to distinguish between ourselves and their monstrous issue, and between the perversion and the good grain from which it came. We continue to admire universal principles and whatever sound logic deduces from them.

Consequently, the problem of assimilation is still with us. It is with us in so very far as all of us – in Israel and in the dispersion, Zionists and non-Zionists – acknowledge Western civilization and lay claim to all that it contributed and contributes to our public and intellectual life, open as it is to the world's expanses. But our belonging to religious, national or linguistic Judaism is not something that can be purely and simply added to our Western patrimony. One of the two terms falls into disrepute. We need to ask ourselves whether there is not a permanent risk of the traditional side of our existence descending, despite the affection and willpower that may be attached to it, to the level of folklore.

The value judgement which falls on the public order to which one belongs is not of the same force as that for which privacy calls. It is the public order that counts. The expression of the Jewish *Haskalah* of the nineteenth century, the Jewish Age of Enlightenment, 'Be a Jew at home and a man outside', was admittedly able to delay the process of assimilation, and ensure for the Jews in Eastern Europe a sort of double culture and thus, in their consciousness, the harmonious coexistence of two worlds. But this had been possible only where the Slavonic civilizations remained both socially and politically closed to the Jews and, intrinsically, did not immediately elevate themselves to the heights of Western universalism. Here, assimilation could limit itself to an adherence. or a superficial adaptation to the surrounding world without the soul being fully subjected to it. The place of folklore was perhaps no longer with the Jews. At times it was the assimilating world which took on its appearances in the popular imagination. The fact that a collectivity could belong to this world while in practice continuing to be excluded from it was seen at times as the unfolding of a masquerade.

Now, at the present time, whatever awareness and knowledge we may have retained or acquired of the spiritual originality and wealth of our Judaism, we could not forget the eminence of the universal of which we are reminded by our passage through the West, where the universal has been made admirably explicit. A civilization, if one may put it like this, which is doubly universal. It reveals itself as the common patrimony of humanity: every man and all peoples can enter it on the same level and occupy a place there at a point that corresponds to their innate capabilities and calling. And at the same time this civilization carries the universal within its content: sciences, letters, plastic arts. It exalts the universal to the point of formalism, finding within it its values and the principle of its will – that is, its ethics. Above all, it also discovers philosophy, which is principally a certain language whose semantics encounters no incommunicable mystery, or any object that is without resemblance, but a language which has also been able to sublimate metaphors into concepts and to express all lived experience, whatever the original language veiled by this experience and whether or not this language were unsayable.

The nations into which the West is divided have as their specific features only what logically appertains to every individual who belongs to a species. The fact that they belong to humanity means precisely the possibility, to which every person aspires and gains access, of being translated into and expressed in this language of philosophy, a type of Greek that is generously widespread in Europe within cultivated discourse. Everything else is local colour. On the other hand, the congenital universality of the Jewish spirit, deposited in the riches of Scripture and rabbinical literature, involves an ineffaceable moment of isolation and distancing. This peculiarity is not simply the fruit of exile and the ghetto, but probably a fundamental withdrawal into the self in the awareness of a surplus of responsibility towards humanity. It is a strange and uncomfortable privilege, a peculiar inequality which compels obligations towards others while not demanding such obligations in return. This is undoubtedly what the awareness of being chosen is. Nevertheless, in the eyes of nations and in our own eyes as assimilated individuals, this inequality happens to take on the appearances of an irremediable particularism, a petitioning nationalism. This is a misunderstanding held in general opinion and a misunderstanding among ourselves.

Despite all the criticism levied against assimilation, we enjoy the enlightened ideas that it has brought, and we are fascinated by the vast horizons it has opened up for us. We breathe in deeply the air of the open sea, while Jewish peculiarity, which is a difficult destiny, constantly risks appearing to us as archaic and, in the growing ignorance of Hebrew's 'square letters' and the inability to make them speak, as narrowing our vision. Nothing from now on would justify this in the modern world we have entered: a world belonging to all where, up until the Holocaust, nothing seemed to call our presence into serious question.

Particularism or excellence? The excellence of an exceptional message, even though it is addressed to all. This is the paradox of Israel, and one of the mysteries of the Spirit. I am convinced of this, and it is at the heart of my present comments. But who, within assimilated Judaism and among the nations, can still imagine that a peculiarity beyond universality is conceivable? That it could contain those Western values that cannot be repudiated, but also lead beyond them? A thought and a peculiarity of which Judaism, as event, history and Passion, is the breach and the actual figure, made manifest well before the distinction between the particular and the universal makes its appearance in the speculation of logicians. But – and this is also an important point – since our emancipation we have never formulated the meaning of this beyond in Western language. In spite of or because of our assimilation. Up until now we have attempted only an apologetics which, without great difficulty, was limited to modelling the truths of the Torah on the noble models of the West. The Torah requires something more.

What have we made of certain other themes? And to mention, by way of example, only the most well-known, what have we made of the theme of this 'people dwelling alone, and not reckoning itself among the nations' (Numbers 23: 9)? Or the theme of Abraham, who is said to be called *hebrew* because 'the whole world was on one side (*me'ever echad*) while he was on the other side' (Bereshith Rabbah 42: 8)? Or the theme of the six hundred and thirteen commandments constraining the children of Israel, whereas seven commandments sufficed for the children of Noah? To owe to the other more than one asks him for! Blinded by the brilliance of the sun of the West, a cursory glance distinguishes here only separation and arrogance. This is a fatal confusion. For one would have every right to ask if this apparent limitation of universalism is not what protects it from totalitarianism; if it does not arouse our attention to the murmurs of inner voices; if it does not open our eyes to the faces which illuminate and permit the control of social anonymity, and to the vanquished of humanity's rational history where it is not just the proud who succumb.

For as long as this confusion lasts, we will not have overcome the temptation of assimilation – and this includes those among us who are the strongest advocates of Hebraism. And this will be the case however tenderly we regard traditional memories and the touching accents of familiar but disappearing dialects, all that folklore which our assimilation will have taught us – and for good reason! – not to see as the most essential.

We Jews who wish to remain so know that our heritage is no less human than that of the West, and is capable of integrating all that our Western past has awoken among our own possibilities. We have assimilation to thank for this. If we are contesting it at the same time, it is because this 'withdrawal into the self' which is so essential to us, and so often decried, is not the symptom of an outmoded stage of existence but reveals a beyond of universalism, which is what completes or perfects human fraternity. In Israel's peculiarity a peak is reached which justifies the very durability of Judaism. It is not a permanent relapse into an antiquated provincialism.

But it is a peculiarity that the long history from which we are emerging has left in a state of sentiment and faith. It needs to be made explicit to thought. It cannot here and now provide educational rules. It still needs to be translated into the Greek language which, thanks to assimilation, we have learnt in the West. Our great task is to express in Greek those principles about which Greece knew nothing. Jewish peculiarity awaits its philosophy. The servile imitation of European models is no longer enough. The search for references to universality in our Scriptures and texts of the oral Law still comes from the process of assimilation. These texts, through their two-thousand-year-old commentaries, still have something else to say.

In presenting these thoughts in the lofty place of the State Presidential Palace in Jerusalem, I am certainly addressing the right audience. Only a Jewish culture called upon to develop out of a new life in Israel might put an end – for Jews above all, but also for nations – to the persistent misunderstanding. It will make us open our closed books and our eyes. This is our hope. To that effect also, the State of Israel will be the end of assimilation. It will make possible, in its plenitude, the conception of concepts whose roots go right to the depths of the Jewish soul. The explanation and elaboration of these concepts are decisive for the struggle against assimilation and are preliminaries to all kinds of effort on the part of generous organizations, and all the self-sacrifices made by noble masters. This task is not only a speculative one, but is full of practical, concrete and immediate consequences.

Notes

Foreword

1 [*Translator's note:* The expression 'plain meaning' is a translation of 'sens obvie', which, to paraphrase, would mean the literal, natural and most obvious meaning (in particular, of a biblical verse, word or, indeed, letter). To avoid such contorsions, 'plain meaning' is used throughout the text whenever Levinas employs the expression 'sens obvie'. Levinas, precisely, explains some of the different categories of meanings that Jewish biblical hermeneutics uses, and which include the 'plain meaning', in Chapter VII, 'On the Jewish Reading of Scriptures'.]

2 Léon Algazi, to whose memory the present volume is dedicated, was one of those who conceived of the idea of these conferences, and contributed much to bringing them about.

3 On this theme, see the prefaces to *Quatre lectures talmudiques* (Paris: Editions de Minuit, 1968) and the volume *Du sacré au saint* (Paris: Editions de Minuit, 1977). [*Translator's note*: Both these works, *Four Talmudic Readings* and *From the Sacred to the Holy*, have been translated into English and published in one volume as *Nine Talmudic Readings*, trans. by Annette Aronowicz (Bloomington and Indianapolis: Indiana University Press, 1990).]

Fidelities

1 Demanding Judaism

1 The Talmud is the written version of the lessons and discussions of the rabbinical scholars who taught in Palestine and Babylon in the centuries preceding and following the beginning of our era, scholars who were probably continuing ancient traditions.

The problems of the morality, the rights and the ceremonial law of Judaism are treated in the Talmud with very acute attention paid to the particular situations of the action, although care for the principles is never absent from this apparent casuistry, and the apologues and parables also extricate the philosophical implications of the Jewish vision of Scripture. One would be right in thinking that the concern for the concrete conditions of the action which characterizes the Talmudic dialectic teaches an art of the most difficult kind: that of protecting the generous and general ideas from the alienation which threatens them when they come in contact with the real; of distrusting ideologies by discerning, in the action they inspire, the precise moment at which the finality of an achievement is overturned and perversion begins.

Talmudic Readings

2 Model of the West

1 See Chapter VI, notes 3 and 4, p. 205.

2 [*Translator's note*: A *baraitha* literally means external matter, and is a teaching or a tradition which was not included by Rabbi Judah haNasi in his *Mishnah*. They are preserved in the *Gemara*, and are usually introduced by special formulas such as 'There is a teaching' or 'Our Rabbis have taught'. Levinas uses the phrase 'Il existe une *braïtha*' ('There is a teaching') in his translations from the Talmud, and this has been indicated in this translation throughout.]

3 [*Translator's note*: Levinas notes that the French version of this verse is a modified translation of the beginning of Job 36: 16, some lines of which are given slightly earlier in the *Gemara* passage. This translation, Levinas states, conforms to the Bible of the French Rabbinate. Levinas remarks that the word *hessitikha*, translated in his version as 'Il te fera passer' ('He will bring you out'), literally means 'Il t'incitera' ('He will allure you out'), an important point to which he will return in his reading. The difference Levinas is highlighting, which is not present in the English translation, can perhaps best be seen by comparing the King James Version: 'Even so would he have removed thee out' with the Revised Standard Version: 'He also allured you out'.]

4 [*Translator's note*: Levinas, of course, gives the French translation as 'pain de proposition'. There are twelve loaves of Shewbread displayed in the temple and renewed every Sabbath, as the verses from Leviticus explain. Levinas himself clarifies the meaning and interpretation of the term Shewbread in his subsequent comments; see pp. 18–19.]

3 Cities of Refuge

1 [*Translator's note*: This verse has been modified in order to conform to Levinas's version: 'Qui aime l'argent n'est jamais rassasié; qui aime la multitude, a la récolte'. The Soncino Edition of Tractate Makkoth 10a translates Ecclesiastes 5: 10 as: 'He that loveth silver shall not be satisfied with silver, and who delighteth in multitude, *not with* increase'. The Revised Standard Version also translates the second part of the verse as a negative: 'He who loves money will not be satisfied with money; nor he who loves wealth, with gain'. Levinas, precisely, will develop the positive and negative interpretations of the same verse in his reading of this passage.]

2 [*Translator's note*: This is a literal translation of the version from the French Rabbinate that Levinas quotes: 'Jérusalem qui est bâtie comme une ville d'une harmonieuse unité'. The three different translations of Psalms 122: 3 that he gives are essential to the idea that he develops of the earthly Jerusalem 'coupled with' or 'compact together' with the heavenly Jerusalem.]

4 Who Plays Last?

1 [*Translator's note*: This chapter was in fact first published in the proceedings from the XXth Conference of Francophone Jewish Intellectuals, held in Paris from 24 to 26 November 1979. See *Politique et Religion. Données et Débats*, edited by J. Halpérin and G. Lévitte (Paris: Gallimard, 1981), pp. 23–47. The 'events' to which Levinas refers, discernible as a reference point throughout the conference on the relationship between politics and religion, are those of the Iranian Revolution of 1979. Hence Levinas's indication of the fortuitous topicality of his reading of the Talmudic text dealing with the war between Persia (Iran) and Rome (the West).]

2 [*Translator's note*: Levinas uses the phrase 'force qui va', which undoubtedly relates to Spinoza's idea of a natural force by which man tries to preserve his own being. Levinas, however, also has in mind the words of Hernani in Victor Hugo's play of the same name: 'Je suis une force qui va' (Act 3 scene 4), in which Hernani exclaims that he is not just a thinking rational being but a blind and deaf agent to the irresistible natural forces within him. Levinas employs the expression here in relation to political power, and in Chapter VII in relation to sexual desire (p. 105) and other natural tendencies (p. 106). 'Outgoing force' has been used to translate this expression in order to indicate the sense of movement that 'natural force' does not contain.]

3 [*Translator's note*: This translation conforms to the French version given by Levinas. The Soncino Edition of Bereshith Rabbah 9: 13 renders the passage as: 'R. Simeon b. Lakish said: ''Behold, it was very good'' alludes to the kingdom of heaven; " And behold, it was very good", to the earthly kingdom.

Is then the earthly kingdom very good? How strange! (It earns that title) because it exacts justice for men'.]

5 The Pact

1 [*Translator's note*: This translation, slightly modified to conform to the version given by Levinas, is taken from *The Mishnah*, trans. from the Hebrew with Introduction and Brief Explanatory Notes by Herbert Danby (Oxford: Clarendon Press, 1933), pp. 300–01.]

6 On Religious Language and the Fear of God

1 *La Révélation* (Brussels: Facultés universitaires Saint-Louis, 1977), p. 40.

2 The commentary on the first sentence of this text was the subject – on our advice, but without our participation – of a televised session which took place on 14 August 1978 on the second channel of RTF within the context of the broadcast: 'Lire, c'est vivre'.

3 The Talmudic Tractates represent the written form – between the second and sixth centuries after Christ – of the oral lessons of the rabbinical scholars, and the discussions they had among themselves. These lessons and discussions, for the Jewish religious tradition, are the teachings which date back to Sinai, completing or clarifying the teachings of the written Torah (the Bible and, more specifically, the Pentateuch) and which, in the oral Torah, theologically signify the Word and the Will of God with the same authority as the written Torah.

4 Like all Talmudic texts, it is made up of two distinct sections which follow on from each other: the *Mishnah* and the *Gemara*. Mishnah signifies 'teaching' or 'lesson to be repeated'. *Gemara* means 'tradition'; it appears as a commentary or a discussion on the *Mishnah*; it is also the term employed to refer to the whole of the Talmud (*Mishnah* + *Gemara*), a term which approximately signifies 'study'. The Talmud (or the *Gemara*) represents the oral Torah through which the written Torah – the Pentateuch and the whole of the Old Testament – is read in traditional Judaism. The *Mishnah* expresses practical teachings or those relating to conduct (*Halakhah*), attributed to the rabbinical scholars of the highest authority – the Tannaim – and written down towards the end of the second century after Christ. The *Gemara*, focusing most often on what is said in the *Mishnah*, is made up of discussions which had taken place in the rabbinical schools of the Holy Land and Babylon from the third century onwards between the scholars called the *Amoraim*; these discussions were written down towards the end of the seventh century.

5 In the Holy Land, which is the West in relation to Babylon, where the present *Gemara* is elaborated. From the third century onwards, the communities in

Babylon achieved the highest authority in the Jewish world, while the rabbinical schools in *Sura* and *Pumpedita* became famous.

6 The ancient prayer of the 'Eighteen Benedictions' constitutes the basis of the daily liturgy of the Israelites, next to the recitation of the *Shema* which begins with the famous 'Hear O Israel: the Lord is our God, the Lord is One' (Deuteronomy 6: 4–9, followed by Deuteronomy 11: 13–21, and ending with Numbers 15: 37–41). It turns out that the interdict of repeating the terms 'We give thanks' refers to the prayer of the Eighteen Benedictions, and that in connection with the interdict relating to the evocation of God for the good that is done, the *Gemara* will refer to the *Shema*. In this formal way there is already an order in the listing of the interdicts. The final section of our text which begins with R. Zera's intervention also compares the 'We give thanks' to the *Shema*. Their inner cohesion is shown in our commentary.

7 The pretext of thinking of 'two impulses' is given by the Hebraic word *levavekha* 'thy heart'), which – in preference to the equally possible form *libekha* – includes the repetition of the letter V.

8 A curious and profound stage of transition: as if 'giving to' could be more difficult than 'dying for' ...

9 There is an untranslatable play on words here on the mysterious Hebraic term *me'odekha*, translated by the 'might', a word which is likened – *licentia rabbinica* – to the word *midot*, 'attributes' or 'measures', in order to permit the translation given here. [*Translator's note*: Levinas translates the phrase 'whatever treatment he metes out to thee' as 'quelle que soit la mesure qu'il t'applique', using the word 'measure' which is footnoted in the Soncino edition of the Babylonian Talmud.]

10 The theme of the religious value of *chok*, an unjustified commandment which provokes the mockery of the rationalists and of 'Satan himself', is familiar to rabbinical thought (see Rashi's commentary on Exodus 15: 26). As part of this thought, it is also to Israel's credit that when they were presented in the desert with the book of the Covenant, the people said: 'We will do, and we will be obedient [we will hear]' (Exodus 24: 7), thus placing the word meaning 'we will do' before the word meaning 'we will be obedient [we will hear]'. The credit for having had the natural tendency to obey before hearing the terms of the law (Tractate Shabbath 88a-88b). Cf. *Quatre lectures talmudiques* [*Four Talmudic Readings*], pp. 91–8.

11 'The great, the mighty, and the terrible God', the words of Moses in Deuteronomy 10: 17, which are also taken up in the first benediction of the prayer of the Eighteen Benedictions, and whose institution is attributed to the 'Men of the Great Synagogue' who are said to have lived at the time of the return from captivity in Babylon. Of these three attributes, Jeremiah drops 'terrible' (Jeremiah 32: 18) and Daniel (9: 4) drops 'mighty'. On this point, see also the Talmudic Tractate Yoma 69b.

12 The metaphor of the heavenly treasury is also suggested by the parable of the 'earthly king [the king of flesh and blood] [who has] a million *denarii* of gold'.

13 [*Translator's note*: Levinas employs the expression 'reconnaissance du ventre', which literally means 'gratitude from the stomach'. In familiar terms it expresses the gratitude felt towards someone who has satisfied our hunger or thirst. By extension, therefore, the gratitude that may be felt towards someone who satisfies our physical (and, indeed, sexual) desires or ambitions. The point Levinas is making here is that the love of God cannot be likened to the physical and interested love one may feel towards another human being.]

14 'You are my witnesses', says the Lord (Isaiah 43: 10). Compare this verse with the commentary of the ancient *Sifre* on Deuteronomy 33: 5: 'When you are My witnesses, I am God, but when you are not My witnesses, I am not God'. [*Translator's note*: This English translation is taken from *Sifre. A Tannaitic Commentary on the Book of Deuteronomy,* trans. from the Hebrew by Reuven Hammer (New Haven, CT and London: Yale University Press, 1986), p. 359.]

15 If it were permitted to mix the commentary of the *Gemara* with a vocabulary which is completely foreign to it, we would say that the height of heaven is given a different meaning to a spatial one from the point where we can think of an absolute *super*lative; that being able to think this bears witness to the idea of the Infinite within us; that its very mode of being within us is precisely the obedience to a Law which remains a heteronomy; and that this way, for the Infinite, of being within us in the form of human obedience is also the way in which the Infinite transcends the finite – that is, the way it accomplishes its actual infinity.

16 Compare Psalms 2: 11: 'Serve the Lord with fear, with trembling', commented upon in the Tractate Berakoth 30b. [*Translator's note*: Levinas's translation reads: 'Réjouissez-vous avec tremblement', while Berakoth 30b has: 'Rejoice with trembling'.]

17 Significantly, the phrase 'to fear God' appears in the Pentateuch in a series of verses which specifically order the concern and respect for one's neighbour. As if the order 'to fear God' were not added solely to reinforce the order not to 'curse the deaf' and not to 'put a stumbling block before the blind' (Leviticus 19: 14), not to 'wrong one another' (Leviticus 25: 17), not to accept interest or increase from the 'brother [who has become] poor, [be he] a stranger [or] a sojourner' (Leviticus 25: 35–6), etc.; as if the fear of God were defined by ethical interdicts; as if the 'fear of God' were the fear for others.

18 It is interesting to note how suitable as a conclusion is the evocation of the *Shema* – whose importance in Jewish ritual we have emphasized. In the structure of the collection of verses it contains, we can find the order of the ideas that we have brought out: the affirmation of God's unity, of disinterested love linked to the fear of God, to obedience, to the study of the Torah, and to education.

Theologies

7 On the Jewish Reading of Scriptures

1 'In rendering legal judgment, [the judge] used to acquit the guiltless and condemn the guilty; but when he saw that the condemned man was poor, he helped him out of his own purse [to pay the required sum], thus executing judgment and charity ... ' Tractate Sanhedrin 6b. [*Translator's note*: Levinas indicates that he is quoting from the translation into French by the Great Rabbi Salzer.]

2 It is against the paganism of the notion of the 'Oedipus complex' that it is necessary to think forcefully about apparently purely edifying verses such as that in Deuteronomy 8: 5: 'Know then in your heart that, as a man disciplines his son, the Lord your God disciplines you'. Paternity here signifies a constituent category of what has meaning, not of its alienation. On this point, at least, psychoanalysis testifies to the profound crisis of monotheism in contemporary sensibility, a crisis that cannot be reduced to the refusal of a few dogmatic propositions. It conceals the ultimate secret of anti-Semitism. Amado Lévy-Valensi has insisted throughout her work on the essentially pagan character of the myth of Oedipus.

3 [*Translator's note*: The Soncino edition of the Babylonian Talmud renders the *a fortiori* argument as 'how much more should one ... ']

4 Curiously, in the final paragraphs of the pages we are studying in the Tractate Makkoth, the distant noise of unsuppressed and triumphant life, the noise of Rome, is heard. 'Long ago, as Rabban Gamaliel, R. Eleazar b. 'Azariah, R. Joshua and R. Akiba were walking on the road, they heard the noise of the crowds at Rome (on travelling) from Puteoli, a hundred and twenty miles away. They all fell a-weeping, but R. Akiba seemed merry. Said they to him: Wherefore are you merry? Said he to them: Wherefore are you weeping? Said they: These heathens who bow down to images and burn incense to idols live in safety and ease, whereas our Temple, the 'Footstool' of our God, is burnt down by fire, and should we then not weep? He replied: Therefore, am I merry. If they that offend Him fare thus, how much better shall fare they that do obey Him!' How much more shall we one day be rewarded or how much better do we who are just fare already, despite our misfortunes? When we are walking on the road and are tired, whether or not we are Rabban Gamaliel, R. Eleazar b. Azariah and R. Joshua, the greatest of the great, the sounds of Rome may for a moment cause us to question, in our minds and in our nerves, the soundness of the just life. R. Akiba alone is able to be merry: despite the failures, he is certain of receiving the best share. He is certain of it not through painful empirical experience, but through an *a fortiori* reasoning that is not here the guarantee of a promise, but of a value.

5 These are the words with which R. Simeon b. Rabbi closes his intervention in the Talmudic text we are commenting upon: 'One who refrains therefrom [shall] acquire merit for himself and for generations and generations to come, to the end of all generations!'

6 On the subject of the interdicts, it would be interesting to quote the lines which figure in what follows in our text of pages 23a and 23b of the Tractate Makkoth: 'R. Simlai when preaching said: Six hundred and thirteen precepts were communicated to Moses, three hundred and sixty-five negative precepts, corresponding to the number of solar days (in the year), and two hundred and forty-eight positive precepts, corresponding to the number of the members of man's body. Said R. Hamnuna: What is the (authentic) text for this? It is, *Moses commanded us torah, an inheritance of the congregation of Jacob* (Deuteronomy 33: 4), *''torah''* being in letter-value, equal to six hundred and eleven, *''I am''* and *''Thou shalt have no (other) Gods)''* (not being reckoned, because) we heard from the mouth of the Might (Divine)'. [*Translator's note*: The ending of Levinas's translation differs substantially from that given here: 'If one adds to this the first two commandments of the Decalogue pronounced at Sinai and which we heard from the very mouth of the Lord, that makes six hundred and thirteen'.] A bizarre sort of accounting! In actual fact, it gives at least three lessons:

(a) Every day lived under the sun is potential depravity and thus requires a new interdict, a new vigilance which yesterday's cannot guarantee.

(b) The life of every organ of the human body, of every tendency (the accuracy or arbitrariness of the anatomy or physiology counting two hundred and forty-eight matters little, since the number of 'positive' precepts divulges the secret of this figure), is the source of possible life. A force that is not justified in itself. It must be dedicated to the most high, to serving.

(c) The code containing the six hundred and thirteen precepts is not met by the number given by the breakdown of the numerical value of the letters making up the word Torah. It is not a system justified uniquely by its coherence. It institutes the order of life only because its transcendent source is personally asserted in it as word. True life is inspired.

7 Cf. *Quatre lectures talmudiques* [*Four Talmudic Readings*].

8 The word of the 'rabbinical scholars', the word setting out or commenting on the Torah, can be compared to the 'glowing coals', to use a phrase from the Pirqe Aboth in the *Tractate of Principles* of the Babylonian Talmud. A remarkable Talmudist, a disciple of the Gaon of Vilna (one of the last great masters of rabbinical Judaism, on the eve of the nineteenth century, the Jewish age 'of Enlightenment'), Rabbi Hayyim Volozhiner, interpreted this remark approximately as follows: the coals light up by being blown on, the glow of the flame that thus comes alive depends on the interpreter's length of breath.

9 The Book *par excellence* of what has meaning. And this is without yet highlighting the testimony given to this book by a people who have existed for thousands of years, or the interpenetration of their history and of this book, even if such communication between history and book is essential to genuine scriptures.

10 Cf. my study 'De la conscience à la veille', *Bijdragen,* 3–4 (1974), 235–49.

11 Ethics – appearing as the prophetic – is not a 'region', a layer or an ornament of being. It is, of itself, actual dis-interestedness,
which is possible only under a traumatic experience whereby 'presence', in its imperturbable equality of presence, is disturbed by 'the other'. Disturbed, awoken, transcended.

12 In the texts invoked, indeed, determined situations and beings – equal to themselves, being held in definitions and boundaries that integrate them into an order and bring them to rest in the world – are passed through by a breath that arouses and stirs their drowsiness or their identity as beings and things, tearing them from their order without alienating them, tearing them from their contour like the characters in Dufy's paintings. The miracle of beings presenting themselves in their being and awakening to new awakenings, deeper and more sober. It cannot be denied that as a disturbing of order, as a tearing of Same by Other, it is the miracle, the structuring – or de-structuring – of inspiration and its transcendence. If purely thaumaturgical miracles seem spiritually suspect to us and acceptable as simple figures of the Epiphany, it is not because they alter the order but because they do not alter it enough, because they are not miraculous enough, because the Other awakening the Same is not yet other enough through them.

13 On the importance attached to this modality of the gift, cf. Baba-Bathra 10b.

8 The Name of God according to a few Talmudic Texts

1 The Bible of the French Rabbinate renders one of the verses in Deuteronomy (18: 13), in which the term *tamim* figures, as: 'Reste entièrement avec l'Eternel, ton Dieu'. [*Translator's note*: 'You shall remain wholly with the Lord your God', which the Revised Standard Version renders as 'You shall be blameless before the Lord your God'.] The strength of this verse – as well as the originality of the notion of *tamim*, very similar to the notion of integrity – consists in its association with the preposition 'with' (*im*): 'you shall be integral [honest or complete] with ... ' The Talmud (Tractate Pesahim 113b) links this verse with the interdiction to resort to astrology. According to its paradigmatic figure of speech, it thus perhaps sees the 'relation with the Lord' as the complete command of one's destiny, the freedom in obedience to the absolutely sovereign Will.

2 The language of the Talmud is justified by its mode of thought and its truth.

Linked to practice, its speculative possibilities are all the more visible, since many of its particulars are grouped around ideas like temple, altar, priest, etc., which are only memories or – but here too it should be qualified – hopes. Moreover, apologues (*Aggadah*) are always mixed in with the discussions of the commandments. They aim at the speculative less directly than the thematizing logos, but more directly than the discussion of ritual (*Halakhah*). Despite everything, is not philosophical thought superior? Must it not be seen as the result of thought altogether, where all its modalities appear as partial views? Is Hegel's attempt a success, or is it itself based on presuppositions that it is incapable of assimilating? The answer here can be only a choice, on account of the good sense still retained in the question.

3 The whole page containing the mistake that justifies the erasure or effacement of the Name must be buried like a dead body. The prohibition to efface or erase the Name of God is linked by the Tractate Sanhedrin (56a) to Deuteronomy 12: 3–4, which orders the tearing down of the altars, the breaking of the monuments and the effacement of the memory of false pagan gods. It adds: 'You shall not do so to the Lord your God'. An addition which admittedly refers to what follows in this biblical text recommending the uniqueness of the cult in the future temple, but which the Talmud, with supreme liberty, relates to what precedes it, considering no doubt that the uniqueness of the Temple cannot be reconciled to the cult of museums and folklore – and that the Temple, even if it is unique, is open to the four winds, to all spirits, to all perversions of the Spirit when it is no longer inhabited by the Letter.

4 According to other opinions and texts, there are seven or ten. We are not going to take account of these variants here. But one comment is essential: the different opinions in the Talmud always conceal a difference of points of view or a difference of aspects in being. This is why a rigorous Talmudic study cannot ignore these differences. Since the multiplicity of aspects is irreducible and open, thought is essentially discussion and polemic, and this in the highest sense of the term – that is, essentially linked to the love of truth. Moreover, this is why humanity itself is said to be multiple, every aspect of the real, accessible through the Torah, requiring, in order to reveal itself, the commitment of a destiny that is spiritual, personal and irreducible to another destiny. Truth is thus simultaneously eternal and historical.

5 Cf. Tractate Kiddushin 71a.

6 The Kabbalah is a way of thinking whose traces and sources can admittedly be found in the Talmud, but the Talmud is quite distinct from it. In the Kabbalah the names constitute a sort of objective sphere – or at least, a sphere which is not subjective – of the revelation of an inaccessible, non-thematizable God. There exists a kind of world of names that determines a separate speculation. A world of names in which names and letters offer to

thought their own dimension and order. I am not capable of leading you into this. In the Talmud the names of God receive a meaning from out of the situations of the person who invokes them. Cf. further on.

7 Among the texts in which the Names are holy there also appears the Song of Songs. The first verse, which attributes the Song to King Solomon, can be read in Hebrew in a less banal way: 'Song of Songs which is sung to him to whom peace belongs'. A Song of Songs, therefore, sung to God. A reading that 'justifies' the mystical interpretation of this erotic song. Consequently, it is forbidden to efface the name of Solomon evoking the Master of peace. But here is a verse that is challenged: 'My vineyard, my very own, is for myself; you, O Solomon, may have the thousand, and the keepers of the fruit two hundred' (8: 12). The thousand coins for Solomon symbolize a thousand people studying Scripture, the 'two hundred for the keepers of the fruit' indicate two hundred warriors. Five intellectuals to every soldier! The proportion is a bad one, the verse is profane, the name of Solomon can here, if necessary, be erased and effaced!

8 [*Translator's note*: Levinas in fact gives the page reference to the Tractate Sotah as 53a. This does not exist. The relevant discussion to which he refers can be found in pages 7a–7b.]

9 Tractate Kiddushin 71a.

10 Cf. my book, *En découvrant l'existence avec Husserl et Heidegger* (Paris: Vrin, 1967), p. 199.

9 Revelation in the Jewish Tradition

1 An invitation to intelligence which at the same time, by the mystery from which it comes, protects it against the 'dangers' of the truth. Here is a Talmudic apologue commenting on Exodus 33: 21–2 ('And the Lord said, "Behold, there is a place by me where you shall stand upon the rock; and while my glory passes by I will put you in a cleft of the rock, and I will cover you with my hand until I have passed by"'): 'Protection was needed, for complete freedom had been given to the destructive forces to destroy'. The moment of truth is the one in which all interdicts are lifted, where the enquiring mind is permitted everything. Only the truth of the Revelation gives protection at this supreme moment against evil, which, as truth, it also risks leaving free.

2 The written Torah refers to the twenty-four Books of the Jewish Biblical Canon and, in a narrower sense, to the Torah of Moses, the Pentateuch. In the broadest sense, Torah means the whole of the Bible and the Talmud with their commentaries and even with their collected works and homiletic texts called *Aggadah*.

3 On this subject, see also Chapter 3 in my *Autrement qu'être, ou Au-delà de*

l'essence (The Hague: Martinus Nijhoff, 1974) [*Otherwise than Being, or Beyond Essence*, trans. by Alphonso Lingis (The Hague and London: Martinus Nijhoff, 1981)], and the study 'Sans identité' in my *Humanisme de l'autre homme* (Montpellier: Fata Morgana,1972).

4 Cf. *Autrement qu'être, ou Au-delà de l'essence.*

5 We are writing this as *essance*, an abstract noun designating the verbal sense of the word 'being'.

6 Freedom would therefore mean the hearing of a vocation to which I alone am capable of responding; or even the capability-to-respond right there, where I am called.

7 The ideas presented in these final pages have already been put forward in 'De la conscience à la veille', *Bijdragen*, 3–4 (1974).

10 *'In the Image of God', according to Rabbi Hayyim Volozhiner*

1 Our references to the text of *Nefesh ha'Hayyim* are confined to a Roman numeral (indicating one of the four large divisions, or 'Gates', of the book), followed by an Arabic numeral indicating the chapter. [*Translator's note*: No translation of *Nefesh ha'Hayyim* is readily available in English, and Levinas does not indicate whether he is using a French or Hebrew edition. Quotations, therefore, are translated directly from Levinas's French.]

2 In the standard rabbinical exegesis of Scripture, *Elohim* always means God as the principle of rigorous justice, in contrast to the Tetragrammaton indicating God as the principle of mercy. In *Nefesh ha'Hayyim* we shall see a vaster perspective open up on this point.

3 By emphasizing the meaning of all its terms, this is how *Nefesh ha'Hayyim* reads the verse from I Kings 18: 39: 'And when all the people saw it, they fell on their faces; and they said, "The Lord, he is Elohim; the Lord, he is Elohim": the God designated by the Tetragrammaton is master of all forces' (I. 2, note).

4 Following his method, Volozhiner bases his argument on a reading that is 'supported' by texts. Here are a few examples: ' "He who [makes] the great lights". Does not Psalms 136: 7 put "made" in the present? In one of the prayers whose institution is attributed to the "men of the Great Synagogue" – an essential link and one of great traditional authority according to rabbinical theology, and located at the return from the captivity in Babylon – is it not written: "He who, in his goodness, renews every day the work of the Beginning?" ' (I. 2).

5 This convention must be acknowledged: authentic humanity is always synonymous with Israel in this text that is conceived and set out from a theological point of view. There is nothing 'racist' about this synonym in a work which refers to the Scriptures, just as there is nothing exclusive in the

notion of Israel in its most common usage, meaning an order which is open to all who wish to join it.

6 In the Jewish tradition there was always the concern with numerically connecting the 'inventory' of human organs with that of both the positive and negative commandments of the Torah.

7 *Nefesh ha'Hayyim* writes: 'This is why the worlds behave according to human deeds which, carried along by their movements, give rise to movements in the root of their superior soul. This soul is above the worlds and is their own life-soul. When the soul moves, the worlds move, and when it stops, they cease to move' (I. 3).

8 Volozhiner refers in particular to Isaiah 51: 16, which in translation means: 'And I have put my words in your mouth, and hid you in the shadow of my hand, stretching out the heavens and laying the foundations of the earth ...' The verse is used to establish a link between the status of the heavens and the earth and the words which leave men's mouths, for they would be put there to that effect. Similarly, the verse in Isaiah 54: 13: 'All your sons shall be taught by the Lord [shall be instructed in the Torah]' is taken up in accordance with the transformation it undergoes in the *Midrash* from the Tractate Berakoth 64a (and also the Tractates Yebamoth 122b, Nazir 66b and others): 'Read not *banayik* (thy children) but *bonayik* (thy builders)'. Those instructed in the Torah are the builders of the worlds. The verse in Isaiah 49: 17: 'Your destroyers, and those who laid you waste go forth from you' is read as: 'Your destroyers, and those who laid you waste proceed from you'.

Finally, here is a characteristic quotation taken from the collection Midrashim Ekah Rabbah: 'Commenting on the Book of Lamentations, R. Akiba said: When Israel does the will of God, it adds strength to the power of the Above, for it is written: "With God we shall do valiantly" (Psalms 60: 12). And when Israel does not do the will of God, it is as if he were to weaken the great strength from above, for it is written: "You were unmindful of [you weakened] the Rock that begot you" (Deuteronomy 32: 18)'. The plain meaning of the word translated as 'you weakened' is 'you were unmindful', but the literal translation is more speculative than the plain meaning.

9 Does not this way of placing man at the bottom teach us that the other as other is always superior and interior?

10 It may even be wondered – I am proposing this question in a strictly personal capacity, but unless we are contented with a pure doxography and the search for its sources, the interpretation is inevitable in a reading that tries to seize the implications of a thought which advances only by repeatedly referring to texts whether prayer, before being the saying of a said, is not a way of invoking or searching or desiring, irreducible to all apophatic or doxic intentionality and to all derivations or types of intentionality. It may be wondered whether prayer is not a way of searching for something that

cannot enter into any relation as an ending, and where we would thus have to make do with a near-reference. For all that, this near-reference would not just be implicit. The fact that it does not reach an ending would not be a way of sinking into indifference either. As a near-reference to an unnameable God, it would be distinguished not only from thematizing and objectivizing intentionality, but even from dialogue's questioning, for it would in no way be equivalent to the position of an ending. The audacity may be taken to the point of wondering whether intentionality is not already derived from prayer which would be the originary thinking-of-the-Absent-One. I have been unable here to develop the particularly rich contributions on prayer expounded in the 'gate'.

11 The subtleness of this 'reference' rejecting reference (see the preceding note), rejecting relation, would thus be expressed in the unusual mutation that takes place in the syntax of the proposition, or by the subterranean, ultra-literal, or, on the contrary, the already symbolic meaning which can be heard beneath the plain meaning.

11. Spinoza's Background

1 [*Translator's note*: Except for the quotation for which Levinas gives no reference and the final quotation taken from Spinoza's *Ethics*, translations from the Latin, which follow the original text, provided by Levinas, are taken from: Spinoza, *A Theologico-Political Treatise and A Political Treatise*, trans. from the Latin with an Introduction by R. H. M. Elwes (New York: Dover Publications, Inc., 1952).]

Zionisms

12 The State of Caesar and the State of David

1 Tractate Sanhedrin 20b.
2 Ibid., 21b.
3 Cf. I Kings 19: 11 and 12.
4 Cf. *Sifre* on Deuteronomy 32: 2, cited by Rashi: 'He knocked at the door of all nations ...'
5 Unless – as has been said in another context, in confusing the Spirit with its presence-to-the-world – civilizations know themselves to be mortal...
6 Temurah 14b.
7 Shabbath 15a.
8 Sanhedrin 21b.
9 Ibid., 21b.
10 Sanhedrin 99a–b: the Messianic epoch has a finite duration.

11 Berakoth 3b.
12 [*Translator's note*: This and the following quotation from Maimonides are taken from *The Code of Maimonides. Book Fourteen: The Book of Judges*, trans. from the Hebrew by Abraham M. Hershman (New Haven, CT: Yale University Press and London: Oxford University Press, 1949), 'Treatise Five: Kings and Wars': Chapter XI, 'The Messiah' and Chapter XII, 'The Messianic Age', pp. 238–42.]
13 Curiously, the expression 'would swallow each other alive' can be found in Psalms 124: 2–3: 'If it had not been the Lord who was on our side …, they would have swallowed us up alive'. The State, even the Roman State, is worthy of expressions praising the glory of God. [*Translator's note*: The English translation from the Pirqe Aboth is taken from *Sayings of the Fathers*, trans. with an Introduction and a Commentary by J. H. Hertz (London: East and West Library, 1952), p. 38).]
14 One of the oldest collections of Midrashic parables and sayings. [*Translator's note*: Levinas's translation of the passage from Bereshith Rabbah 9: 13 is a variation of the passage already quoted in Chapter IV, 'Who Plays Last?', p. 66. The English translation here is adapted to the translation given by Levinas.]
15 Baba Mezia 83b.
16 Sanhedrin 99a–b.
17 Ibid., 99a.
18 'The eye hath not seen' oddly calls to mind the strange passages where Marx expects socialist society to bring about changes in the human condition, frustrating any prediction by virtue of their actual revolutionary essence.
19 Sanhedrin 99a.
20 During the IXth Colloquium of Francophone Jewish Intellectuals, held in Paris on 25–26 October 1970.

13 Politics After!

1 Throughout her work, Eliane Lévy-Amado maintains this almost ontological structure of anti-Semitism.
2 [*Translator's note*: Levinas gives the page reference (p. 115) to the Russian edition of this book, and translates the title as *L'Avenir radieux*.]

Index